2<sup>50</sup>

# RESTORING PROSPERITY

# RESTORING PROSPERITY

## HOW WORKERS AND MANAGERS ARE FORGING
## A NEW CULTURE OF COOPERATION

## WELLFORD W. WILMS

TIMES BUSINESS

RANDOM HOUSE

Copyright © 1996 by Wellford W. Wilms

All rights reserved under International and Pan-American Copyright Conventions. Published in the United States by Times Books, a division of Random House, Inc., New York, and simultaneously in Canada by Random House of Canada Limited, Toronto.

Library of Congress Cataloging-in-Publication Data

Wilms, Wellford W.
    Restoring prosperity : how workers and managers are forging a new culture of cooperation / Wellford W. Wilms. — 1st ed.
      p.    cm.
    Includes bibliographical references.
    ISBN 0-8129-2030-9
    1. Reengineering (Management) — Case studies.   2. Corporate reorganizations — Case studies.   3. McDonnell Douglas Corporation — Personnel management.   4. Hewlett-Packard Company — Personnel management.   5. USS-POSCO Industries — Personnel management.   6. New United Motor Manufacturing — Personnel management.   7. Joint ventures — Case studies.   I. Title.
    HD58.87.W55   1996
    658.4'063 — dc20                              95-43145

*Printed in the United States of America on acid-free paper*
9  8  7  6  5  4  3  2
FIRST EDITION

TO BENSON MUNGER,

A sage and teacher

who, like Lao-tzu, knows that a leader is best

when people barely know he exists

# ACKNOWLEDGMENTS

LITTLE DID I KNOW in 1989, when my research team and I started working on the assembly line at NUMMI, that we were witnessing the end of mass production in America. Over the next five years, as we also studied USS-POSCO, Douglas Aircraft, and Hewlett-Packard, the magnitude of this revolution and its requirements for new and cooperative human relationships became crystal clear. Because what we were discovering had consequences for workers, union leaders, managers, academics, and policy leaders alike, I decided to write a book that might transcend these points of view. I am grateful to my old friend, journalist Robert Scheer, for leading me to Steve Wasserman, editorial director of Times Books. Steve quickly saw the broader implications of our early findings and offered to publish such a book—just the outlet I wanted.

This book grew from research sponsored by the California Worksite Research Committee—a bipartisan organization of men and women in senior positions in business, labor, government, and education. A number of individuals helped lead this effort, not the least of whom is Benson Munger, senior consultant to the California Senate, to whom this book is dedicated. Without Ben's guidance and encouragement through the twists and turns of the past years, I would have surely given up or self-immolated. I also wish to acknowledge the leadership role played by Dennis Cuneo, vice president of NUMMI, who chaired the committee and helped open the doors of industry to us. I wish to pay special tribute to retired UAW organizer and officer Marvin Brody, who helped guide us successfully through the political minefields that lay between management, labor, and government. Elizabeth Kersten, director of the Senate Office of Research and one of the instrumental members of the Worksite Research Committee, recognized the policy implications of this study and played a critical role by fashioning bipartisan support among key legislators. I am also indebted to Robert Monagan, former Republican speaker of the California Assembly and a respected policy leader, who helped stimulate early interest in the project with progressive business executives just when it was most needed.

Hirsh Cohen, vice president of the Alfred P. Sloan Foundation, quickly saw the value of ethnographic research, contributed financial support, and led us to an expanded network of academics who were also working to improve America's economic health. His provocative questions, however discomforting, invariably led to new and deeper insights for which I am grateful. Finally, I am indebted to Carnegie-Mellon University professor Herbert Simon for encouraging me to stay close to firsthand observations and for the many examples from his own long and productive career.

At first these large, complex companies and unions were complete mysteries to us. But we were blessed with help from countless men and women—production workers, executives, managers, and union leaders, many of whom appear in the book—who let us into their lives and became our teachers. I am extremely grateful to each and every one of them.

The hard day-to-day work was done by members of my research team, who spent years with me digging into these companies and unions while writing thousands of pages of field notes, as well as their own books and dissertations. I am especially indebted to members of the original research team—Alan J. Hardcastle, Sergio Sotelo, Kimberly Ramsey, and Deone M. Zell—as well as to anthropology professor and friend Harold Levine, who taught us how to become careful participant-observers.

Thanks also to researchers Loralee Olias and Cui-Jiu Ping, and to Laurel Davis, Cathy Dawson, Sarah Kincaid, Maritza Rubio, and Joke Zell, who helped transcribe the field notes.

Many people read drafts of the manuscript and offered useful comments or were sources of inspiration in other important ways. They include Alexander Astin, Helen Astin, Bob Baker, Stephen Barley, Sara Beckman, Gordon Berry, Christoph Buechtemann, Ada Carrillo, John Cotter, Richard Cyert, Michael Damer, Rodger Dillon, Steve Duscha, Gerald Geismar, Bill George, Joel Fadem, Richard Florida, Douglas Fraser, Jack Fujimoto, Peter Gaarn, Paul Guenzel, Stephen Harrison, Kathy Hendrickson, Cao Hong, Sanford Jacoby, Dan Katzir, Xandra Kayder, Jan Klein, Archie Kleingartner, Thomas Kochan, Jimmy Lewis, Karen Lewis, Claudia Luther, John McDonough, John McNeil, Ruth Milkman, Ted Mitchell, Richard Moore, James Quillin, Dan Roos, Janis Rosebrook, Joyce Ryan, Josh Scheer, Peter Scheer, Warren Schmidt, Marvin Spiegelman, Nevzer Stacey, Deborah Stipek, Adam Urbanski, Piet Van de Mark, Auggie Wilms, Hermann P. Wilms, Jr., and Thomas C. Wilms.

It took more than a million dollars to bring this project to fruition, and I am deeply grateful for financial support from the Alfred P. Sloan Foundation, the California Economic Development Corporation, the California Employment Training Panel, the California Senate, the Carnegie Bosch Institute, UCLA's Center for International Business Education and Research, and private donors including ARCO, Hewlett-Packard, Pacific Bell, Pacific Gas and Electric, Rockwell International, Safeguard Health, Santa Fe Pacific, and the United Auto Workers.

Academic writing has a structure and symbolism all its own, and complexity is usually regarded as a virtue. But much of what is published in academic outlets is impenetrable and obscure to most readers except those in the inner academic circle. To write for an audience beyond the academic community requires a different set of tools that many of us lack, and I was no exception. I am indebted to Times Books associate editor Geoffrey Shandler, who suggested an initial architecture around which to craft the book and who spent many hours editing the manuscript with me. Thanks also to editorial director Steve Wasserman for his early encouragement and his insistence that every word be in the service of a point.

Thanks also to Lynn Anderson for such careful and painstaking copy-editing. Finally, I owe a large debt of gratitude to my friend and colleague, UCLA professor Sol Cohen, for helping me try to strike a balance between these divergent demands.

# CONTENTS

# PART I

# INTRODUCTION

# CHAPTER ONE

# THE ECONOMIC
# ENGINE OF
# CHANGE

I MET YOH SANG WHAN on a blustery December day in 1991. A cold wintry rain misted across the rugged South Korean mountains as the clouds scudded off in an eastward direction toward the Sea of Japan. Yoh, then executive vice president of Pohang Iron and Steel Company, Ltd., known as POSCO, a company that had grown from a speck on the industrial map to the second largest steelmaker in the world, leaned back in his chair.[1] His office overlooked the massive Pohang steelworks, which spread below as far as the eye could see. For a moment he pursed his fingers before saying "United States Steel was once the symbol of American strength. But your country gave it all away—the industry, the technology, everything!" A look of urgency spread across his open face. "Without steel you can build nothing. A country without steel has no backbone! Without steel a country will lose everything—its automobiles, shipbuilding, electronics!"

Yoh's point was clear. Those of us who grew up in the postwar years were blissfully unaware of the wealth we took for granted and what might happen if we ever lost it. We had never experienced a serious economic downturn. All of our institutions—our companies, labor unions, schools, and government agencies, as well as the cultures that supported them—

were constructed on the assumption of eternal prosperity. But gradually, our appetite for public schools, prisons, roads, health, and welfare began to outstrip our ability to pay for them. A new, grim reality is dawning: either we restore our economic prosperity, or we will surely lose the economic war and become a second-rate power.

Few American industries were prepared to compete in the new, fast-moving world economy. Autos, steel, and electronics were the first to be decimated by the Japanese and then by the South Koreans. Behind them lay an army of rapidly industrializing countries—the "little tigers," like Taiwan, Thailand, and Malaysia—whose hardworking citizens were fast to adopt the newest production technologies and would work for one tenth the cost of American wages. They were hungry, unfettered by excesses of a glorious past, and poised to exploit any opportunity that appeared. That opportunity appeared in the 1980s.

POSCO was one of the many companies that arose in this new economy. With just twenty-five years of steelmaking experience, today it is the world's lowest-cost producer of steel, and it is poised to overtake its Japanese competitors—Nippon Steel, NKK, and Kawasaki Steel. Formed in 1968 under the guiding hand of its visionary former chairman Tae Joon Park, an ex–army general, two thirds of the company stock is owned by the government.[2] The rest is held by employees or other private investors. Its public stature vests the company with a mission that extends far beyond the bottom line. Just days before I met with Yoh in Pohang, news came that North and South Korea were seriously discussing reunification for the first time in forty years. Yoh told me that reunification would cost $200 billion over the next decade. "Who is going to pay?" he asked, raising his eyebrows but making the answer abundantly clear. "So we are working for something bigger than profits. For a big idea!" But Yoh is no ordinary steelmaker. To him, making steel is more than just a business—it is a national calling. It is steel, he is convinced, that will enable unified Korea to take her place next to Japan as an industrial world leader. And Yoh is convinced that it is POSCO that will make all this happen.

Criticizing America comes hard for Yoh. He likes Americans—particularly American workers—whom he came to know during a four-year tour in the United States in the late 1980s. He was then executive vice president of a new joint venture between POSCO and USX (the American conglomerate that had formerly been U.S. Steel Corporation) called USS-POSCO Industries, in Pittsburg, California. Yoh personally interviewed each of the plant's eight hundred American workers, and the experience affected him profoundly. "I came to know many of the American workers well," he recalled. "There were families that had been steelworkers for three generations. They were experienced, but they had no leadership." Yoh explained how the financial gap between exorbitantly paid top executives and the workers at the bottom breeds a paralyzing antagonism. "Conflict is costly because events are moving more quickly than ever," he said. "In this global economy everyone must depend on the other. Everyone must take an expanded view. But in our joint venture I saw how the average American worker had no room for a long-term perspective without security. He was forced to live day to day because the plant may close tomorrow. The question for him was 'How do I keep my job today to escape being laid off tomorrow?' "

Just a few weeks earlier, in Tokyo, I had met with Jinnosuke Miyai, president of Japan's influential Productivity Center, who had expressed a similar point of view. Upstairs in his comfortable offices overlooking the bustling Shibuya district, Miyai described how, after the Second World War, Japan's business and labor leaders had developed three principles that would guide its industrial development over the next half century: employment security for workers, cooperation between management and labor, and sharing of the fruits of production fairly among consumers, owners, managers, and workers. As Miyai stubbed out a cigarette, he told of going to work for Shell Oil in Japan in 1948. Ultimately, he had become a vice president at Shell, the highest-ranking Japanese to do so. Like Yoh, Miyai was perplexed by the inflated salaries paid to many American executives, which are roughly twice those paid to CEOs in other industrialized countries and 180 times more than those of production workers.[3] Bloated salaries are symptomatic of a deeper malady, he insisted, of short-term, individualistic thinking—thinking that creates an unnecessary divide between top managers and workers. "In Japan," he said, "it is immoral for top-level executives to make such huge salaries. Most often, top executives of big Japanese companies make no more than ten times that of the lowest-paid individual."

Miyai lit another cigarette and told me a story about the 1973 Arab oil embargo, which had hit Japan with great force. "At least twenty-five percent of our biggest companies reported losses. But in these companies there were no layoffs. Akio Morita, who was head of Sony, flashed a cable to America saying there were to be no layoffs or reductions in wages for employees." Whatever wage reductions there had been, said Miyai, had started at the top. "At most big Japanese companies, top management's salaries were reduced between twenty and thirty percent, while employees were given raises of more than thirty percent to protect them from inflation. At Shell, my salary was reduced by twenty-five percent and we gave our employees a thirty-three percent raise." The show of good faith had helped to unite management and labor, which in turn enabled them to pursue their mutual economic interests.

Though these principles are now being tested as Japan and South Korea adjust to persistent and deep recession, there is something to be learned.[4] By uniting the interests of society and industry as well as those of management and labor, these two countries were able to move aggressively into the emerging world economy and leapfrog America's industry, whose leaders had become arrogant and insulated from the world around them.

## ECONOMIC DECLINE (1973–1993)

Even though a few experts had seen the warning signs years before the economic slide began, most American executives shrugged them off.[5] Even the 1973 oil crisis failed to raise more than a few eyebrows. Japan, however, read the signals accurately and quickly. Japanese manufacturers were forced to shed wasteful operations, and together with the government they planned for a more energy-efficient future. Consequently, when the second oil crisis hit, the economy was ready and little damage was done.[6]

Furthermore, Japanese automakers quickly saw that fuel-efficient cars were the future. Executives at Chrysler, Ford, and GM, on the other hand, remained unmoved. They took comfort from the fact that American cars accounted for almost 80 percent of the domestic market and, as they saw no need to change, their factories continued to pound out cars around the clock while thousands upon thousands of well-paid autoworkers formed a new middle class.[7]

But the Big Three became increasingly disconnected from their customers and insulated from the larger world around them, unconcerned about the mounting pressure for safer cars that would get better gas mileage. Also, quality began to suffer. Smart buyers learned to avoid cars built on Fridays and Mondays because they frequently lacked parts or were assembled poorly. Autoworkers joked about how they would "lick 'em and stick 'em," meaning "do a lick of work and stick the dealer with the shoddy product." David Halberstam, in his book *The Reckoning*, concluded that American auto industry executives had become so arrogant and so shielded from the world that "when they sinned in the construction of the cars, they did not seek to correct the sin but rather sought to find the flaw in their accuser."[8]

By 1979 Japanese automakers had increased their share of the American market from 10 percent to 30 percent, and American automakers were suddenly awash in red ink.[9] Between 1980 and 1982 GM, Ford, Chrysler, and American Motors lost more than $7 billion. In a defensive move, Congress threw up trade barriers, but the damage had already been done. By the early 1980s one out of five U.S. autoworkers was unemployed and four out of five western U.S. auto plants had been closed.[10]

Over the next ten years, Japan cut even more deeply into American auto markets, establishing ten highly automated plants in the Midwest and Canada. The Big Three were caught overextended and burdened with expensive manufacturing facilities that no one wanted. For GM, 1991 was the worst year ever; it posted losses of nearly $4.5 billion and announced it would shut twenty-two plants and lay off 75,000 employees.[11]

American steel followed much the same course. The Japanese, Germans, and South Koreans had rebuilt their postwar steel industry with efficient basic oxygen furnaces, but their American competitors, assuming their world dominance would continue, still relied on energy-intensive open hearths that depended on huge volumes of steel. Costs soared, and by 1981 the industry had started to collapse. The large integrated U.S. mills were running at just 44 percent of their capacity, while the Japanese, South Koreans, and Brazilians had grabbed 25 percent of the steel market in the United States. By the end of the 1980s only about one in twenty steelworkers was left employed in western Pennsylvania as the once famous mills owned by U.S. Steel, Wheeling Pittsburgh, and Jones and Laughlin were shuttered forever.[12]

Other industries followed a similar path of decline. Until the late 1980s the United States had a virtual monopoly on commercial aircraft, controlling nearly three quarters of the world market, with Boeing claiming 55 percent and McDonnell Douglas 18 percent.[13] But Airbus Industrie, a European consortium subsidized by the governments of France, Britain, West Germany, and Spain, undercut Boeing and McDonnell Douglas in an attempt to gain a greater share of the market by selling aircraft at a loss. The strategy worked well, as Airbus quickly claimed about 28 percent of the world market.[14] Domestic defense cutbacks were also a huge blow not only to Boeing and McDonnell Douglas but also to their thousands of suppliers. For instance, in 1992 the U.S. Air Force canceled a contract for A-12 fighter planes, a cut that alone cost McDonnell Douglas $67 *billion* in revenue.

Like autos, steel, and aircraft, American manufacturers once dominated the world's computer market, and exports to Japan and Europe grew steadily through the 1970s. In the mid-1970s American semiconductor manufacturers, who produced the memory chips used in computers, accounted for 60 percent of the world market and 95 percent of the domestic market.[15] In fact, until the mid-1970s the United States imported no computers at all. But in 1981 a recession jolted the industry, marking the beginning of a downward slide. By the late 1980s IBM, which had once had 40 percent of Japan's computer market, saw its share slip to less than 15 percent. By 1987 America's share of the world semiconductor market had shrunk to only 40 percent.[16] Meanwhile, during the 1980s, Japan claimed 36 percent of the world's computer market.[17] Many large American electronics companies, such as IBM, Apple Computer, National Semiconductor, and Seagate Technology, Inc., belatedly realized that they had overexpanded during the 1970s and 1980s and began to restructure themselves by cutting deeply into their workforces.

## EXPLAINING AMERICA'S FAILURES

As competition from Japan, South Korea, and Europe intensified in the early 1980s, the Reagan administration and Congress, seemingly unaware of the larger pattern of economic change, responded to the pressures caused by growing unemployment and sagging industrial productivity by borrowing money, thus laying the foundation of an enormous national debt. In 1981 U.S. indebtedness passed the $1 trillion mark for the first time in history. A decade later it had quadrupled.[18] New phrases—"the Pacific Rim," "the Tokyo stock market," "the European Community"—suddenly came into use, but few grasped how revolutionary the changes really were. Some blamed the economic downturn on the multinationals—runaway companies, which, they claimed, were moving their operations overseas to exploit cheap labor. Others pointed the finger at the Japanese. A rash of new spy-thriller-*cum*-industrial-espionage books, complete with crafty Japanese agents, Swiss banks, and Iranian middlemen, appealed to those who thought the Japanese were simply stealing American trade secrets.[19]

Other less sinister explanations claimed that the Japanese were taking unfair advantage of American business through their *keiretsu*, industry groups with interlocking relationships among large manufacturers such as Mitsubishi, Toyota, and Nissan, their suppliers, and the Japanese banks. Some warned that Japanese investments were only the first step of a carefully orchestrated attempt to infiltrate and weaken the U.S. economy. Others, like corporate raider T. Boone Pickens, alleged that Japanese companies and their "transplants" had developed exclusionary relationships with Japanese suppliers that froze out potential American suppliers, complaints that led to federal investigation of trade practices.[20]

## THE NEW ECONOMIC ORDER

Though by the mid-1980s nearly everyone had felt the effects of the changes in the economy, few of us understood their root causes. Peter Drucker offered what was perhaps the first explanation about the rapid transformation that was reshaping the world's economy in a 1987 article that quietly appeared in *Foreign Affairs*.[21] According to Drucker, nations' productive capacities had become uncoupled from capital, which was sweeping independently and with lightning speed through international financial markets. Steady, linear industrial growth had been replaced by volatile, fast-moving change, now directed by the movement of capital. Around the same time, a flurry of state and federal reports appeared warning that American manufacturing was being eclipsed and our standard of living was being threatened. The 1990 *Economic Report of the President* noted that manufacturing's contribution to the U.S. GNP had dropped from 28 percent in 1947 to 19 percent in 1988.[22] A report by the Massachusetts Institute of Technology's Commission on Industrial Productivity confirmed that American productivity had been eroded markedly over the past decade. Slow economic growth and poor product quality had opened the doors to hungry international competitors, which had quickly gained a foothold in American markets. The commission noted that this was not a situation that could be fixed easily. The roots of the problem, the commission said, lay deep in organizations' inherent weaknesses and in individuals' attitudes and beliefs, both of which thwarted attempts to diffuse new ideas and manufacturing practices.[23]

Some were unconcerned, saying that the loss of manufacturing was simply a predictable step in America's evolution toward a service and information economy—a "postindustrial economy" as then-President Ronald Reagan called it.[24] This view, which was shared by Republicans and conservative Democrats alike, is consistent with an American belief that government should stay out of industrial policy, which is best regulated by markets and the hidden hand of supply and demand. However, as falling American wages and buying power have shown, depending on a "postindustrial" economy to restore the country's health is unwise. In fact, the demand for services and information *depends* in large part on the demand for manufacturing.[25] In other words, manufacturing is the locomotive that pulls much of the economy behind it. On its front end are the highly skilled researchers, scientists, engineers, and technicians who create products. In fact, it is companies that make things—manufacturers—that account for almost all research and development done in the United States.[26] It is manufacturing that creates millions of jobs for production workers, jobs that have become stepping-stones to America's middle class, as well as employment for manufacturing engineers and managers.

But these stepping-stones are now gravely threatened. Millions of blue- and white-collar workers—men and women who had assumed they would stay with their employers for the rest of their working lives—have found themselves out of work. Between 1979 and 1992 the *Fortune* 500 companies handed pink slips to 4.4 million employees.[27] The consequences of this restructuring are now being painfully realized. The disappearance of high-paying manufacturing jobs has helped create a gulf in earnings between what Labor Secretary Robert Reich calls the "fortunate fifth" (the 20 percent of Americans who are most highly educated and better employed) and the less fortunate lower four fifths. The numbers speak for themselves. Between 1979 and 1989 high-paying jobs in the goods-producing sector, which includes manufacturing, shrunk by nearly 10 percent. During the same years, low-paying jobs in service industries mushroomed by nearly 110 percent.[28] Real wages have fallen for workers of every level of education, except the most highly educated.[29] The effect has been to polarize society into "haves" and "have-nots" at a time when resources need to be poured into improving standards of living *for everyone*. Furthermore, disenfranchising a significant proportion of men and women from the American Dream is sure to have catastrophic consequences by creating growing levels of unemployment and poverty, which ultimately translate into higher levels of drug abuse and violent crime.

But a strong manufacturing sector has other effects than creating employment. Manufactured products that can be exported to foreign markets help maintain a balance of trade because exports of automobiles and television sets generate more income than do exports of oranges or apples. Manufacturing has another subtle but important impact: the creation of new technologies and products ensures a steady stream of economic opportunity. Consider how America's commanding lead in space exploration generated a vast array of new technologies—superconductors, fiber optics, and advanced lightweight materials—that are now in wide use in consumer products.

The financial impact of America's manufacturing losses is now being felt throughout society as counties, hospitals, and school districts go bankrupt and are forced into receivership. California, which had been hit perhaps harder than other states because of losses sustained by its huge manufacturing and defense bases, actually faced insolvency. In 1994 then–Assembly Ways and Means Committee Chairman John Vasconcellos warned that "California is on the verge of a breakdown—headed toward bankruptcy, and rapidly and perilously approaching a point of no return with respect to our future."[30]

Though the national economy has rebounded, its gains may prove to be more illusion than fact. The Competitive Policy Council—a blue-ribbon committee that advises the president and Congress—reports that, although the economy has been improving, government and household debt has continued to grow to record levels and the distribution of income between men and women who are fully employed and those who are not is getting worse.[31] It echoes Labor Secretary Reich's warning that the disparity in earnings and employment between the "fortunate fifth" and the rest of society is widening.

There can be little doubt that turbulence in the world economy will only continue. And as more and more countries develop new technologies to copy products invented elsewhere, the speed of change is sure to increase. In his book *Head to Head*, Lester Thurow explained how, throughout the 1960s, the United States' dominance in manufacturing made it impossible for Japanese and German companies to compete by inventing and making products. Instead, they were forced to develop new production processes, investing twice as much as Americans in process R&D. As Thurow says, "The moral of the story is clear. Those who can make a product cheaper can take it away from the inventor."[32]

Not everyone agrees with Thurow. Paul Krugman, a Stanford economist, thinks that America's manufacturing slowdown is due to domestic problems rather than to international competition.[33] He maintains that people are buying relatively fewer and less expensive manufactured goods. Manufacturing jobs are being lost, he says, because employers are replacing workers with machines and using the workers they keep more efficiently. Wages are stagnating because economic growth has slowed.

Regardless of which side one takes in the debate, almost everyone who has studied the issue concludes that if our economic productivity is to be restored, companies will have to learn to change quickly to take advantage of shifting circumstances. They will have to depend on a solid core of employees who have learned to work together cooperatively under pressure. That sort of change, however, will take a cultural shift of massive proportions. Old beliefs, developed through years of adversarial labor-management relationships, will have to go. They will have to be replaced by a new covenant—one that says "We are in this together."

Some executives scoff at the idea that anything has to change, pointing to figures that show that the economy has finally turned the corner and is coming back. Indeed, production of goods and services surged by 7 percent in the last quarter of 1993, the strongest performance in a decade, while capital investments grew by 47 percent between 1992 and 1995.[34] Companies are restructuring themselves at a rapid rate, slashing payroll costs and adopting new "lean production" methods so they can produce more with less.

## THE HIGH COST OF RESTRUCTURING

But despite the good news, the current restructuring and cost-cutting have a darker side. According to *Fortune*, and a recent series of articles in *The New York Times*, any sense of security that companies may once have offered their employees is quickly becoming a thing of the past.[35] A growing number of companies report that they can no longer afford to offer their employees any hope of lifetime employment. Moreover, some executives regard such belt-tightening as long overdue, claiming that their employees have come to regard job security as an entitlement that only encourages them to resist change. This "new deal" insists that job security is history and that employees' best hope lies in making sure they continue to add value to their employer. In return, they can expect broad new freedoms to set their own hours and create their own working conditions. But the safety net that so many employees once took for granted would be gone. In its place would be a new philosophy that everyone is responsible for his or her own career. *Fortune* acknowledges that few managers realize how debilitating this new agreement would really be, but the fact of the matter is that the hopes American workers may have had about trading loyalty to their employers for security are "virtually dead."

If *Fortune* is right, this new arrangement is revealed as somewhat of a hollow bargain, at least for most employees. One of the clearest indicators of this is the more than seven thousand temporary employment agencies that act as intermediaries between temporary workers and employers, who are hiring permanent employees only cautiously. Stanford management professor Jeffrey Pfeffer reports that the temporary employment industry outgrew the U.S. GNP by nearly two to one between 1970 and 1984.[36] Manpower, the biggest of the agencies that supply temporary help, has grown at a phenomenal rate, adding 80,000 temporary employees to its payroll in 1993 alone and boosting its U.S. payroll to 640,000 temporary employees.[37] The very presence of this booming industry makes it abundantly clear to workers that they are now entirely on their own.

Lest there be any doubt about this new arrangement, Congress's refusal to grant unions more power made it abundantly clear. In July 1994 it rejected legislation that would have strengthened unions by prohibiting companies from firing striking workers and replacing them with nonunion workers. This further reflected the growing support for a Horatio Alger–like philosophy to govern the American workplace, where luck, pluck, and personal responsibility define the winners. Unfortunately, this point of view is a formula for economic disaster.

Instead of this hypercompetetive individualism, we should be looking toward a more positive scenario. Five years of hands-on research inside some of America's most critical industries—aircraft, steel, electronics, and autos—has convinced me that the winning combination lies in a new alliance between employers and their workers, an alliance based on mutual self-interest, fairness, interdependence, and trust. By "trust" I do not mean a naïve or blind faith that managers will look out for their employees or vice versa. Rather, I mean the development of a mutual confidence and respect that reflects the new reality that neither side can go it alone. Put another way, I am not primarily moved by a humanitarian impulse, although my viewpoint is humanitarian. Quite simply, such change is a matter of economic survival. To weather the uncertain and rapidly changing conditions that will surely characterize economic life in the future, American companies must learn to adapt.

But the transition will be no Garden of Eden. For employees to give their utmost so that their companies can become responsive and nimble, they must be assured that everyone is in the same boat—executives and employees alike. By the same token, executives must recognize that without the hard work and commitment of their employees, a company cannot prosper. Thus, companies that will have the advantage in the turbulent times ahead are those whose executives, union leaders, and workers recognize that they are bound at the hip in the race to survive and prosper. If one partner fails, the entire enterprise will fail.

Companies that currently practice these principles in the United States often run into problems. As employees learn to share responsibility for a company's survival and to work smarter by eliminating wasted effort, they also learn that they can work themselves out of their jobs. This is not the basis of successful long-term policy. To remain loyal to a company, employees must feel secure. Security, however, can take many forms. At its extreme, security can mean guaranteed lifetime employment, a policy that few corporations can carry through in today's environment. But security can also flow from a dynamic environment in which employees feel they have a say in decisions that affect them and in which they share fairly in the fruits of their labor and their company's continuing success.

Companies that want to be successful have to learn that to foster such interdependence and to unlock their employees' full potential, they must integrate the productive work of the organization into manageable systems that *employees can control*. Total quality management (TQM), Toyota's "lean production" system, and sociotechnical systems (STS) work design are examples of how companies can weave interdependence into the fabric of the enterprise by starting with the customer and then systematically working back to each supporting operation. But implementing a new system is not easy. A company may falter because its executives fail to recognize that changing one part and failing to make corresponding changes in others is to invite failure. Also, executives may overlook the resistant power of an organization's culture and assume that change can simply be driven from the top down.[38]

Companies that learn how to create this new pact between management and workers will be harder to manage because they are dynamic and thus less predictable. In truth, conflict becomes the rule once employees taste decision-making power and unions take on roles that were once reserved for management. How conflict is managed between these divergent interests is of crucial importance. Conflict that degenerates into hostility or lies submerged beneath the surface saps an organization's energies. On the other hand, conflict that is well managed is healthy. Not only does creative conflict resolve issues quickly and openly, it also produces a mutual confidence that is an indispensable resource of any organization. This form of trust acts like a shock absorber, enabling diverse opinions to be considered and drawn together for the larger good.

I am convinced that companies that are able to restructure themselves at this deepest level will have the competitive edge. Energies that in the past were poured into conflict and strife will instead be channeled into productive work. As companies prosper, so will the men and women who make them run and who share in the fruits of their labor.

There is a counterargument—that success will go to lean and mean companies that run off the labors of nomadic workers and managers. This argument is gravely flawed. Its key assumption is that the kind of knowledge now required can be stored up and easily transferred through waves of short-term employees. But the knowledge required to prosper in today's environment runs far deeper than mere skills, and it permeates an organization from its top to its bottom. The abilities to work interdependently, to sublimate one's ego for a larger good, to value and trust others' opinions, and to take risks are not learned easily. They develop as the result of successfully working with others under pressure and are resources of immeasurable value.

This book provides a window into the makings of this new culture in four emblematic companies: Douglas Aircraft, a subsidiary of McDonnell Douglas; USS-POSCO, a joint venture between USX and the South Korean steelmaker POSCO; Hewlett-Packard; and New United Motor Manufacturing, Inc. (NUMMI), a joint venture between General Motors and Toyota. Most accounts of America's economic decline have been refracted through the lens of macroeconomics—a tool that is particularly useful for describing broad patterns but whose value is limited in the subjective or qualitative arena of human affairs. By portraying human behavior in its natural setting, from the shop floor to the executive suites to which we enjoyed unprecedented access, this study offers an insider's view of these companies and their employees, captured in the midst of transformation. By revealing how men and women cope with the pressures of the changing world in their day-to-day lives, we can better understand the problems and rewards in the new American economic order. We can also understand how the forces that are re-forming the industrial sector can be harnessed to reclaim education and help steer America into the twenty-first century as a world leader rather than as a second-rate power.

## THE MYSTERIOUS WORLD OF INDUSTRIAL AMERICA

When I first became a professor nearly twenty years ago, I realized that the hardest part of teaching was to get a student to ask a question. Only then, it seemed, could education really begin. The more I studied education, the more convinced I became that schools were failing in this most essential task. Instead of provoking students to ask "Why?," most schools simply push information at them just as industrial mass production companies mindlessly push products down assembly lines. My research led me away from mainstream education to institutions that lie on the margins of society—private vocational schools and work-study programs—where the lack of formality and resources seems to help teachers engage students more creatively. In these institutions I rediscovered a principle I had learned from my own education—that individuals ask the best questions when they really want to know something. Over the next decade I published a number of books and articles on education and training that immediately became controversial because they revealed that some of the best educational practices are found outside of the formal educational system.[39] In the 1980s I was drawn to job training, where I discovered that it, like education, had turned inward and become largely disconnected from larger social needs. The lesson was clear: education and training were in serious need of revitalization, but what was needed even more immediately were more good jobs and increased public revenue. But by the early 1980s millions of manufacturing jobs began to vanish as public revenue dwindled. Few academics or policy makers fully grasped the enormity of the wrenching economic transformation that had begun and the implications it would have for America.

I wanted to know how companies and unions were being reshaped by economic forces and what it meant for our survival. I also wanted to find out how education and training were being affected and ultimately what the implications for public policy would be. I knew that doing another survey based on questionnaires was not the answer, because we didn't even know the questions to ask. The world was changing too quickly, and what was called for was a fresh, unorthodox kind of study. I knew it could certainly not be done from my comfortable university office. In 1988 I found a few colleagues and four graduate students who were equally fascinated with what was happening. A year later we had rounded up a small amount of seed money from the California Senate, and we set off to discover this new industrial world for ourselves. There were no theories to guide us since we were literally witnessing the unfolding of a brand-new era, so we would have to rely on our own observations.

The only way to gain such a firsthand view was to work at close range like industrial anthropologists. So, armed with notepads, hard hats, steel-toed boots, and employee badges, we went to work inside these four big manufacturing companies, which were in the throes of change. Over the next five years we helped build aircraft at Douglas and worked in the steel and tin mills at USS-POSCO. We worked at a Hewlett-Packard division that designs and builds sophisticated electronic instruments, and we built Geo Prizms and Toyota Corollas at NUMMI. We sat in on all kinds of meetings and grievance hearings, where we observed not only what people said but what they did. We listened to the stories workers and managers told while we asked an endless stream of questions. We tried not to take sides or to judge but to remain open to all points of view, while writing thousands of pages of field notes. In time we came to be trusted. As it turned out, the personal relationships we built over the years proved to be of immense value: not only were they pleasurable, they also opened doors to information rarely revealed by studies of this kind. This vantage point as insiders treated us to a special view of this new chapter in America's history as it was being written.

As we examined these companies, we glimpsed the unmistakable remnants of an old American industrial culture—an amalgam of beliefs and behavior—that at one time had steered industry toward immense power and wealth but that today finds itself estranged from a rapidly changing world. At the same time, we uncovered evidence that a new industrial culture is struggling to be born—one that recognizes that without new and interdependent bonds between worker and manager, we will suffer. This book is about the painful birth of this new culture and why the old one is so resistant to change. It is an intimate view of these four companies that reveals what they have done to rid themselves of the burdens of the past and begin to create a new future.

Douglas Aircraft's is a story that reveals what can happen when a large, mature organization tries to transform itself in the midst of crisis. This huge aircraft builder appears to have managed to recover just in time to embark on a more successful long-term strategy. The case of USS-POSCO shows how an infusion of South Korean cash and technology was blended with American grit to begin a painful transformation that saved a failing U.S. steel mill. But its achievements have come at a high cost, because the company remains hobbled by century-old antagonistic labor-management relations that are changing very slowly. Hewlett-Packard's story is from the leading edge of international electronics, where the rate of change is dizzying. To restore profitability to one of its oldest divisions, HP redesigned it from top to bottom to foster flexibility and teamwork. The redesign freed the division from its old organization and culture and helped point it toward new growth opportunities in telecommunications. NUMMI's is a story of how General Motors, Toyota, and the United Automobile Workers of America (UAW) together transformed one of GM's worst assembly plants into a world-class auto-manufacturing facility. In turn, NUMMI created a new culture that takes the best from both its American and Japanese parents.

This book is about these four companies as they navigate their way out of the old world into the new. It is an account of individuals and organizations compelled to change by the forces unleashed by economic pressures almost beyond their ability to control. It is about what people do—and don't do—when change is demanded of them and how a new bond between managers and workers is being formed. It also points to the future by drawing out lessons from which policy makers, business and labor leaders, and educators can begin to redesign American education to produce the human qualities that will most assuredly be needed. It is an encouraging view—one that is informed by the voices of the men and women who are creating a new template for America's future.

# CHAPTER TWO

# THE CULTURE OF MASS PRODUCTION

A CENTURY AGO, mass production—a wondrous arrangement of men and machines that enabled the production of vast quantities of goods at low cost—led America out of nineteenth-century craftwork into a new era of boundless prosperity. Mass production became the gospel of the twentieth century and efficiency its creed, and no one saw it coming better than Henry Ford. Ford carried this new religion to dizzying heights, constructing a production system the likes of which the world had never seen. He drew together iron ore and coal mines, ships, railroads, and assembly plants into a single operation that could turn a lump of iron ore into a car in just eighty-one hours. Ford declared, "If you shoveled a building full of dollars, you would not have the same capacity for production and use as you would have if you filled that same building with machinery and an organization of human skill."[1]

The wealth-producing capacity of companies like Ford—and of Du Pont, Firestone, Carnegie, and Swift, to name but a few—was truly awesome. But mass production would also lay the foundations for a powerful middle class. The more men worked and the more they earned, the more they would consume. This was the road, many thought, to economic freedom. But mass production also needed an industrial culture to support it, a corresponding system of human relationships and beliefs that would justify the division and specialization of labor. It would have to provide a rationale for why managers should be entitled to direct workers in the tiniest details of how they did their jobs. It would have to provide a corresponding rationale for why workers should submit to management's authority.

The system of behavior and beliefs that began to emerge in the early twentieth century was the human side of mass production. It was well adapted to the demands of rapid industrial expansion, and it propelled American industry to the pinnacle of success and world domination. Yet, as we will see, seeds of discord were sown by its very structure. The same beliefs that led America to world leadership etched a deep and angry divide between managers and workers. Though these beliefs would basically be ignored for nearly a century, they would cripple American industry in the 1980s.

## THE PRINCIPLES OF MASS PRODUCTION

Mass production had a long, fitful birth. French and English water-powered silk and spinning mills first used assembly-line techniques, which are basic to mass production, in the eighteenth century. But the ideas failed to spread because of opposition by powerful guilds and a strong tradition of craftwork.[2] It would take the insatiable demands of an expanding post–Revolutionary War America to bring it fully to life. Here was a country that had a seemingly unlimited demand for food, housing, and transportation but lacked the industrial infrastructure to supply them. The conditions called for something new.

It may have been Oliver Evans, a miller on a creek outside Philadelphia, who in 1780 developed the first true American assembly line.[3] Evans's mill substituted machines for human hands in funneling grain through a series of continuous operations during which it was ground into flour, packed into bags, and shipped to customers. Later, in the 1860s, inventor Linus Yale, whose name still appears stamped into the steel of modern locks, devised a mass production system for assembling locks for bank vaults. As America continued to expand, mass production techniques slowly caught on. The modern American assembly line, which evolved from these nascent techniques, had its origins in the great meat-packing houses of the Midwest.[4] Machines had been invented to butcher hogs, but none of them worked particularly well because of the animals' irregular shape.[5] What evolved was the next best thing: a continuous over-head conveyor that saved precious time by speeding hanging hog car-casses past rows of standing workers.

While the division and specialization of labor had improved the as-sembly process, most work was still done by hand and was slow and ex-pensive. What was needed to truly launch mass production was a means of mechanizing the assembly process, and the key to mechanization lay in the use of identical and interchangeable parts to build identical products. Until about 1830 parts had been made individually by craftsmen, as had each finished product. By the 1830s the development of industrial dies made it possible to stamp out identical parts — saw teeth, gun parts, gears for clocks, parts for reapers and threshers, and whatever else was needed — and continuous assembly started to become a reality.[6]

Still one question remained: How could workers' body movements be precisely controlled so they could work in concert with their machines? The answer came from Frank Gilbreth, a production engineer. In 1909, with his psychologist wife, Lillian, Gilbreth began to figure out how to vi-sualize hand movements in the tiniest detail. By photographing the hand movements of girls folding handkerchiefs and men swinging rapiers, Gilbreth learned to represent hand movements precisely in time and space.[7] His discovery of how to visualize human movement was a giant step toward the total control of mass production. It was now only a matter of time before industrial engineers would be able to program workers' hand and body movements uniformly to eliminate waste and reduce fa-tigue.

By now a growing number of social critics began to forcefully express reservations about mass production. Karl Marx correctly foresaw the dan-ger of specialization and control. In *Das Kapital*, he cautioned, "If [such a division of labor] develops a one-sided specialty into a perfection at the expense of the whole of a man's working capacity, it also begins to make a specialty of the absence of all development."[8] Marx believed that man's ability to conceptualize set him apart from animals, who work on instinct. He wrote, "What distinguishes the worst architect from the best of bees is this, that the architect raises his structure in imagination before he erects it in reality. At the end of every labor-process, we get a result that already existed in the imagination of the labourer at its commencement. He not only effects a change of form in the material on which he works, but he also realises a purpose of his own that gives the law to his *modus operandi*, and to which he must subordinate his will."9 Other social theorists, including Friedrich Engels, Thorstein Veblen, and John Dewey, also decried the idea. To them, work was more than simply tending a machine or doing repetitive assembly jobs: it was a reflection of man's marvelous inner capacity for imagination and thought. Mechanizing work would ultimately strip people of their human quality.10 However, even if industrialists read Marx, Engels, Veblen, and Dewey, they remained indifferent to their warnings. Nothing could hold back the advance of mass production.

## FREDERICK W. TAYLOR AND SCIENTIFIC MANAGEMENT

Frederick Taylor was born in 1856, and by the 1880s he had become a shop foreman at Philadelphia's Midvale Steel Company, where he laid the foundations of a new and revolutionary science of management.11 Taylor's discovery that steam hammers ran with optimal efficiency just before they snapped convinced him that systems usually ran best under stress, a conviction further supported by his observations of cutting tools, which cut most sharply when they were red hot—just before they melted.12 These were principles he would extend to attempts to stretch human capacities.

Taylor appeared at precisely the right time in America's economic development. In the first decades of the twentieth century, the competition to supply steel, agricultural implements, lumber, rope, wire, and other industrial products was intense. Companies had no choice but to cut costs and expand production in order to achieve economies of scale. Industrial workers, hired from waves of Irish and eastern European immigrants, had to be directed and programmed for high-speed production. The continuous assembly line became the new master. Although Taylor believed that work should be done easily and without fatigue, it would soon become clear that high levels of mass production could not be achieved without transforming the human worker into a mechanism.

Taylor was convinced that labor would have to be specialized and organized around continuous processes if industry were to advance. It would take a militarylike organization to control such operations. Orders would flow from the top down, from superior to subordinate, from department to subunit. The planning of work would have to be segregated from its execution. In this way, workers would become extensions of their machines. He felt that workers should be paid precisely what they were worth, or they would become shiftless and extravagant; if they realized they could earn more by working harder, he claimed, they would produce more.

Taylor's convictions rested on a powerful American belief, popularized in the late nineteenth century by the prolific popular writer Horatio Alger, that determination, luck, and courage were what it took to get ahead.[13] "First-class" workmen, said Taylor, would be able to move up the job ladder while new immigrants filled in behind them. His vision was confirmed by what he saw happening around him. He wrote, "The type of man who was formerly a day laborer and digging dirt is now for instance making shoes in a shoe factory. The dirt handling is done by the Italians or Hungarians."[14]

## THE UNDERSIDE OF AMERICA'S INDUSTRIAL CULTURE

Thus mass production and its supporting belief system were born. Guided by the principles of scientific management and the fact that it was a more efficient and productive system, mass production became the means by which American industry grew and prospered. But the complex of beliefs that supported mass production included assumptions about human motivation that would ultimately prove to be the system's very undoing.

As political ideology and fundamental beliefs about human development became inextricably interwoven, the great divide between management and labor became defined even more starkly. Practical industrialists like the conservative Ford believed that mass production truly freed men from the stultifying world of handwork. Only brains and ambition would limit how far a man could rise in this newly industrialized nation. But trade unionists and social activists dissented, claiming that mass production stripped workers of their humanity. In their view, it was only the industrialists and the new class of professional managers who benefited from the labor of the working man. "Industrial democracy"—a twentieth-century term that involved extending civil and political rights into the workplace—further polarized labor and management because managers regarded attempts by unions to foster worker participation as little more than thinly veiled plots to control the workplace.[15]

Perhaps the inadequacies of the system were clear from the very beginning. Even before Taylor developed the concepts of scientific management, the great strikes of the 1890s had crippled coal mines, railroads, and steel mills—a forewarning that the mass production system and the adversarial human relationships it created might one day become unworkable. Nowhere could its debilitating effects be better seen than at the Homestead Works, a steel mill that lay along the south bank of Pennsylvania's Monongahela River. The mill had been bought by Andrew Carnegie in 1883, and his cash and technology had established Homestead as a beacon of America's prospering steel industry. But Carnegie did not want to share the mill's wealth with its workers. He firmly believed that they were already getting more than their fair share of profits—and, after all, it was *his* money that had purchased the new open hearths and automated rolling machines. Furthermore, these brand-new technologies allowed an unskilled man to rise up to the level of an accomplished melter in just a few weeks.[16] Carnegie was convinced that the workingman already got plenty in return for his labor.

Even though the steelworkers' union, the Amalgamated Association, claimed only about 800 of Homestead's 3,800 workers as members, it broke with Carnegie over wages and equipment-manning levels. In July 1892 the union decided to strike. Undaunted and secure in his own beliefs, Carnegie hired 300 private detectives from the Pinkerton Agency to seize the mill from the armed and angry workers who had taken it over. This was, in fact, the chance Carnegie had been waiting for to rid his company of the union once and for all. The small army of Pinkerton guards sailed silently down the Monongahela River toward the mill in the dead of night. But the workers had already learned about Carnegie's plan, and they were waiting. As the Pinkerton captain stepped off the barge onto the gangplank, two shots rang out and he fell back into the arms of his men. The Pinkertons did not hesitate to respond. As the New York Herald reported, "A row of rifles gleamed an instant from the side of the shoreward vessel and in an instant more a sheet of flame ran all along her clumsy hulk from stem to stern."[17] A full-scale battle that broke out between the Homestead workers and the Pinkerton guards raged for an entire day. Finally, the Pinkertons surrendered. They were marched from their barges and forced to run a gauntlet between rows of men, women, and children who beat and spat on them. By the time the Pennsylvania militia finally arrived on the scene and restored law and order, twelve men were dead.

In the end Carnegie won, but it was a mixed victory. On the one hand, the state militia kept the strikers off the streets, enabling the company to resume production with nonunion workers. But on the other, Homestead would become not only a symbol of industrial injustice but a touchstone that would unite trade unionists against management for the next hundred years.

The Homestead conflict was repeated many times over in America's industrial history. No industry was immune. The auto industry frequently saw management and labor pitted against each other. John Allard, a veteran UAW member who had helped organize the aircraft industry before going to work for UAW president Walter Reuther, once described to me the conditions at Chrysler's huge plant just south of Los Angeles in 1936.[18] Allard, who was then a strapping twenty-one-year-old, had just moved west from his native Kansas, where drought had destroyed the family farm and the bank had taken what was left. Working at Chrysler was rough. "When I first signed on, I didn't think about the union one way or another," Allard said. "But then I saw the guys I worked with having to take a licking just like my mom and dad, who had worked hard all of their lives. So when these old boys from Detroit started talking to me about a union to protect ourselves and gain some respect, I was all ears." Allard described how ideological divisions had further widened the rift between management and labor. He had begun by working on a "bull gang," moving parts from the railroad cars into the plant. He recalled, "Before we organized, we were completely at the mercy of management, and they did some unmerciful things to us. They were the bosses. But after we organized, we began to feel that we owned the place and our union's membership was big enough to take it. There were just two distinct forces—management and the union. The only rules of the game was 'No holds barred!' "

The idea that workers had simply to be told what to do became the norm for managers, and the notion of sharing decision making with them was unthinkable. Courses offered through new university-connected business schools, the American Management Association, and the Young Men's Christian Association (YMCA) rationalized these beliefs as they taught generations of future managers how to give orders, how to standardize work and conduct time-and-motion studies, and how to motivate workers to produce more.[19] They were also taught how to defeat unionization and how to break strikes when necessary. Foremen were the front line in the battle since they were closest to the workers, and they were taught how to head off unions.[20]

The real teaching, however, was done on the shop floor, where seasoned veteran managers instructed trainee managers how to behave. They were taught to stick together and to remain aloof from their crews, fearful that any personal relationships with the workers might compromise their authority.[21] Workers were also socialized, but into a blue-collar culture that sustained the beliefs that companies were exploitative and bosses couldn't be trusted. All a company wanted, they believed, was a workman's strong back. The autocratic style of management that had naturally evolved from the mass production system reinforced the stereotypes on both sides. In time these adversarial relationships would form the cornerstones of America's industrial culture.

"We fought with companies like cats and dogs," recalled Art Mullett, a former steelworker and organizer.[22] "It was open war. We would hold organizing meetings on the hillsides at night, because people would be scared to be seen with us. We'd have to meet undercover, because if you went to people's houses, someone would snitch on them. The next thing you knew they'd have a watch put on them. All of the big companies had company spies—those Pinkerton guys the steel and automobile companies hired. They'd chase down our union leaders at night. When they caught them, they'd lay them down in the street and stretch their legs up over the curb and jump on them to break them. Then they'd beat them half to death. The violence was terrible."

## THE DEEPENING DIVIDE

With the onset of the Great Depression, more and more political leaders concluded that it was critical to direct energies into productive work and to reach a more cooperative accord between management and labor. The National Labor Relations Act, also known as the Wagner Act, which was passed in 1935, gave workers and their unions the right to organize. It also improved working conditions and wages, but it did nothing to establish even a modicum of trust between management and labor. Instead, the act merely shifted the battleground to the question of who was in control. Collective bargaining finally gave unions the tool with which to achieve a balance of power with management, but it also replaced human relationships—bad as they may have been—with contractual ones, exchanging one ill for another. The very law that had sought to find a productive balance between labor and management now formalized the adversarial relationship between the two warring sides.

If adversarial collective bargaining failed to divide the interests of management and labor completely, the rigid job classifications of the Wagner Act did the rest. They spelled out in tiny detail precisely what workers could and could not do. Job classifications were used by both companies and unions for their own ends, for reasons that frequently had little to do with productivity or safety. "In the early days the steel companies had *fifty-five thousand* different classifications!" Mullett said. "They used them to control the plant. Let's say you was an oiler and I liked you. I'd give you a special rate because you'd report to me what was going on in the plant. I'd figure, 'Well, hell, he's a great guy. I'll give him an extra fifty cents an hour to keep me informed.' So you'd get a special classification. At bargaining time we'd agree to cut the classifications way down, but we'd get the company to agree to higher pay rates in exchange. This was the entire deal in negotiations. Maybe we didn't win in the wage bargaining, but we'd get more money for our members in other ways. We got what we wanted one way or another!" Pay systems were negotiated in much the same way, in such tiny and complex detail that they could be interpreted only by specialized lawyers retained by both sides. So it went for sixty years, as each new labor contract heaped layers of regulations onto an already inflexible system of production.

Thus, even with federal intervention and the recognition of the trade-union movement, the great divide between management and labor widened. Although the Second World War temporarily united management and labor in a common goal, the truce necessary to keep up with war production schedules was short-lived. When the war ended in 1945, the old wounds broke wide open as waves of industrywide strikes swept the nation. In fact, that year companies were shut down by strikes 4,750 times, losing 38,000 workdays.[23] Ford, Chrysler, General Motors, U.S. Steel, and other big manufacturers were all embroiled in continual conflict with their unions over wages and working conditions.

That same year, a young man named Marvin Brody was mustered out of the navy and went to work for Ford's Maywood plant, where, a few years later, he was elected president of the UAW local—of which he would remain a member for the next five decades. Today, though he is officially retired from the union, Brody works equally long hours as a lobbyist for NUMMI, representing the company's interests in Sacramento. We met one day in the UAW hall, across the street from NUMMI, in Fremont, California.[24] He described to me how the postwar years had marked a watershed when workingmen and -women became even more deeply alienated from their employers. "The direction of the trade-union movement after the war had nothing to do with the product. It sold itself in the marketplace. Ford had no competition other than GM and Chrysler, and no one cared! We played hell with management, organizing on the job, stopping work just to show them who was really in control. We'd strike the company over anything, just to show them how militant we were. Christ, once we struck over coveralls—coveralls, can you believe it?" Strikes over such frivolous issues were common, and they had nothing to do with product quality or making cars. In fact, questions of product quality never surfaced. The strikes were simply about power, about who was going to run the union to keep management in line.

Brody threw himself into organizing at Ford and was promptly fired. "Even though I was seen as left wing, the union wasn't going to tolerate it," he recalled. "You know, you just don't allow the company to screw around with organizers, no matter what their ideology." But in the end Brody couldn't maintain his position within the union. Ford had bused in enough retirees opposed to Brody to cost him the election. Adding insult to injury, the company put him back to work on the assembly line. "I'd been off the line for a number of years now," Brody remembered. "I'd enjoyed all this freedom to move around, doing the work I wanted to do. But now they put me on the lousy jobs on the line. I mean the lousy jobs! Working overhead, bolting on those heavy bumpers. Well, management loved it, you know. And the guys from my caucus would come around

and laugh at me." Brody took it for a few weeks and then met with the industrial relations manager. "Okay," I told him, "you've had your fun. I've
given you a bad time, and you've given me a bad time. That's enough. I
want you to know that two years from now I'm going to run again [for
the presidency of the local] and I'm going to win. I'd suggest that you'd
be wiser to get off my back now and treat me like an ordinary worker."
The manager took the advice and put him back to work in his classification. Two years later, Brody won the presidency. Later that year, the company and the union negotiated a new contract and reached agreement
easily.

However, in a surprise move, Brody pulled the local out on strike in
retaliation for the company's having meddled in the election two years
earlier. "We had a contract, and everybody was happy to go. It was like vacation. We set up picket lines, and everyone had their time on the line and
then they could go home or go fishing. We went to the motel across the
street and played poker and watched. They kept asking us to come back to
the table, but we took a four-week vacation. It cost the company millions."
By the fourth week, Brody felt he'd made his point. He agreed to go back
to the negotiating table. He remembered sitting across from the manager
who had been responsible for busing in the retirees two years before. "I
told the jerk, 'Okay, we're coming back to work, but don't you ever fuck
with me again!' " Brody sat back and whistled through his teeth, remem-
bering. "It was fun. It didn't hurt the workers, and the company passed on
the cost to the consumer, who was hungry for the product."

## A GROWING INDUSTRIAL WEAKNESS

Though it was not obvious on the shop floor that something was wrong, a
weakness was growing deep within American industry. Across the country,
productivity began to sag as workers became increasingly alienated from
their specialized, mind-deadening jobs. In response, management simply
tightened control, setting off new cycles of conflict.

There was no reason for industry leaders to wait to be told by the
South Koreans or the Japanese that the angry division between American
workers and managers was inherently unhealthy. Social scientists such as
Harvard's Elton Mayo and MIT's Kurt Lewin had been writing about it for

thirty years. Since the 1920s study after study had shown that both managers and workers wanted control over their own destinies, to be treated
fairly, and to participate in decisions that affected them.[25] For instance,
Lewin's famous study of small groups revealed that work groups following
democratic principles outperformed those that were run autocratically. In
the autocratic groups (which mirrored contemporary industrial practice)
members argued with one another and tried to find scapegoats to blame,
while in the democratic groups members worked cooperatively.[26] Later, in
1943, Mayo studied the airframe industry in southern California and
found that, despite the antagonism between management and workers,
conditions that would foster teamwork could be established. Mayo documented such teamwork, or "spontaneous cooperation" as he called it, as
managers and workmen transcended conflict and focused their energies
on the common good.[27] Though industrial leaders remained blind to it,
the evidence was compelling that workers wanted more than just a job
and a paycheck. Abraham Maslow, founder of the human potential movement, was convinced that developing the capacity for trust, openness, risk
taking, joy, and empathy were essential human qualities, without which
humans would surely atrophy.[28] His insights encouraged others to look for
ways to restore meaning to factory jobs.[29] Frederick Herzberg, a noted job
satisfaction expert, echoed Maslow, saying that workers wanted "growing
room" in their jobs and that a paycheck and fair treatment were not
enough. All money and fair treatment could do was to prevent *dissatisfac-
tion* on the job.[30]

In 1960 MIT professor Douglas McGregor went a step further, developing a new management theory that started with the assumption that
workers were eager to work and that they wanted to develop themselves to
levels never envisioned by Frederick Taylor.[31] McGregor was convinced
that by using traditional forms of management and rewards (a style he
called "Theory X"), employers were tapping only a fraction of their employees' talent. He formulated a set of management principles to foster cooperation and individual growth on the job (called "Theory Y").
McGregor believed that workers could become self-managing, making
external direction and control unnecessary. But even though landmark
studies like those done by Mayo, Lewin, Maslow, Herzberg, and McGregor forcefully contradicted the belief that workers naturally shirked hard

work and avoided responsibility, the antagonistic beliefs that supported mass production were already etched too deeply in the psyches of industrial leaders and managers for any real change to occur.

By the beginning of the 1970s it should have been clear to America's industrial leaders that something was seriously wrong. The evidence was overwhelming that America's adversarial form of labor relations was fast becoming a liability. During the 1960s absenteeism at General Motors and Ford had doubled. In 1969 the quit rate at Ford was 25.2 percent.[32] At one Ford plant, the quit rate ran 8 percent each month, requiring the company to hire 4,800 new workers every year to maintain a workforce of 5,000.[33] A 1972 federal task force studied the roots of worker discontent and reported that they lay in the structure of work itself, which for many workers was routine and mind-deadening. The report validated research done earlier by Mayo, Lewin, Maslow, and others by showing that worker morale and productivity improved when workers were allowed to participate in decision making and their jobs were enlarged.[34]

But industry leaders were unmoved and pressed onward, installing robots and other advanced technologies to maintain levels of production in the face of growing worker discontent.[35] General Motors led by designing the most highly automated plant the world had ever seen. The plant opened in 1970 in Lordstown, Ohio, but, far from setting new standards for productivity, it became the symbol of everything that was wrong with American industry. Young workers, who wore long hair and bell-bottoms and questioned authority, were forced to keep up with an assembly line that ran twice as fast as average. The results were disastrous. Absenteeism and drug use soared. Workers sabotaged the plant, hiding spare parts inside closed compartments, where they would rattle but never be found. Others set fire to the assembly-line control panel to stop production. Autoworkers snapped off keys in the ignitions, put the cars into gear, and locked the doors, thus jamming up the assembly line. The more GM tried to bypass the workers with automation at Lordstown and other plants, the worse things became.[36]

Some union leaders now saw that the disastrous course that management had set could end only in a massive collision. UAW president Walter Reuther warned industrial leaders that they were creating a monster that was sure to completely alienate generations of young autoworkers. In an interview in *Fortune*, he said, "The prospect of tightening up bolts every two minutes for eight hours for thirty years doesn't lift the human spirit. The young worker feels he's not master of his own destiny. He's going to run away from it every time he gets a chance."[37]

## FUTILE REFORMS

In 1967 Irving Bluestone, a noted authority on labor-management relations, was an assistant to Walter Reuther. He pressed the UAW for action to relieve the mind-deadening routine of the assembly line. Bluestone told a convention of UAW officers, "The work place is not a penal colony; it must be stripped of its air of coercion and compulsion; imaginative new ways must be found to enable workers to participate democratically in decisions affecting the nature of their work."[38] But little changed.

As worker unrest continued, a variety of reforms was advanced, including labor-management participation teams (LMPTs) in the steel industry and quality of working life (QWL) initiatives in the auto industry. QWL, for instance, was based on the idea that cooperation between management and labor was favorable to conflict and that trust and mutual respect should replace antagonism.[39] But sharing authority with employees and substituting trust and mutual respect for caustic human relations flew in the face of the prevailing beliefs. When the idea of collaboration was first brought up, GM negotiators scoffed.[40] However, by 1973 GM had softened up, as its executives found themselves mired in conflict with unions in plants across the country. Nevertheless, because QWL represented such a radical break with the past, it was implemented slowly and failed to spread very widely.[41] Once again, GM's executives had missed an opportunity to find a common ground with the union on which a new relationship could have been established.

In truth, as long as the economic tide continued to rise, the growing illness within American industry could remain concealed. Because America's industry leaders' own wealth rose with the nation's prosperity, they were unable to comprehend that the problems were the fault of the mass production system itself. Instead of facing up to the root causes of growing worker alienation and worsening productivity and quality, management blamed the unions and workers. By 1990 the beliefs that separated management and labor had been gestating for a century and in a very real sense had become fundamental truths.

But in some other countries, progress was being made on restoring meaning to assembly-line jobs.[42] Much of it was based on work done years earlier by British social scientist Eric Trist and his coal-miner colleague Kenneth Bamforth. In 1949 Trist and Bamforth had stumbled onto the fact that English coal-mining companies and unions had discovered a superior system of self-managing teamwork that put decision-making power into the miners' hands and restored human relationships to the workplace.[43] Later, Trist and his Australian colleague Fred Emery refined the idea and developed a theory called "sociotechnical systems" (STS) theory, which aimed at optimizing the social and technological elements of the workplace.[44] STS had a large impact in Norway and Sweden, where the political environment was more conducive to extending democratic principles into the workplace than that of the United States was.[45] By the mid-1970s both Swedish companies (especially Volvo and Saab) and German companies recorded some success in enriching jobs by forming "quality circles"—voluntary work groups whose members took responsibility for figuring out ways to improve quality.[46]

Still, concepts such as STS and quality circles found their way into accepted use in America very slowly.[47] During the 1960s and 1970s several blue-chip companies such as General Motors, Bethlehem Steel, U.S. Steel, General Electric, Exxon, Alcoa, and AT&T launched some promising pilot projects, but they failed to take root. Harvard Business School's Richard Walton, who spent more than thirty years following the diffusion of such ideas, noted that even though many pilot innovations had produced improvements in productivity and morale, few had successfully been diffused into the industrial mainstream.[48] Just as the development of the assembly line had stalled in Europe three centuries earlier, the time for a complete overhaul of mass production and the adversarial relationships that were dividing worker from manager had not yet arrived.

Other ideas about how to reform the relationships between employees and managers were short-lived and failed to take root. For instance, electing union leaders to corporate boards—an idea aimed at giving unions a vote on strategic decisions—took hold for a while at some companies such as Chrysler, Eastern Airlines, and Weirton Steel. But the results were mixed (actually, both sides disdained the idea) because the union leaders were usually elected under stressful conditions at a time when the companies were facing bankruptcy and because American corporation law had no provisions for board members' acting as agents for the workers.[49] Employee stock ownership plans (ESOPs) were another attempt to broaden employee influence at the strategic level. Though ESOPs grew steadily over twenty years and were shown to result in somewhat higher productivity when the employee-owners truly participated in decision making, they were in fact terminated faster than they were formed.[50] Although such reforms were well intentioned, the reformers underestimated the resistant power of the existing order. But if American industrial and union leaders could not change the system, who could? Was there any hope?

## A NEW INDUSTRIAL CULTURE?

As we shall see in the chapters ahead, it would take a crisis of massive proportions to shake America's industrial and labor leaders out of their complacency. Japan's assault on America's once impenetrable auto industry in the 1980s provided just the precipitating event. By 1990 the Japanese economic invasion had finally jolted America's industrial and labor leaders into reality. What had become clear was that the Japanese had rediscovered the importance of satisfying customer demands for quality and that they had invented a radically different production system to achieve high quality and low cost, the likes of which the world had never seen. Called "lean production," the Japanese system contained many of the human elements missing from America's system of mass manufacturing.[51] Managers in Japanese plants relied on workers to make sound decisions, and they worked together in relative harmony, enabling Japanese companies to act with a singleness of purpose. The implication of Japan's achievements was inescapable: American industry would have to change.

Within a year, a rash of books on quality, teamwork, and reengineering the corporation flooded bookstores.[52] The principles fundamental to "lean production" became part of America's lexicon—"just in time," *kaizen, kanban,* and others swiftly came into popular use. With the door to change now wide open, would American industry finally respond?

Most of the evidence says "Yes." For the first time in history, companies and unions are beginning to take these ideas seriously.[53] A broad consensus appears to be growing that America's combative style of industrial relations can no longer be tolerated. In a new preface to their book on industrial relations, MIT's Tom Kochan and his colleagues write, "All of the evidence we have seen since 1986 reaffirms our conclusion that arm's-length collective bargaining, with its tightly written work rules and clear separation of the authority of management and the rights of workers, no longer meets America's economic needs. . . . We continue to believe that the U.S. industrial relations system is in a period of dynamic transformation."[54] Soon after President Clinton took office, these issues were thrust into what is fast becoming a national debate when the Commission on the Future of Worker-Management Relations was formed under the chairmanship of former U.S. Labor Secretary John Dunlop.[55] The commission spent twenty months taking testimony around the country, and in January 1995 it recommended that new ways be found to boost productivity through management-labor cooperation and employee participation and that a new legal framework be developed to guide labor-management relations.[56]

Thus far the evidence seems clear and compelling: mass production and the adversarial labor relations that evolved to support it have now become grave liabilities in today's fast-changing, unforgiving economy. Though new and more productive ways of organizing work are now emerging, their definitions so far remain unclear. By examining companies that have been forced to change, we have found clues to the future of mass production and its adversarial labor relations. We have also discovered important lessons that can be applied to redesigning American education.

A few words about the road map for the journey ahead: I have portrayed each company in a three-chapter case that allows the reader to draw comparisons, though each story has an integrity of its own. In the opening chapter, after a brief introduction, I take the reader into the company's history to witness the events that led to its crisis. In a second chapter, the obstacles the company faced are laid bare. The reader sees each story unfold from multiple viewpoints—through the eyes of production workers, managers, and union leaders. In a third chapter, the actions the company took to overcome them and their results are described. Finally, I discuss the conclusions that can be drawn from each company's story. Such is the layout for the company cases. In the book's final chapter, I propose an all-inclusive set of conclusions and discuss how the experiences of these companies and unions can be applied by others in similar circumstances. But, more important, I examine what the actions taken by these companies and unions portend for America's future.

This is a unique view into the heart of America's industrial engine. It is a strenuous journey—and a rewarding one. The blend of voices of men and women on the shop floor, in the union hall, and in the executive suite portray the way in which a new industrial culture is being forged. While each of the four stories stands on its own, the whole is greater than their sum. Together they have a cumulative impact that conveys a message of signal importance—the steps that must be taken to restore America's prosperity.

# PART II

# DOUGLAS AIRCRAFT

# CHAPTER THREE

# FROM BOOM TO BUST

OUR STORY BEGINS in Long Beach, California, on the sprawling site of Douglas Aircraft, a subsidiary of McDonnell Douglas, one of America's largest defense contractors. It is a story about how a once proud company—an American Thoroughbred—narrowly averted disaster. For decades workers had swarmed over aircraft frames with rivet guns, installing noses, tails, wings, engines, and thousands of component parts as they assembled some of the largest and most complex aircraft in the world. Each week shiny new aircraft emerged from the massive hangars in a steady stream and were wheeled out onto a runway, where they waited to be flown away by Douglas customers. By 1990 Douglas was one of the largest companies in California, employing more than 53,000 men and women. Just five years later, however, the company had fewer than 13,000 employees working in its immense hangars.

What happened? As we shall see, there is much to be learned from the story of Douglas Aircraft. It is a stark example of how many years of earlier success translated into a sense of complacency that caused managers to overlook the company's growing problems. It is also a dramatic illustration of how adversarial relationships between management and labor can

virtually paralyze an organization at the very moment when it desperately
needs to harness every resource to set a new and productive course.[1]

## DONALD DOUGLAS'S FOUNDING VISION

Failure was nowhere in the mind of Donald Douglas when he founded
his company in 1920. Just before going off to the U.S. Naval Academy in
the summer of 1908, Douglas had seen the Wright brothers fly at Fort
Myer, Virginia. It was love at first sight. Later, at the academy, he became
absorbed in designing gliders and models, using rubber bands to work out
lift and drag.[2] After three years at Annapolis, Douglas left the Naval Academy. He had decided that he didn't want to become a naval officer after
all—he wanted to design and build aircraft. He enrolled in the engineering school at MIT, after which he got a job with the pioneer Glenn L.
Martin aviation company in Cleveland, Ohio, where he rose quickly. By
the time he was twenty-eight, Douglas was a vice president and chief engineer.

But Douglas wanted to design and build his own airplanes, and his
work at Martin did not allow him to. So, on a gamble, he quit and moved
west to Los Angeles. There, Douglas and a new financial partner, David
Davis, formed the Davis-Douglas Company in the back of a barbershop.
They later moved to an abandoned movie studio on Wilshire Boulevard
in Santa Monica, where in 1920 Douglas designed and built his first plane,
dubbed the "Cloudster." The Cloudster was significant because it was the
first plane able to carry a load that weighed more than itself. The following year, Douglas designed a new torpedo bomber for the navy, which led
him to his first military contract. Three years later, he produced a modi-
fied version, the Douglas World Cruiser, which was the first plane capable of flying around the world. It was the beginning of a pattern the
company would follow successfully for years, deriving commercial applications from military designs. Douglas himself would soon become the
undisputed leader in aircraft design and construction, and his success
would fascinate other inventors and businessmen in this new market: by
1929 more than a hundred American firms with names like Autogiro, Edo,
Moth, and Birdwing were building aircraft, though only a handful survived for long.[3]

Mass production had not yet come to this fledgling industry, and while there was a division of labor between design engineers and mechanics, there were no interchangeable parts or assembly lines. Instead, these early airplanes were constructed entirely by hand. Designers and mechanics worked in teams, remaining with each new airplane from its first drawing to its maiden flight. Teamwork occurred naturally as designers and mechanics developed close working relationships around their common interests.[4] Harvard professor Elton Mayo, one of the first researchers to study the emerging airplane industry, noted how teamwork produced "spontaneous cooperation" between managers and workmen, aligning their efforts in a common endeavor.[5]

The small design and assembly plants also allowed frequent personal contact between mechanics on the shop floor and their legendary owner-designers. Donald Douglas and the other men whose aircraft companies bore their names (such as John Northrop and T. Claude Ryan) were heroic figures, and their employees bestowed godlike qualities on them. Not surprisingly, the relationships that formed between these larger-than-life men and their admiring workers often took on a paternalistic quality. That quality was one of the hallmarks of Douglas Aircraft's early culture. Douglas knew that his employees were the backbone of his company, and he consistently inspired and rewarded their loyalty and dedication. Once, when the company went through a four-month period without an order, Douglas absorbed the costs and kept the company's nearly six hundred engineers, managers, and workers employed doing gardening and maintenance to keep busy, rather than laying them off. Hearing from his banker-father that the banks might close in 1932, Douglas paid his employees in silver dollars to make sure they would not be hurt.[6] The company also had a Welfare Department whose policies were extraordinarily enlightened:

> If a worker is sick for longer than a day or two, Welfare sends a visiting nurse to see if the man is being adequately treated. If the man needs treatment, but cannot afford it, Welfare lends him the money. If the illness is protracted and the worker cannot keep up his insurance payments, Welfare pays them. If the man dies, Welfare helps his

widow, if possible tries to place her in the Douglas organization should she need work.[7]

Douglas's benevolence notwithstanding, he ran his company with a tight grip. Unions were anathema.

## THE SPECTER OF UNIONIZATION

While many of the employees appreciated Douglas's generosity, they also wanted more control over their own work and a larger share of the company's growing prosperity. Douglas did everything he could to keep these feelings—and, more specifically, the potential for unionization—at bay. In 1933 he sidestepped an organizing drive by the American Federation of Labor (AFL) by forming a company union that he himself controlled. However, once Congress passed the Wagner Act in 1935, the union movement took on new legitimacy. In 1937 a series of sit-down strikes swept the auto industry and spilled over into the budding aircraft industry as aircraft mechanics demanded wages equal to those paid to nearby autoworkers, who often produced the parts used in aircraft assembly. As John Allard, a soft-spoken UAW veteran who helped organize southern California's aircraft industry in the 1930s and 1940s, recalled, "Workers were getting twenty-five, thirty cents an hour more at Chrysler building parts for Douglas. Where's the justice and fair play there? We wanted workers to be able to affect the direction of their own lives inside the shop."[8]

In 1937 the UAW staged a sit-down strike at Douglas that turned ugly. Nearly four hundred workers were jailed and later indicted by a Los Angeles grand jury for conspiracy. Years later, Donald Douglas, Jr., explained his father's feelings: "Dad didn't hate the union, but he fought it. He didn't want some shop steward telling him how to run his company. Dad suffered personally, which made him resist all the more. During the sit-down strike they treated him pretty damn rough, putting sugar in his gas tank and threatening his life. He drew the line at violence and destroying personal property."[9] Though the workers ultimately got their jobs back, a divide began to open between Donald Douglas and his workers. In time the company would become unionized, but it would take the UAW seven years to do so.[10]

But nothing, it seemed, could put a damper on the company's prospects. The aircraft industry continued to boom. In 1934 Trans World Airlines (TWA) had bought twenty DC-2s from Douglas. The DC-2 was so advanced that it could fly fourteen passengers across the country in just eighteen hours.[11] But American Airlines, seeing the enormous passenger and air freight markets beginning to open, turned to Douglas for something larger and faster. The redesigned and stretched DC-2 became the famous DC-3, powered by twin 1,000-horsepower engines and containing sleeping berths and a galley that turned out hot meals. The plane proved a phenomenal success, and by the mid-1940s it carried 90 percent of all civilian U.S. air traffic, propelling Douglas into the premier position among aircraft builders.[12]

The great demand for the DC-3 meant that Douglas Aircraft had no choice but to adopt mass production. Specializing labor and assembling identical aircraft in a planned sequence would greatly increase productivity. As it turned out, it would also create a new culture within Douglas. Soon assembly lines, three shifts, rigid job classifications, and a formalized reporting system replaced natural teamwork. The fact that jobs were narrowly defined meant that workers could be trained for them in a matter of weeks.

The switch to mass production was accelerated by the entry of the United States into the Second World War. In 1940 President Franklin D. Roosevelt announced that fifty thousand new military planes would be needed each year. As a principal military contractor, Douglas grew at a breathtaking pace. The gigantic increase in military orders, combined with the company's new and fast-growing commercial business, quickly outstripped its productive capacity. By 1943 Douglas was turning out one C-47 (the military version of the DC-3) every half hour, as well as other military planes such as the mighty B-19 bomber, from six plants from Chicago to Long Beach. It had become one of the largest companies in the world, growing from 7,589 employees in 1939 to a whopping 156,000 just four years later.[13]

Working conditions in the aircraft industry were harsh during the war years. Turnover averaged 85 percent annually, and Douglas was no exception. But somehow the company managed to maintain peak efficiency and to meet its production schedules on time.[14] In a cover story on Donald Douglas, *Time* marveled at his success, noting that he was a "hard-headed manufacturer, with no room in his head for nonsense."[15] Douglas's secret, apparently, was his genius for organization and efficiency. *Time* also reported that "Douglas has not achieved this efficiency through any golden-rule-and-free-showers treatment of workers"[16] James Douglas, the youngest of the Douglas sons, who had directed the company's strategic planning, described his father's demanding philosophy: "I remember getting the blankets wet on the boat. I didn't get to sail it for a year! Ain't no bullshit about that. You did the right thing. You did your duty . . . or boy, that was *it*! You had to earn trust, and you had to take responsibility. Dad lived by his own code, and it permeated the company."[17]

But Douglas himself was ambivalent about his company's meteoric rise, claiming that he had never intended to become such a big-business man—his love lay in designing aircraft. He had, in his own words, been "shanghaied" by his company's phenomenal growth. Douglas worried that such uncontrolled growth could one day extend the company beyond its means and lead it into financial insolvency. He also feared what would happen if the company ever fell into the hands of bankers, for whom he had considerable contempt. Finally, he worried that such growth might sap the company's inventive spirit, the very quality that had propelled it into the vanguard of aircraft design.

After the war, the unions wanted Douglas to keep thousands of men and women on the payroll, but it was clear to him that orders for new aircraft would shrink as excess military airplanes were converted to commercial use. This sense of realism overcame any paternalistic feelings Douglas might have retained. As *Time* reported, "Douglas himself, at 51 president of the biggest aircraft company in the world, has a very simple postwar plan. Last week he stated it: 'You shut the damn shop up.' "[18]

Not surprisingly, his decision to lay off thousands of workers put him onto a collision course with the UAW. John Allard recalled, "Douglas Aircraft wanted it its own way, paying workers less and working them harder. All during the war years it was produce, produce, produce. The union wanted production too. We needed those planes. Our country was at war. But after the war, the workers and the unions felt they needed some recognition too." Allard remembered that Douglas kept a little ceramic skunk on his desk. "Whenever I'd walk in, he'd point to that skunk and grin, saying 'Whenever I look at that little guy, I think of the UAW!' "[19] But Douglas wasn't predictable. He surprised union leaders by resolving thousands of backlogged grievances in record time and seemed to accept the UAW as a rightful partner at the bargaining table.[20] He wanted to convince the union that it was in its best interest to lay off thousands of extra workers to save the company. Even though Douglas Aircraft had a backlog of orders worth $129 million, its immense workforce threatened to drag it under. Douglas decided to cut the workforce in half. After much discussion the union agreed, and in an unusual act of cooperation Douglas and the UAW together steered the company through a wrenching shrinkage. In one week alone, the Long Beach plant laid off 15,000 workers. Not a single grievance was filed.[21] It looked as though Douglas had succeeded in positioning his company to take advantage of the new environment created by the war's end.

## BOOM TO BUST

In the early 1950s orders for new aircraft again began to pour in, and Douglas expanded on this new wave of prosperity. Little by little, mass production, unbridled growth, and a growing sense of complacency strained the human relationships that had established Douglas as the world's premier aircraft company. According to one veteran engineer, "Douglas rewarded his favorite executives with generous stock options, while other salaried employees were paid more and more for doing less and less. Getting something for nothing became an expectation." Feelings of entitlement and permissiveness among the salaried employees produced a growing bitterness and animosity between management and labor. But for a while the company's growth and prosperity concealed the angry feelings, while its advanced aircraft designs kept it ahead of the competition. Orders piled up for Douglas's new pressurized DC-6 passenger liner and the Globemaster II (C-124) and Cargomaster (C-133) transport planes. In 1953 Douglas introduced the DC-7, its last propeller-driven airplane, which could fly across the country twice without refueling. But trouble lay just around the corner.

By 1957 it became clear that Donald Douglas could no longer afford to run his company in the hands-on manner that had been his habit. Douglas was, as *Fortune* claimed, "one of the last great individualists." No fewer than twenty-seven executives reported directly to him, and he had always conducted the company's business personally over the telephone with his military-general and airline-president cronies.[22] But the company had simply outgrown his single-handed grip. In response to growing criticism that the company needed new leadership, Douglas promoted his son, Donald Douglas, Jr., who had been vice president of testing, to become the company's president, though Douglas Sr. retained veto power as chairman of the board.

It was with the introduction of its first passenger jet, the DC-8 in 1958, that Douglas Aircraft's fortunes began to wane seriously.[23] Though the airlines regarded the DC-8 as a superb plane, Douglas had waited too long to introduce it. Most of the airlines had already signed up for the new and comparable Boeing 707, which had been introduced a year earlier. American Airlines president C. R. Smith, an old friend of Douglas's, advised him to delay production of the DC-8 because American had just bought a fleet of DC-7s.[24] But a Douglas engineer said the real reason for the delay had been that the DC-7 had been so profitable. He said, "Every DC-7 that came off the line represented a $750,000 net profit to the company. It's pretty hard to go to the president and say, 'Stop building these DC-7s and build this new one instead.' The company had simply become complacent." For the first time in its history, Douglas failed to exercise its characteristic nimbleness and lost out to a main rival.

Douglas had already invested more than $300 million in the DC-8, and it had to sell 250 airplanes just to break even. But by the close of 1961 it had sold only 47. In the same period Boeing had sold nearly three times the number of 707s. Suddenly Douglas was awash in red ink, posting losses in excess of $100 million in 1959 and again in 1960. Boeing furthered its lead in 1963 by introducing another new jet—the twin-engine 727, which the airlines bought in record numbers.[25] It was a quick and complete reversal of fortune for Douglas, which was forced to rely on military orders to stay solvent. By 1965 some Douglas executives advocated what had previously been unthinkable—that the company should abandon producing commercial aircraft altogether.

## DISASTER STRIKES

For a moment in 1965, it looked as if Douglas Aircraft might make a dramatic comeback by pulling a winning design off its drawing tables. The DC-9 was a short-range jet with unmatched efficiency that flew with a crew of only two and had the lowest operating costs of any plane in existence. Its design was so advanced that an engine could be replaced in just twenty-eight minutes, compared to four hours for a DC-8. Within a year, Douglas had 400 firm orders and 101 options averaging $3.3 million each for the DC-9, making it, in the words of *Fortune*, "the hottest Douglas product since the DC-3."[26]

But Donald Douglas, Sr., who as chairman of the board still wielded enormous power, made a costly gamble by deferring the DC-9's development costs into future years, when Douglas assumed, business would have improved. But instead of improving, conditions worsened when the company lost a $2 billion contract for a military transport (the contract went to rival Lockheed). The transport, the C-5A, would have provided Douglas with badly needed cash to help finance the DC-9 launch, and it would also have provided a shortcut to developing a new jumbo jet to catch up with Boeing's newest, the 747.

In addition, interest rates rose and cash advances from customers failed to materialize, further strapping the company. Parts costs soared and labor costs ran out of control as the company began a massive buildup, causing the company to fall behind on deliveries of the DC-9. Losses for the third quarter of 1966 exceeded $16 million. Douglas stock plummeted from $112 to $30 a share. A vicious financial circle developed: Bankers were frightened and cut off the company's line of credit, demanding that the company do whatever was necessary to regain control. But without access to credit, the company had no way of getting back on its feet. It was the very nightmare that Donald Douglas, Sr., had worried about in *Time* twenty-three years earlier.

"I think we had about a fifty-million-dollar line of credit in Canada and a hundred million in this country, but our projections showed that we needed more money than that to make it," remembered Donald Douglas, Jr. "My father and I went to New York to talk to the bankers. But they waffled. We made the mistake of telling the truth—a mistake that Lockheed and Chrysler didn't make. I learned from the Lockheed case that you don't tell the banks you need money until you've borrowed every goddamned dime that you can. *Then* you tell them, 'Oh God, I can't pay it back.' *Then* they want to help you. It's an absolute fact, goddamn it. Well, my straightforward honest Scotsman father, he and I went to the banks and told them, 'We're going to need a couple hundred million, a hundred million isn't enough.' They tossed us to the wolves. The bankers said, 'Well, you've got to raise more equity. We're just not going to lend you no goddamned more money. You're just going to have to merge with somebody.' "

Douglas said he and his father talked with scores of potential investors in hopes of raising cash. But none would commit to making the tremendous investment required to restore the company's financial health. The picture of the company as portrayed in a 1967 issue of *Fortune* was anything but flattering:

> Douglas expected to lose $50 million before taxes in 1966 and was likely to show a substantial loss again in 1967. It had a backlog of $3 billion but lacked most of the modern techniques of management, particularly those associated with controls and long-term planning. Its productivity problems were immense: Douglas' sales per employee reportedly averaged about half the rate of the other big aircraft companies. The annual payroll of $640 million was excessively burdened with employees hired three to six months in advance of any work they could do. Quality was good but being achieved at an exorbitant price.[27]

*Fortune* acknowledged that Donald Douglas, Jr., had inherited a deteriorating situation, but it laid much of the blame at his feet. *Fortune* charged that the younger Douglas had lived for too long in the shadow of his genius father and had failed to develop an adequate sense of himself. *Fortune* characterized him as impetuous and brash—not up to the task of managing this huge, important company.[28] Despite the criticism, Douglas Sr.'s support for his son was unflagging. Douglas Jr. recalled, "He never put the blame on people. He was willing to take whatever came along. That's why he was such a great person. That's why he had the loyalty people had for him."[29]

Blame aside, the situation at Douglas was grim. Investors insisted that the only solution was to merge with another growing company that could furnish badly needed cash and a new top-to-bottom management. Many Douglas executives agreed, and a merger committee, headed by Donald Douglas, Jr., was formed. Douglas Jr. recalled how he tried to protect his father: "It was terribly hard for us. It was like a train running downhill, and I had no goddamned brakes. There was nothing I could do except try to do the best job I could. I ended up being the good boy and making the merger happen. It was a crushing blow. It was like committing hari-kari." Invitations to merge were extended to a number of likely partners, including General Dynamics, North American Aviation, Martin Marietta, Signal Oil and Gas, and McDonnell.

## ENTER McDONNELL

James S. McDonnell, who already owned a large block of Douglas Aircraft stock, had wanted to buy the company outright for a number of years, but the time had never been right. Now events seemed propitious. McDonnell had known Donald Douglas, Sr., for years. They had been friendly competitors ever since McDonnell had founded his own aircraft company in 1939. McDonnell's specialty was jet fighters, and by the mid-1960s, during the Vietnam War, he had made a fortune building the F-4 Phantom II for the navy and air force. McDonnell, who referred to himself as "Old Mac," was portrayed as an extroverted supersalesman, who like Douglas would go to any lengths to keep control of his company.[30]

In 1967 McDonnell held 300,000 shares of Douglas stock (the Douglas family held only 9,000 shares—the rest was held by employees and investors), and he promised Douglas's board of directors that he would spend whatever would be required to restore Douglas's financial health. According to *Fortune*, the board was also drawn to McDonnell's proposal because there seemed to be a good fit between the two companies. McDonnell had recently reorganized his own company into three autonomous divisions, and adding Douglas as a fourth to work independently within the larger company seemed natural. McDonnell offered to pay $68.7 million for 1.5 million shares of Douglas common stock—a substantially higher price than the company would get in the market—despite having no guarantees that the Justice Department would approve the merger.

The merger saved Douglas from bankruptcy, but the next twenty-five years would not be kind. After a brief honeymoon, a Douglas engineer remembered, "McDonnell's top executives in the Saint Louis headquarters watched Douglas managers very closely and gradually weeded out the ones they didn't like and replaced them with their own people." Donald Douglas, Jr., recalled the transition in a less kindly fashion: "You couldn't take a pee without checking with Mac or his financial guy. They exerted total price control, total top decision control. There was just no flexibility whatsoever."[31]

The lack of price flexibility, according to Douglas Jr., cost the company dearly. In 1970 Douglas Aircraft became enmeshed in a costly struggle with Lockheed over competition between the Douglas DC-10 and the Lockheed L-1011. Although Boeing had captured most of the market with its new 747, there was still room for another company to claim the remainder. But the market was insufficient to support all three companies, and the fierce battle drove prices below production costs. Douglas Jr. claimed that if McDonnell had made some price concessions, the L-1011 could have been stopped. But "It just didn't happen. Mac was totally in charge, and even his own guy couldn't get him to make the decision." Douglas was able to hold on, however, ultimately forcing Lockheed out of the commercial aircraft business, but at great cost. The DC-10 never truly caught on, and Douglas's strategy of undercutting Lockheed's prices had left it financially vulnerable.

At the same time, competition was threatening Douglas's DC-9 market. Starting in the early 1970s, Airbus Industries, a heavily subsidized consortium of English, West German, Spanish, and French companies, deliberately sold its planes at a loss as a temporary strategy to capture a share of the middle-range aircraft market. Being forced to sell its planes at a loss to ward off Airbus almost ruined Douglas. The corporate office in Saint Louis now began exerting even stronger financial and management control. According to *Fortune*, Douglas lost "buckets of money" in the 1970s and the early 1980s as it struggled with growing competition and the effects of a DC-10 crash in Chicago that killed all 273 people aboard.[32] In fact, Douglas failed to show a profit for the seventeen years between 1974 and 1991.[33]

In 1981 the company was awarded two huge military contracts for the air force's C-17, the world's largest transport, and the navy's T-45 pilot-training jet. It looked like a reprieve. But unfortunately for the Long Beach plant, the T-45 project was transferred to Saint Louis and the C-17 quickly ran up enormous cost overruns. Despite backlogs of billions of dollars in commercial orders, quality problems increased and delivery schedules continued to slip, costing the company thousands of dollars each day in contractual penalties as overall costs began to rise. In 1982, after eight consecutive years of losses, McDonnell Douglas executives finally drew up plans to close the commercial side of the business once and for all.

## THE "FIVE KEYS TO SELF-RENEWAL"

Sanford "Sandy" McDonnell, nephew of the founder, took over as chairman in 1980, after his uncle's death. He knew that McDonnell Douglas needed a new set of management principles to guide the company, especially to fill the void left by the death of James S. McDonnell. Sandy and John McDonnell (son of James S. McDonnell) had been following Japan's massive economic upswing with great interest. In 1981, long before most American executives had begun to grasp the significance of the Japanese model of cooperation and teamwork, they had already understood the implications for their own company. John McDonnell was convinced that failure to adapt to the rapidly changing world would threaten the survival of the company. "We are in the midst of a business revolution that is invading one industry after another," he wrote in the mid-1980s. "Already well along the way are such industries as electronics, computers, and automotive. The common denominator of each is that they have direct, intense competition from the Japanese."[34]

Sandy McDonnell developed a McDonnell Douglas strategy he called "Five Keys to Self-Renewal."[35] The first key was "strategic management," a process McDonnell was convinced was needed to identify the company's strengths and weaknesses, its competitive situation, and its customers' needs. The second key was "participative management," a style of management that would ensure that all points of view were considered, enabling employees to contribute fully in decision making. The third key, "human resource management," would ensure the company's future by identifying and developing future leadership from within. The fourth key, "ethical behavior," when practiced by management, would win the trust of workers and customers alike. Finally, "productivity," the fifth key, would be "the banner" under which all the keys would come together in the service of continuous improvement.[36] The Five Keys were an implicit recognition that employees should be considered as assets and be given opportunities to contribute to the extent of their abilities. Management, the strategy suggested, should lead by example. McDonnell was convinced that these principles would build personal trust throughout the company. John McDonnell, who would become chairman in 1988, agreed with his cousin. More than anything, both McDonnells wanted the Five Keys to become embedded in the company's culture and to guide its behavior in the turbulent world they were entering.

The McDonnells spent millions of dollars in training and development to further their strategy. By 1985, well ahead of most American companies, more than ten thousand McDonnell Douglas managers had been trained in the philosophies of management gurus W. Edwards Deming and Joseph Juran. Throughout the corporation (though, interestingly, not at Long Beach) there was a flurry of activity as eager managers launched more than a thousand "quality circles" and experimented with "participatory management" and innovative "just-in-time" manufacturing systems. The McDonnells knew that this kind of change would take time and that they would have to lead it personally. Their devotion took on a near-religious fervor. As Sanford McDonnell exhorted his managers:

> As you get into the guts of what must be done, you find you must change the management style, corporate culture and many of your policies. Only top management leadership will be able to get these done. Mutual respect and trust must be established between management and labor, employer and employee, the company and its suppliers and customers. And this will only happen as a result of *ethical* behavior throughout the company.[37]

Teams of managers were sent from Saint Louis to Long Beach to try to help Douglas regain control and to implement the Five Keys, but to no avail. The once nimble and inventive company continued to stagger under layers of bureaucratic management and an extraordinarily complex production system. Conflicts with its unions continued to divert energy from productive activity. To most observers, the huge subsidiary seemed impervious to change. A McDonnell Douglas vice president concluded, "Management teams that had been sent out from the corporate offices to Long Beach were swallowed up like platoons sent to China! No one ever saw them again!"

Still the McDonnells persisted in the belief that Douglas could get onto its feet. They searched for answers, hoping to find a model in another company that had successfully been turned around. They were soon drawn to NUMMI, the GM-Toyota joint venture in Fremont, California. That joint venture had succeeded in transforming a facility that General Motors had closed into a world-class auto-assembly plant using the "lean production" system pioneered by Toyota. McDonnell wanted to see how it had been done and what lessons it might hold for Douglas Aircraft. In 1987 a large group of McDonnell Douglas executives and union leaders toured the Fremont plant and saw how NUMMI's production system united managers and production workers in the common pursuit of quality.

The job of arranging the tour fell to Joel Smith, a UAW International representative. Smith is a large, silver-haired man in his early fifties with a boyish face and an unusual rolling gait. His friendly manner and irreverent humor make him seem open and accessible. Smith is articulate, and he has the gift of being able to translate ideas into language and images that others can easily grasp. A born communicator, his background is also unusual, combining years of experience both in the UAW and in corporate management in the United States and the Far East. In 1983 Smith had gone to work for UAW International, only to find himself in the middle of the GM-Toyota start-up.

While leading the tour of NUMMI, Smith told the 150 McDonnell Douglas executives and union leaders that it was his feeling that many of NUMMI's concepts could be transferred to the aerospace industry. His ability to communicate with executives as well as with his UAW colleagues made a lasting impression on the McDonnell Douglas emissaries. Smith stayed with the delegation through two days of tours and through hours of question-and-answer sessions.

A few months later, a smaller group, headed by president Gerald
Johnston, returned to NUMMI, ostensibly to gather more information. In
reality, Johnston had come to hire Smith. A few weeks later, Smith was invited to John McDonnell's house in Saint Louis, where the new chairman and CEO said he wanted Smith to bring NUMMI's experience to
McDonnell Douglas. He indicated his desire to "change this company
from top to bottom, to dedicate it to continuous improvement." He
wanted Smith to spearhead the effort.

Joel Smith agreed, and he took on his new assignment enthusiasti-
cally. *The Wall Street Journal* praised the company for its unusual appointment, saying that in Smith, McDonnell Douglas had found a man
who could cut through the "total quality" jargon and get to the root of the
industry's quality problems.[38] Little did Smith know, however, that his
final assignment would be to lead an eleventh-hour attempt to rescue
Douglas Aircraft.

# CHAPTER FOUR

# TQMS AND THE PROMISE OF RENEWAL

JOEL SMITH WAS CONFIDENT that the principles he had learned at NUMMI could be transferred. McDonnell Douglas president Gerald Johnston decided to try to transform a small plant in Columbus, Ohio, as a test case. One day in August 1988, just five months after Smith had been hired, Johnston called him into his office and said, "Douglas wants to acquire an old Rockwell plant in Columbus to make parts for the C-17. I want our team to take it over, and I want you to do another NUMMI there. Can you do it?" Smith felt sure he could, provided he was given a free hand. Johnston assured him he would have everything he needed.

Smith brought his trusted assistant, George Nelson, with him. Nelson, a cheerful, talkative man with a large handlebar mustache, also had impeccable union credentials, and like Smith he had been a part of the impressive start-up of NUMMI. Smith and Nelson flew to Columbus to assess the site, a plant that Rockwell had closed two years earlier, when the B-1 bomber had been canceled.

They agreed that it would work, and soon a management team was assembled at Columbus. Managers came from McDonnell Douglas locations all over the country—Salt Lake City; Grand Rapids, Michigan;

Mesa, Arizona; Saint Louis; Titusville, Florida. Some members of the start-up team had also played important roles in the successful Salt Lake City start-up in 1985—in particular, Dick Thomas, who would become the Columbus manager, and Ron Berger, a twenty-five-year veteran Douglas human resources manager. Berger believed that Columbus offered a chance to refine the principles he and Thomas had used earlier at Salt Lake City, where they had tried the principles embodied in the Five Keys strategy. At Salt Lake City, Berger had seen how, by making the company's purpose clear and choosing the right people, the adverse human relationships engendered by mass production could be replaced by mutual trust, high productivity, and high quality.

Smith and Nelson, on the other hand, saw Columbus as a chance to replicate what they had learned at NUMMI. Nelson recalled, "The president was serious. This was their pilot test of the NUMMI concept. If it flew, they were going to do it companywide."[1] Smith would provide the link between the company's top management and the UAW International, while Nelson would work with the local management team, helping to set up the system and configure training.

Everyone assumed that the union was going to be the stumbling block. But, Smith recalled, "it wasn't. Once the leadership saw the logic in what we wanted to do, they developed an attitude of 'We've got a lot on the line, and we're going to make this thing work.' " After conversations with the UAW western regional director and others in the International, Smith was assured of union support. He and his staff worked up an outline of how the human and production systems would be organized at Columbus to produce subassemblies for the C-17 similar to the "lean production" methods Smith had seen used at NUMMI.

Columbus was an ideal site. It was small and manageable. It would start up with an initial complement of just four hundred employees. Laid-off workers were anxious to get back to work, and the UAW local and International were both in a cooperative spirit. The union's leadership trusted Smith and Nelson because of their long-standing union credentials. And now, for the first time, a trusted former union official was a key executive.

Smith and his team put together a local management structure, making sure that the union was included at every step. Once the plan had been worked out and the management team and union were on board, Smith forged a consensus on the terms of an agreement between the union and management. "We put together a letter of intent which was very similar to NUMMI's, with language assuring employment security and a wage agreement," he said proudly. "We blew right through all of that in four hours one afternoon. Next we negotiated the job classifications. The union wanted fifteen categories, but we agreed on just three. It was a one-two-three punch."

Members of the team, which now included managers and specialists drawn from Douglas's Human Resources and Manufacturing Departments, developed an assessment system to choose the first four hundred employees from the pool of applicants to be rehired from the old Rockwell workforce. Nelson, plus Ron Berger and others from Douglas, developed a screening program for "Hi-Pots"—McDonnell Douglas jargon for managers with high potential—and they designed training to indoctrinate all employees in the principles of total quality management systems, or "TQMS," as the new system was called. Nelson candidly acknowledged that much of what was used at Columbus had been borrowed from NUMMI, including Lego models and exercises adapted to assess aircraft workers' abilities to plan and coordinate the flow of work. The start-up team developed a battery of questions to assess Columbus workers' abilities to work in teams, as well as case studies that would assess their analytical capabilities, to help select workers who would ultimately be hired. Most important, said Nelson, was the 120 hours of on-the-job training that was carefully designed to help workers to apply the principles they had learned in formal classroom training. Once back on the job, they were helped by specially trained coaches in ways of doing their jobs most effectively.

Before long, Columbus was heralded as the prototype of reform for all of McDonnell Douglas. It was regarded as an unqualified success, a model of labor-management cooperation and continuous improvement. Smith laughed as he recalled how the union had gone from cynical reluctance to outright support. "Some of those UAW folks thought this cooperation was a lot of bullshit. But once the thing really got going and people saw they had some control over their own destiny, management could not deviate because the union wouldn't let 'em! I'm sure they'd strike the place before they'd make poor quality."[2]

John McDonnell and his top executives were impressed with the transformation they saw taking place at Columbus. They were eager to extend the effort to the entire company. Joel Smith soon found himself on an airplane with George Nelson, heading to California for a meeting with Douglas executives.

Nelson was shocked by what happened at the meeting. "Gerry Johnston and Senior Vice President James Henry MacDonald were there, Joel, myself, and some others from Columbus. The guys from Corporate told the Douglas folks that they had to make some serious changes in how they were doing business. Douglas was becoming a dinosaur. But, in their characteristic way, they just dug in deeper. They wouldn't listen. Trying to convince these guys that they had to change was like shoveling sand on the beach.

"So here was all the brass in one room. The guys from Columbus and Saint Louis tried to cajole them at first, and then things got heavier as Saint Louis began to lean on them. Finally, one of the Douglas vice presidents threw down the glove. He basically told us to forget it and go home. When he finished giving all the reasons, he added, 'We are *not* going to be a playpen for the latest fads from the corporate office.' No one said a word. You could have heard a pin drop in the room. I was stunned. I couldn't believe what I'd just witnessed. We'd been completely stonewalled. On the way back to Saint Louis, I was spilling my guts to Joel, and he said calmly, 'Don't worry about it, George. These guys have been doing this to each other for years.' "[3]

The stonewalling only hardened the McDonnell Douglas executives' resolve to bring Douglas under control. They knew that Douglas was hemorrhaging financially and that if left alone it would bleed to death. By the end of the first half of 1989, Douglas was projected to lose a quarter of a billion dollars, and each of its aircraft programs was seriously behind schedule. The Air Force C-17 cargo jet was more than $400 million over budget, and the MD-11 wide-body commercial jet, on which Douglas had pinned its hopes, was four months behind schedule. Even the MD-80 twin jet, which had produced profits year after year, was now losing money.[4]

But that wasn't the worst of it. The prospect that Douglas could pull down the entire corporation was real. In a series of meetings in the Saint Louis headquarters building, a core of McDonnell Douglas executives, led by James Henry MacDonald and including Smith, began to craft options to save Douglas. Just weeks later the alternatives were presented to John McDonnell. The only path that seemed to be open was taking control of Douglas by whatever means necessary. Quickly, the group moved to find a leader to direct the mission, selecting Robert Hood from the company's missile subsidiary.

## THE TAKEOVER

In the early hours of one cold February morning in 1989, a half-dozen cars converged on a fashionable Saint Louis neighborhood, parking in front of a large white house. By ones and twos, ten casually dressed men knocked at the door, where they were greeted and escorted into the house and down the stairs to the family room. The greeter was Robert Hood, who had just been appointed president of Douglas Aircraft. The men included McDonnell Douglas Chairman and CEO John McDonnell, President Gerald Johnston, and eight trusted executives who had been secretly brought together to plan a revolution. The meeting had been planned so carefully that three of the men who had just flown in from California had thought they were going to a total quality management seminar.

John McDonnell told the men that they were now charged with taking over Douglas Aircraft and reforming it completely. It would take extraordinary measures to save the once proud aircraft company, which was now perilously close to ruin. For twenty-two years, every effort that McDonnell Douglas executives had made to turn Douglas around had foundered. McDonnell was now gambling that the group he had assembled would be able to jolt the company's 53,000 employees out of their complacency and infuse them with the urgent desire for change.

For the next two weeks the executives would spend their days sequestered in Hood's basement, with only one unlisted portable phone to call out on. In the days ahead, a plan would take visible form on lengths of butcher paper plastered on the walls. They would physically seize control of Douglas. Next, they would fire nearly half of its 5,200 managers, restructure the organization, and streamline the production system. They would implement a new total quality management system that had been developed from principles drawn from the Five Keys strategy, from lessons learned at Salt Lake City, and more recently from the great success at Columbus. They would also create what McDonnell called a "new culture" at Douglas, one that was built on mutual respect, trust, and teamwork. It was a huge—and daunting—challenge: every previous attempt had failed. McDonnell was determined to succeed.

The sprawling Long Beach facility was the assembly site for the massive C-17, a four-engine Air Force jet cargo plane that can carry twice the payload of any plane in existence and land in half the space; the $100 million MD-11, a jumbo wide-body passenger jet that was in development; and the $30 million medium-range MD-80 twin jet.[5] Building one of these modern airplanes is one of the most complicated tasks imaginable, requiring a demanding combination of skill, experience, motivation, and teamwork—conditions hard to meet even under the best of circumstances. The system that Douglas used in 1988 to build airplanes had changed little since 1958, when it had moved civilian production from Santa Monica to Long Beach. Between 1941 and 1958 the Long Beach plant had been used exclusively for the construction of military aircraft, and the military influence had been lasting and powerful: early on, a top-down military management style and a stifling bureaucracy had bogged down the Long Beach system in red tape and costly delays, and over time these inefficiencies had been multiplied by an increasing number of requirements imposed by the Federal Aviation Administration and California regulatory agencies.

Though Douglas airplanes met the highest quality standards, such quality came at an exorbitant cost. The production system was burdened with multiple inspections, a staggering amount of paperwork, and small armies of managers who checked and cross-checked decisions made at lower levels. Mistakes were almost always caught, but the costs of rework were staggering. Computer systems kept track of hundreds of thousands of parts. Computers also documented each step in the construction of each airplane to ensure that correct procedures were followed and to compile a record in the event that a plane should crash. Meanwhile, informal networks of workers who had known one another for many years worked quietly to circumvent the unwieldy formal system so that production quotas could be met. New managers quickly learned that their careers depended not so much on their ability to develop teamwork as on their ability to control crises. New workers were socialized into a slow pace of work, and waiting around had become the norm. The cantankerous, mistrustful UAW local played a role in keeping the company off balance as well. To the extent that the union's leadership spoke with a unified voice, it was a voice of opposition to any changes management tried to make.

The manufacturing process began in an area known as PCO, or Product Center Organization, where parts were made for later assembly. In another area, called the Chem Mill, the great wing surfaces and skins for the C-17 were dipped in an enormous vat of gooey green protective latex called "maskant." Elsewhere, a variety of parts, including long aluminum spars, landing-gear assemblies, and window panels, was fabricated in machine shops. Emergency replacement parts were fabricated in Department 403, known as "Quick Fix." Enormous hangars housed the assembly of the MD-80, MD-11, and C-17 aircraft. A steady stream of trucks, jitneys, cars, and forklifts bumped up and down the streets that ran between the massive buildings that made up the complex.

Without well-developed informal teamwork, it would have been impossible to coordinate Douglas's paper-laden, bureaucratic system to ensure the timely delivery and installation of the thousands of parts shipped in from all over the world. For instance, wing sections were built and shipped by rail to Long Beach from a McDonnell Douglas plant in Canada. Other components intended for wing assembly came from Saab Scandia of Sweden, Aeritalia of Italy, and Mitsubishi of Japan. The tail section, or *empennage*, was shipped from Saint Louis, while floor units came from Macon, Georgia. Design specifications, procurement of myriad small parts, shipping schedules, and unforeseen emergencies all had to be efficiently coordinated if assembly was to go smoothly. Douglas's informal network of trusted associates who had worked together over the years was vital.

Inside a cavernous 1,100-foot hangar known as the "bird farm," the MD-80s are assembled. The hangar dwarfs everything in sight, including the huge airplanes themselves. Sparrows fly in and out through the gaping doors from their nests high up in the hangar's girders. Hundreds of suspended incandescent lights provide a surprising amount of light in this windowless structure.[6] The complexity of building an MD-80 is staggering, making automobile assembly look like child's play. More than 160,000 different parts must be made to exacting specifications, and they must arrive at the right time and the right place as the plane creeps through an assembly process that takes ninety-five days from start to finish.[7] Before an airplane is test-flown, more than a *half-million* fasteners — rivets, bolts, and screws — will be driven into its body and *sixty-five miles* of electrical wire will have been threaded through its interior. Workers squeeze themselves into tiny spots to install the electrical, hydraulic, air, and fuel systems, which are made in the PCO or fabricated by thousands of subcontractors all over the world.

By the late 1980s Douglas Aircraft was losing money on each plane it sold. According to one top official, "We had thirty billion dollars in aircraft orders, but it was going to cost us thirty-five billion dollars to build them."[8] Even so, management had little choice but to meet the expanding production demands by hiring 43,000 green employees. By 1988 Douglas's Long Beach workforce stood at nearly 50,000. Most employees were new and inexperienced. Not surprisingly, productivity sagged and quality problems grew, while deliveries slipped further and further behind schedule.

Douglas's precarious financial position began to threaten the entire corporation. Though McDonnell Douglas's revenues topped $15 billion each year, it began to feel the effects of the growing defense cutbacks caused by the end of the Cold War, and the corporation was beginning to see losses in both its military and commercial operations.[9] Corporate analysts predicted that Douglas would soon account for 55 percent of the parent corporation's total revenue. "Douglas was choking us to death," a McDonnell Douglas vice president explained. "It was getting bigger and bigger, and it was being managed worse and worse." Profits were also badly needed to speed the development of the MD-11, Douglas's new jumbo jet derived from the DC-10, which was only on the drawing boards — far behind schedule. Executives back in the Saint Louis headquarters knew that the parent corporation could no longer carry Douglas's mounting losses.

It seemed increasingly clear that the halfhearted attempts to bring

Douglas around in the 1980s had had little or no effect. A veteran Douglas manager explained, "When Saint Louis wanted a new program, Douglas managers would give the appearance of compliance. They would get terribly busy, but their activity had no relationship to results. Few new ideas ever penetrated to the production floor, where they should have started in the first place. When we hired new managers, they wouldn't listen to what had already been done because they had their own ideas that they wanted to implement."

Conditions continued to worsen. California's economy began to weaken, and the cost of doing business in California soared. The state's strict environmental regulations added to the already escalating costs of building aircraft. John Van Gels, vice president of Long Beach's Product Center Organization, was livid about southern California's environmental controls and furious with the regulators' arrogance and inability to understand that companies like Douglas were critical to California's future. "Since 1986 the yearly costs of complying with environmental and safety regulations, workers' compensation, and local assessments have doubled," he asserted. "They've gone from fifteen million dollars to more than thirty million. I don't want to fight these regulations, but goddamn it, I don't want to have them forced on me and be given no time to comply. They pass these laws and say, 'Now you go figure out how to do it.' Our Chem Mill is cleaner than the goddamn San Diego Freeway, but I can't run it but eight hours a day. Because of the new regulations on solvents, I have to fly planes out of the state to paint 'em! Tell me that makes sense!" Rising worker's compensation costs also added to the costs of building aircraft in California. Van Gels estimated that worker's compensation costs alone added $500,000 to the price of every airplane.

Van Gels was in the vanguard of the business executives who began to give up on California. He laid much of the blame at the feet of the state's policy makers. "These folks are going to wake up one morning and find everybody gone," he predicted. "We're pulling out of here. We're going to Utah and to other states where they want a company like McDonnell Douglas." The long-term corporate plan, according to Van Gels, was to carve up manufacturing and move it out of California to other, more hospitable states. Many of them, such as Utah, Georgia, and Arkansas, were "right-to-work" states, where employees could choose whether or not to join a union. Van Gels explained, "Long Beach will shrink and become a final-assembly operation. The era of the forty-thousand-employee plants is over. They're too inefficient, and they can't be managed. We're aiming for plants that run at a maximum of a thousand."

## MASS PRODUCTION, DOUGLAS STYLE

Douglas's cumbersome mass production system and the bureaucratic military structure it had inherited stifled individual initiative and creativity. James A. Moore, a thirty-seven-year veteran Douglas engineer, described the suffocation: "The move to Long Beach in 1958 created a single Engineering Department that included Santa Monica commercial engineers, El Segundo naval aircraft engineers, and the Long Beach air force engineers. Everyone was forced into Long Beach's military paper system. The Long Beach engineers had been there since the war, and they were firmly entrenched. They were complacent in their ways, and nobody was going to change them. It was a muscle-bound, military environment. Santa Monica engineers, who were the only ones who knew how to put an airplane together, were pushed aside by the air force. Their knowledge was lost. It took forever to get anything done at Long Beach, because every decision was made by committee. Individual contributions were devalued. No single individual was responsible for anything. To get a single purchase order approved, it would go through twenty-eight different people. The red tape drove costs through the roof. It took me four or five times longer to get something done at Long Beach than it did at Santa Monica."[10]

One general manager described the production system as a case of "grand suboptimization." "It runs on brute strength," he said. "If you took the system apart and laid it out piece by piece, it would make sense. But it is impossible to hand off quality between the pieces, because it doesn't work as a system. For example, the planners pump out the paper based on the drawings they get from the designers. The paper gets passed onto the mechanics, who scream when something doesn't work. Problems get fixed on the shop floor instead of being traced back to their root cause. So there is no gain for the system. Nothing improves, it just gets fixed in crisis after crisis. Assembly gets killed with hours and hours of rework and extra costs. They have to do everything three, four, five times to get it right. We build quality aircraft because they get built four or five times over. That's the joke around here. Build in quality the first time — the fifth time around! We can't compete that way anymore. The rework costs are astronomical, and the competition's beating our pants off. We've got to develop the production and human systems to do it right the first time."

In the 1960s management encouraged the proliferation of review committees, and it also centralized engineering design and assembly in a single office. The goal was to curb escalating costs, but the actual effect was to add a new layer of management and barriers between departments that in the past had communicated frequently and easily with one another. At the Santa Monica facility, for example, individual aircraft project teams had always taken full responsibility for their success or failure, and team members had dealt with everyone from customers to component suppliers. They knew exactly how to design and assemble their aircraft and how long it would take. But under "program management," decisions were increasingly made by committees of men who were divorced from the actual work.

The rigid and hierarchical military style intensified the disintegrating forces that had been introduced by mass production decades earlier. The Engineering, Manufacturing, Sales, and Accounting Departments became fragmented and isolated from one another. Far from gaining control, program management created needs for *more* control, leading to even more layers of management, which in turn translated into higher costs. "The program office became the front office," Moore explained. "It dealt with the customer and got all the attention, all the cameras and lights. The project people who really did the work were isolated and pushed into the background. The only way Engineering could now talk to Manufacturing was through the program office. Manufacturing began making decisions that really should have been made by Engineering. It created a situation that I called 'hole-in-the-wall engineering' — Engineering makes the drawings, stuffs it through a hole in the wall, and Manufacturing has to make it work. The engineer becomes divorced from manufacturing and from the responsibility for the configuration of the final product. There was no coordination between the Sales and Engineering Departments. Imagine a customer coming through the plant with an engineer, watching his DC-8 coming down the line. He says, 'Hey, I didn't order it this way. I didn't order that plane. The configuration of seats and lavatories is wrong.' The Douglas guy says, 'Why didn't you tell us?' The customer says, 'I told your salespeople.' He says, 'Well, they never told us.' So the system caused us to deliver airplanes to customers that they never ordered. There was no longer any single point of control."[11]

The costs of building an airplane can quickly get out of control because of the complexity, the cost of the parts, and the requirements imposed by the FAA for an elaborate and expensive paperwork trail. Though Douglas had a sophisticated electronic system that documented each step in the assembly of each aircraft, it lacked a reliable system of cost accounting. Thus, it was nearly impossible to track the costs of each aircraft as they accumulated.

Without individual responsibility, accountability, or control, internal politics became rampant and all-consuming. Moore described the debilitating effects: "One department would tell another, 'You just mind your own business, and we'll worry about ours.' Little by little, everyone started taking on a defensive frame of mind. Problems were attacked by committee. People would be frozen. They would be horrified at the thought of taking any individual responsibility. The only way you could get anything done was to do it informally, outside of the system."[12]

An antagonistic relationship with its union, the rebellious UAW Local 148, only intensified Douglas's problems. Engineers and managers who came to the Long Beach complex from the Santa Monica facility had been accustomed to working cooperatively with the machinists' union and had a hard time adjusting to the style of Long Beach's militant UAW local. Moore remembered that "At Santa Monica, when we'd have an electrical problem, a mechanic and an electrical guy would work together. One would string the wires, and another would power it up. But when we got to Long Beach, the union would insist on having five or six guys do the work of one. It made no sense at all."[13]

Although the UAW International tried to maintain a constructive relationship with management, getting any cooperation from Local 148 was difficult at best. Bruce Lee, a pragmatic man who retired as the UAW's western regional director in 1995, knew that if Douglas went under it would mean the loss of tens of thousands of high-paying jobs, and he tried to persuade the local to see his point of view. But the fractured and combative local was more concerned with union politics and broad social issues than it was with the company's survival, causing it to veer between halfhearted cooperation and out-and-out warfare.

In 1981 Robert Berghoff was elected to head the local. Berghoff's aim was to fight the company at every opportunity. He established a militant caucus within the local that called itself the Responsible Action Party (RAP); it took a dim view of anything approaching cooperation. A general manager recalled, "The Berghoff motto was 'We're going to bring the company to its knees.' He would do anything he could to cause us to fail. It was a personal vendetta with him." For the next six years problems increased as Berghoff's demands (and the frequent work slowdowns and a brief strike in 1983) overrode any movement toward reform and improvements in productivity and quality. By 1987, however, support for Berghoff's confrontational methods had eroded, and he and his followers were voted out in favor of a more cooperative caucus. For a short while, the relationship between management and labor improved as the new local president, Doug Griffith, patched up the local's relationship with the company and the International. But even his efforts did little to change the company's stagnant culture.

## USING A SHARP AX

John McDonnell knew he had to do something dramatic to shake Douglas out of its lethargy. "It's the old story about the mule," he recalled. "You've got to get its attention first. We decided, because of Douglas's condition and ingrained culture, that it was better to try to do it on a massive or dramatic scale. We recognized it would create a big disruption, but we hoped we could get through it and then get on with business."[14] Joel Smith knew what a Herculean task McDonnell had set for himself. "I had been on a picket line at Douglas in 1983," he recalled. "Local 148 was probably the most disorganized, fragmented local union that's ever been around. Their attitude was nothing but 'Gimme, gimme, gimme.' Management was equally wacky. They were hopelessly fucked up. I didn't want to have any part of the goddamned thing." But at that meeting in Saint Louis at

Robert Hood's home, there in the basement, Smith could see that McDonnell's executives had run out of patience. "They were also very, very frustrated by the years of poor performance," he said. "Time had run out. Their feelings were clear: 'We gotta move now. We gotta be swift.' Once that decision was made, I knew there was going to be pain no matter what we did. I figured that we should move as swiftly as possible. We shouldn't use a rusty pocketknife. We should use a sharp ax and get on with it."

Within days, the team flew to Los Angeles to prepare for the takeover. Smith remembered that they arrived in a cold drizzle—perhaps a portent of the events that would soon follow. To keep their activities under wraps, the executives took rooms in a waterfront hotel in Long Beach, a few miles from Douglas headquarters. They used the hotel as a staging area to plan the takeover. "We got to Long Beach a week in advance to work out the operational details, to make sure this thing was well choreographed. No one at Douglas knew we were there or what was happening," Smith said. The operation was so secret that they had to pilfer badges from Douglas security so they could get through the gate the morning of the takeover. Back in their hotel rooms, the executives took Polaroid snapshots of one another that they sealed onto the badges with a portable iron.

According to Smith, the takeover was to be executed as "a one-two-three series of punches." First, they intended to put an immediate stop to Douglas's uncontrolled hiring. Next, they would radically trim and reorganize management to restore control. The number of vice presidents would be slashed from 275 to 75, and middle managers' jobs would be reduced by 50 percent. John McDonnell knew he had to drive home the message that this was not just another reorganization—it was now a matter of the company's very survival. He planned to call all of Douglas's 5,200 managers together and tell them that nearly 2,500 of their jobs would be cut. If they wanted to keep their jobs, they would have to reapply. The others would be placed in jobs elsewhere in the company.

In a dramatic first step, Douglas would be reorganized from a "matrix" form (in which Human Resources, Engineering, and other departments were centralized to provide companywide services) into a "vertical" form. A vertical organization would, it was hoped, give more authority to general managers over nine new divisions (five divisions that would build aircraft and manufacture parts, plus Quality, New-Product Development, Support Services, and Marketing).[15] Each of the new divisions, including Human Resources, Customer Support, and Engineering, would be self-contained. The reorganization would also flatten the top-heavy company by removing three layers of management from the eight that existed. Decision making would be pushed downward to business-unit managers, who would organize their units into teams. The responsibility for quality would ultimately rest with workers on the shop floor.

Second, it would be critically important to select a new group of managers who could radically alter the old bureaucratic, militaristic culture and infuse the company with a new philosophy of cooperation, teamwork, mutual respect, and trust. McDonnell said that he had been convinced that without a new cultural foundation, it would be impossible to restore the company's profitability. Smith had detailed a plan for managers to undergo rigorous screening and assessments to make sure they had the desired new traits—the ability to work in teams and the capacity to develop trust and mutual respect. Managers who exhibited these qualities would be critical to forming Douglas's new culture. They would stand a much better chance of being selected for the reduced number of jobs than would those who clung to the old authoritarian ways.

Third, a massive investment would be made in establishing new training facilities, where managers, union leaders, and production workers would go through eighty hours of classroom training in total quality management systems (TQMS). They would return to their departments, where they would get an added forty hours of hands-on training to help them apply what they had learned to their jobs.

The union was to play a key role in implementing the new plan. Smith's union credentials and his long-standing relationship with Bruce Lee created a direct link between Douglas's top management and the union. Lee had already laid a considerable amount of groundwork for change with the local, and he recognized that Douglas's worsening financial condition required that something dramatic would have to be done soon. He also knew that joint action between the union and Douglas management would be required. Lee had already brought the local's leadership together with Douglas managers in an off-site meeting the year before to develop plans to work together. Subsequent meetings had led to a pledge between the union and management to work cooperatively to help ensure the survival of the company, and Doug Griffith, who had been elected to the union's presidency on a platform of cooperation, could be counted on to support the effort. But Smith and Lee knew that other factions within the cantankerous 18,000-member local would be harder to win over. For the time being, however, it seemed as though the union was on board.

While the principles that were to be followed at Long Beach had already been tested at Columbus, a struggle now broke out among McDonnell Douglas executives about whether or not it was advisable to try to replicate the small Columbus greenfield experience at Long Beach. Ron Berger said that he and others had implored Smith to go slowly, to take the necessary time to modify the Columbus model to fit Douglas. Berger said that neither Smith nor anyone else would listen to him. Smith claimed that things had run beyond his control. "There were no more options but to move fast," he said. "The impatience at the top of the organization was simply overwhelming. So we ended up bringing the whole damn thing out here and jammed a four-week training program into two weeks. It was compromise, compromise, compromise."

George Nelson worried that McDonnell Douglas executives' plans to impose the Columbus model on Long Beach would be sabotaged. He explained, "They talked about empowering people at Long Beach, but they weren't going to practice it—they were just going to *do* it. I'd already gotten to know some of the managers at Long Beach, who knew something was coming from Saint Louis. Their attitude was 'Oh well, that's okay. Just go along with it, because in six months they'll just cancel it anyway.' And I'm sitting there with my fingers in my ears saying to myself, 'Oh, no, this can't be! I'm not believing what I'm hearing!'" Despite misgivings, the McDonnell Douglas executive team made its final preparations to occupy the huge Long Beach subsidiary.

# CHAPTER FIVE

# DISASTER OR MIRACLE?

ON MONDAY, February 13, 1989, the day before Valentine's Day, all of Douglas's Long Beach managers were summoned to a mass meeting in a huge C-17 paint hangar. The event would be remembered as the "Saint Valentine's Day Massacre"—a reference to the infamous murders of the Chicago police by Al Capone's gang in 1929. Joel Smith, who had arrived early, recalled his feelings as he looked out over a sea of 5,200 empty chairs. "It was very impressive to see those empty chairs in that damn hangar and the two big video screens that lit up the stage. I was feeling a whole lot of things. One, I suppose, was the fear of the unknown. I thought to myself, 'Jesus, do you guys realize how big this is?'"

A few minutes after 10 A.M., when all the managers had taken their seats, John McDonnell walked briskly onto the stage. A hush fell over the audience. He said, "Hi, I'm John McDonnell. As of this moment every one of you is out of a job. We're going to start from scratch!" The audience reacted with a stunned silence. Then McDonnell continued speaking from a series of overheads that flashed up on two huge screens, showing how the organization was going to change and how it would look when McDonnell and his men were through.

The feelings of the managers who attended the meeting were mixed. Some felt that the change, harsh as it was, was long overdue. Others reacted angrily to the message and to the way it had been delivered. One manager said he had been shocked to hear McDonnell Douglas executives talk about teamwork and empowerment while holding themselves out as saviors. "They didn't say, 'We're going to work together to rebuild this place.' Hell, no! They said, 'We're going to *save* you!' This was just overblown egos and heroics!" James S. Douglas, the youngest son of founder Donald Douglas, said, "We were dumbfounded. Absolutely stunned. We had all lost our jobs, and management was going to be cut in half. For now we would stay on and maybe even get our jobs back after we'd been shown how to do this TQM."[1] He said that once he had heard that half of them would find jobs in the new structure while the other half would be given something else to do, the message had been clear. "That immediately told everybody that, for half of us, our asses are on the street. There was an attitude of 'Well, here's another invasion of gumshoes from Saint Louis.' " The impact of the mass demotions raced through the organization, creating a climate of fear and anger. "It became a dog-eat-dog atmosphere," said one manager. "It nurtured antagonisms that had always existed between managers and the workforce. It was humiliating. Some of the workers thought it was funny and pointed fingers and laughed at us." Other managers were anxious and fearful as they returned to their offices to wait to see what would happen next.

In the weeks that followed, Smith and his staff hurried to enlist old managers to analyze their departments and to recommend criteria for selecting the new managers who could carry out their vision. Naturally, because TQMS sought to drive decision making downward in the organization, a heavy emphasis was put on managers' abilities to work cooperatively and develop teamwork. One by one, managers were brought together in groups of eight to play games like those developed at Columbus that simulated stressful situations. A game called "Lunar Colony," for instance, simulated life on the moon. Players had to negotiate with one another to decide how to allocate limited resources for libraries, roads, hospitals, transportation, and other services. Members of assessment teams, which included students from local universities, sat at one end of the room, carefully observing and documenting individuals' styles. Assessments based on the role-playing exercises, results of other tests, and ratings by former employees became part of the record for each of the 4,878 managers who applied for the 2,800 new positions. Managers who failed would keep their benefits and salaries and were assured of being placed elsewhere in the organization.

## RETRAINING FOR THE NEW CULTURE

John McDonnell knew that, at its root, the problems at Douglas had grown from its permissive culture. "When you get successful, you build up a culture around that success and then the world changes around you," he said. "It's very difficult because, like the frogs in the water that just gradually warms up, you don't realize it until it's too late. Success doesn't end overnight. Signs come up, but you've got this culture that doesn't see those signs. So it's very important that an organization keeps learning and changing. The question is how to do it. I know one way to do it is to get into a crisis from time to time."[2]

McDonnell was convinced that in the emergency conditions he and his executive team had created, a massive infusion of training would break down the old culture and instill a new set of beliefs and behavior into the workforce. Soon Douglas managers began to talk in terms of the "old culture" in contrast to the desired "new culture." "New culture" managers were those who would become coaches or mentors to their employees. They would foster teamwork among employees, who would have greatly expanded roles and authority.

A multimillion-dollar retraining effort was launched to indoctrinate employees in the new principles. More than two hundred instructors selected from the Douglas training staff, the union membership, and outside consultants were trained in the TQMS principles. Classroom facilities were leased in two local schools, one dedicated to training managers in the new principles, the other aimed at training production workers how to implement the principles on the job. As at Columbus, two weeks of initial training was done in classrooms, while the remaining week was done with employees on the production lines.[3]

Douglas employees were bused to the training facilities, where they went through a carefully scripted ten-day curriculum. They learned how

TQMS was essential to Douglas Aircraft's survival, and they were drilled in techniques to improve quality and reduce costs. They learned how to improve the flow of work between operations and how to identify the next "customer" in an assembly operation. They learned statistical process control techniques to help control production, as well as a six-step problem-solving process. They were taught how to identify and remove waste, which was causing quality to suffer and costs to rise. They worked in teams and did role playing to improve their communications and to learn how to develop teamwork and build trust.[4] Team members were instructed in the company's business operations and finance as the first steps to taking control. Once back on the job, the plan called for trainees to go through another forty hours of carefully structured on-the-job training to help them transfer the new principles to their jobs. In all, $17 million was invested in such training, which began plantwide in November 1989.

## TQMS STALLS

Though this kind of training had worked at Salt Lake City and at the small Columbus plant, Long Beach was another matter. Douglas was a huge facility, the size of a small city, running day and night to meet production schedules. If the company could not continue building aircraft to keep up with customers' orders, it would simply not survive. As Jesse Salazar, the UAW bargaining committee chairman, quipped, "Trying to make these massive changes at the same time we're being forced to get planes out the door was like trying to rewire your house while the power's on." As time passed, the decision to try to repeat the Columbus experience began to be revealed as a mistake.

Compounding the problem, it was becoming clear that the TQMS concept lacked coherence even among members of the executive team. Though TQMS had evolved as a composite of ideas drawn from quality guru W. Edwards Deming, the Five Keys, and NUMMI's production principles, Joel Smith felt it had been only loosely defined. There had been very little serious discussion of the concepts themselves and how they should fit together. He recalled his first meetings with the McDonnell Douglas executive team: "These were the movers and shakers, but our meetings were little more than one-way conversations. I explained the ideas I'd taken from NUMMI and how they could be applied to aircraft, and I tried to bring them up to speed. I tried to explain the importance of trust and of open communication and of sharing a vision. I explained that we had to redesign the production systems.

"But as soon as they heard the word 'system,' they tuned out. They just wouldn't get it. To them, 'system' meant automation. When I used the term 'standardized work,' they assumed that meant the end of their creativity and their intellectual freedom. These were engineers. Standardizing and systematizing production was a demeaning idea to many of them. They thought of McDonnell Douglas as an engineering company. In private I'd tell them, 'We're a goddamned manufacturer! We assemble stuff, and we sell it. We don't do any real engineering here—we farm out the high-tech stuff to General Electric, Honeywell, and other subcontractors!' These guys in the aircraft business talk a lot of bullshit about planning, but they really don't do it."

The lack of conceptual definition and integration confused and diluted the reform effort, as did the lingering presence of previous efforts. "As we began to develop TQMS, it became clear that each of the operating units had already invested a lot of time in adapting the Five Keys and SBI (an earlier McDonnell Douglas improvement effort called "strategic business initiative") to their own operations," Smith said. "They tried to fit what they heard from me into what they'd already done so there would be a minimum amount of disruption."

But George Nelson said it was worse than Smith made it out to be: "Joel and I were floored when we found out that we were actually in *competition* with SBI! With our own people!" Douglas was so huge and disjointed that apparently an entire unit, which had once been charged with implementing SBI, had continued unnoticed for years. Nelson exclaimed incredulously, "It had a life of its own! We couldn't believe it! These people were supposed to have been cleaned out a long time ago! Their operation was supposed to have been shut down. But here we had two campaigns going, TQMS *and* SBI! SBI still carried the blessings of Sandy McDonnell. It was a sacred cow. Worse, it turned out to be the basis of opposition to anything new. Lots of people wanted us to fail before we'd ever even started!"

The lack of clarity in the TQMS concept and the lack of overall commitment to it, Smith said, fragmented support from the beginning. He said, "By the time we began seriously negotiating the concept with the executives, it became clear that everyone had his own version of continuous improvement. No one wanted to change corporate principles or anything that would affect their own operations. So we wound up in endless conflicts. I wanted John McDonnell to take a stronger role. I wanted him to say, 'Look, this is what I want and your job is to figure out how to do it,' but he didn't want to go that way. He wanted everyone to talk it through. He wanted consensus. But it was like taking a bunch of seventeen-year-olds who have never welded anything before and asking them to design a welding curriculum. You would end up with all kinds of weird shit, and that's exactly what happened. We had all the TQMS principles spelled out, but in the end it was a real hodgepodge."

The feelings of fear and anger about the sudden demotions and reorganization cost support where it was sorely needed—among middle managers. Bob Connolly, a grandfatherly-looking group leader in "Quick Fix," who had worked at Douglas since 1939, said he had known that something dramatic had to be done, but he had thought the strategy was too severe. "Management cried wolf too often, and they wore it out," he recalled. "If people were going to listen and take it to heart, management was going to have to give this place a pretty good jolt. But they went too far and destroyed the trust that had taken years to create. It sure beat hell out of a lot of good people."

As apprehension spread among the workers, support for TQMS began to plummet. Despite the new emphasis on teamwork and cooperation, many Douglas managers persisted in their authoritarian style. One mechanic on the MD-80 said, "Here they talk about cooperation and empowerment, and then they try to ram it down our throats!" Salazar complained bitterly that Douglas executives rarely consulted with the union before making important decisions. "They keep on making decisions without asking us. They say 'Just do it!' They never ask us anything. They just give orders, and bang, bang, bang!" he exclaimed, hitting himself on the forehead. "Bang, bang, bang, how do you like that? I know where we've got to go as a company and as a union. The Jimmy Hoffa days are over. If this place goes under, we go with it. I told [Robert] Hood that if he doesn't get the union on board, there won't be any fucking company! It's gotta change, or we're not going to make it."

Though many of the authoritarian managers had been demoted in the reorganization, an unexpected problem emerged among the new younger managers, who had been chosen for their ability to work cooperatively in teams: many of them lacked technical and managerial experience. One team leader in the Chem Mill said, "These new guys don't know shit. They quake in their boots when their bosses tell them to do something. Instead of saying 'I'll try my best', they'll promise anything to get off the hook. Then they freak out and come down on us to deliver. The group leader gets no support from the BUM [the improbable acronym for "business unit managers"], and the BUM gets no support from the general manager. The general manager only wants cut-and-dried answers—'Yes sir' or 'No sir.' No bullshit. You know he's getting his ass kicked by the vice president, who's getting his ass kicked by the air force. Nobody in the whole chain of command will admit anything's wrong. Everyone just protects his own ass, and to hell with everyone else. It's management by intimidation."

The reform effort began to stall. Team leaders were to have been a critical link between production workers and management. To help empower the teams, executives agreed that they should elect their own leaders. Once elected, team leaders' hourly pay would automatically jump to the top of the rate, with an assurance from the company that if they were demoted, they would retain it. These jobs were naturally prized by younger workers, who had fewer years of seniority and lower hourly pay rates. Older people with more seniority and higher earnings had little to gain. Phyllis Brown, a veteran Douglas employee, said, "There's nothing in it for most of us except headaches. Who'd want to beat your brains out for a few more cents an hour?" But most of the young team leaders who were elected had had only minimal experience on the job. One production worker complained that his team leader knew nothing: "The clown who was elected to head my team came over and asked me to help him do his job. If he's going to be a team leader, then he should goddamned well know the job. Shit, he went from about twelve to eighteen dollars by becoming a lead man. Show me the fairness in that!"

## THE LIMITS OF TRAINING

Though John McDonnell was convinced that training would be the means by which TQMS would be implemented at Douglas, the pressures of production caused it to be done in a piecemeal fashion: since the company had to produce planes, it couldn't shut down production to train everyone at once. In fact, most workers could not be spared from their jobs long enough to attend the training at all. Those who did go found, once they returned to their jobs, that little had changed and that they were unable to apply the principles they had learned. Smith knew that attempting this massive retraining effort in a high-pressure environment where production took precedence over everything else was risky. Still, he was shocked by the reality that confronted him. "We were forced to go out on the floor with big nets and scoop up employees who weren't doing anything. They were sent away for two weeks of training. It was like punishment. Then they were sent back to their jobs, where nothing had changed and there was no follow-up training to translate what they'd learned to their jobs. You might find some pockets out there where it worked, but damn few."

By mid-1990 only 8,000 employees—a fraction of the company's 50,000-strong workforce—had gone through the training program. While most employees said they had liked the training, their evaluations of the TQMS effort were, at best, mixed. Sue Walshe, a young woman who had recently been promoted to team leader in the Chem Mill, said, "Most of the people from the Chem Mill who went through the training said it was good and they came back bubbling with enthusiasm. But they were sent one by one, and their bosses never went with them. The effects wore off quickly, because there was no support on the floor for their new ideas once they came back."

Others said that training was fragmented but, worse, that it failed to translate back to their jobs. Andy Hyde, a team leader, complained, "People came back from training with a different attitude, but then they'd hit a brick wall. Their bosses hadn't been through any training, and they never got any on-the-job training once they came back." Jerry Aspin, a production worker, described how his boss and coworkers had mocked him when he had returned from the training. "They said, 'Where the hell have you been while we've been doing your work? Oh, you're converted now, ho, ho, ho!' It didn't make me feel too good." Aspin said he had liked the training but that his fellow class members had not taken it seriously. "There've been so many programs at Douglas that everyone figured, 'Oh, here comes another one.' "

Ralph Simms, a team leader in "Quick Fix," said that training had been wasted on the older workers, many of whom were cynical and refused to share their knowledge. "Some of those guys came back from training with their minds made up that anything they learned wouldn't work. I purposely sent some of my older problem workers, hoping that they might change. But they came back worse off than before they went. A lot of these older guys don't give a fuck. Look at that," he said, pointing to an older mechanic's red toolbox. On its side were three-inch letters that read, I DON'T KNOW. DON'T ASK. "What kind of signal do you think that gives to new workers in here? You think they're gonna go to him with a question? There's an old guard here, and they want to keep all they know for themselves! Most of these old farts just keep to themselves anyway. They don't lift a finger to help. That rubs off on the young guys, who pick up bad habits. Most of these old guys would never make it on the outside. They've gotten used to the easy life."

## THE SUPPORT OF THE LOCAL UNION ERODES

Though the union was supposed to have been a partner in the TQMS initiative, the local was sidelined because of political infighting. At issue was whether or not the union should cooperate with the company. Because the union caucus known as New Horizons supported TQMS, its president, Doug Griffith, was accused by dissident union factions of being a sellout. Richard Rios, an aggressive leader of Responsible Action Party, had long been an outspoken critic of cooperation between labor and management. His angry sentiments touched a responsive chord among many union members who harbored long-standing antagonisms against the company. The feelings surfaced in a runoff election for the union's presidency in May 1990, when a record thirteen thousand votes were cast. The election was close. The union members who were supporting the reform effort were stunned: Rios beat Griffith by a few hundred votes. Though the other key union leadership positions were won by New Horizons members, the presidency gave Rios a visible pulpit from which to assail the company and any union members who spoke in favor of cooperation.

Still, Rios lacked sufficient support to call a strike, and even if he could generate support for a strike he knew he would encounter stiff opposition from the International. He decided instead to try to extract concessions from the company in the upcoming contract negotiations by tying it up in its own red tape. He boasted publicly, "We can slow this place down to a standstill and bring the company to its knees." Bruce Lee knew of the danger that lay in Rios's strategy, because Douglas was now operating on the slimmest of margins. If conflict between the union and the company caused production to come to a halt, Douglas could easily fail, and thousands of high-paying jobs would be lost. Lee's own reelection bid was not far off, and he knew Local 148 represented the largest bloc of votes in his region. Whatever steps he might take to help management and the union find common ground, he would take them at great peril. Nevertheless, in many meetings and in mailings designed to bypass the local, Lee cautioned the workers that their jobs were at stake and urged them to challenge the local's leadership.

## POCKETS OF SUCCESS

Despite the growing conflict over TQMS and the erosion of the union's support, there were some isolated successes. For instance, John Wolf, a vice president who had been part of the original takeover, made significant improvements to the MD-80. Wolf was widely regarded as a capable leader, and he brought together a team of managers who were eager to prove themselves and to help save the company. Within months the MD-80 began to show improvement. An increasing number of aircraft were delivered on time. Quality improved as costs began to decline. Ron Berger, who was in charge of human resources for the MD-80, observed, however, that Wolf had brought these changes about through his own leadership, "Sure, his message was TQMS," Berger said, "but it could have just as well been Charles Dickens! What he accomplished, he did through common sense and personal leadership."

Wolf brought in Mike Young as general manager for the MD-80. In just a few months, Young doubled the weekly production rate of the MD-80 from 1.5 aircraft to 3.0. But even Young felt that TQMS—though a good idea—had been implemented too fast. "Most of the managers who got axed hung around for months," he later said. "Many of them were bitter, and they weren't motivated to do anything. On top of it, we had to bring in new people to fill the positions. In many cases they didn't know much about their new jobs and they had no informal networks to rely on, so it took another six months before they got up to speed. The bottom line was, we more or less just stopped what we were doing here for about a year."

## THE SUMMER OF HARD REALITY

By the summer of 1990 it was clear that TQMS had failed to penetrate Douglas's culture. Down in the shops the management shake-up was for many just a painful memory. Aircraft continued to be built largely as they had been in 1958. The revolution that John McDonnell had tried to spark had never happened. Most managers continued in their authoritarian ways, and permissive behavior persisted. The complex production system that governed daily life in the plant remained untouched. Joel Smith said he had tried to alter the production system—but, he conceded, "It was impossible. It was too complex. Too many people had vested interests in keeping things as they were." Smith felt that he had made some headway on standardizing some of the MD-80 assembly operations by providing precise timetables for each day's work. But, as Smith joked, "It had no effect on improving the process. All we did was sequence the waste!"

Meanwhile, things went from bad to worse. In the first quarter of 1990 Douglas posted losses of $84 million on sales of $1.1 billion. By the next quarter, losses had climbed to $117 million. McDonnell Douglas's stock dropped steadily in value, and its credit rating was downgraded. At the same time, the C-17 slipped further behind schedule and cost overruns grew, causing the air force to suspend payments. Rumors of mass layoffs swept through the plant, creating mass apprehension. It was a period John McDonnell calls "the summer of hard reality."[5]

For Smith, the Long Beach experience was torment. "It was like trying to save a drowning person," he recalled. "The closer you get to going under, the more frantic you get. You wind up doing crazy things, whatever it takes just to stay afloat. You paddle madly. None of us believed this place couldn't be turned around, but by this time no one could focus. It's very hard for a drowning guy to realize that he's just got to take a nice, deep breath and concentrate on floating, not on swimming."

John McDonnell agreed, "By summer it was clear that we had to cut costs drastically and quickly. The process of trying to get systemic improvement through TQMS was just not fast enough. Our markets were starting to fall out from under us. We had a number of fixed-price development programs, and they were not going well. We were significantly overrunning, and we were potentially even above ceiling price. It would all be on us! We had customers that were withholding progress payments, and we knew that we had to dramatically reduce costs to make sure that financially we wouldn't get into a position where we had no alternatives. So that's what happened."

The saga was followed closely by reporters, who speculated on whether the company would survive. As the financial crisis spilled out into public view, executives squabbled over whether to continue the TQMS training. An air force colonel publicly castigated Douglas in the press, charging that its executives had lost control and that they didn't know the difference between "participative" and "permissive" management. A brisk underground of cartoons and jokes sprang up as Joel Smith and other executives were regularly denounced on posters and flyers that began to appear on company hallway and bathroom walls. John Capellupo, Douglas's deputy president, was featured in one as a homeless person wearing a large sign that read, WILL BUILD AIRPLANES FOR FOOD! Workers joked that TQMS really meant "Time to Quit and Move to Seattle," the home of rival Boeing, which was flourishing.

On July 16, 1990, John McDonnell announced that, despite his hopes, TQMS had failed to restore the company's financial health. He was now going to take extraordinary measures to cut costs. Seven hundred million dollars would immediately be cut from the corporate budget. At least 17,000 jobs would be eliminated, 8,000 of them at Long Beach. The multimillion-dollar training budget would be cut in half, gutting the reform effort and forcing layoffs of all two hundred of the TQMS trainers.

Whatever hopes there had been of improved relationships within the ranks began to vanish as fears that the company might fail altogether caused some managers to commit desperate and panicky acts. Bill Skibbe, who had taken over as vice president of the MD-80, excoriated employees about their work areas and their bathrooms in a memorandum. It read, in part, "Why do you need or feel the urge to act like a pig or a pervert or a bigot by being a slob or writing your silly crap on the restroom walls? . . . CLEAN UP YOUR ACT OR LEAVE! FRANKLY, WE THINK YOU'RE CHILDISH, YOU'RE AN IDIOT, YOU'RE SICK AND YOU'RE BORING . . . GROW UP!"[6]

## DOUGLAS'S FORTUNES SINK

A few weeks later, on August 10, Joel Smith was fired. The experiment with TQMS was finished, and Smith had become the symbol of its failure. While the company tersely described his abrupt departure as a "resignation to pursue an advanced degree," it was clear that Smith had become a liability. Not everyone agreed, however. One industry analyst portrayed Smith's firing as a case of "the messenger who got shot."[7]

By September, a pall fell over the company as thousands of employees were laid off. Each week RIF (reductions in force) notices were issued that identified employees who had lost their jobs. Morale sunk to an all-time low as workers marked time, waiting for their names to be called. Managers were similarly dispirited but for different reasons. Though they were held accountable for meeting production goals, they were never sure if they would have the employees they needed to get the job done. A manager said, "We're running blind. We're trying to build airplanes, but we don't even know if we'll have the people to do the work tomorrow morning."

The company now entered a steep decline as it cut deeply into its workforce to reduce costs. Over the next three years 40,000 Douglas employees lost their jobs. Commercial contracts for both the MD-80 and the MD-11 slowed dramatically. In Building 13, where 7,200 workers had once produced three brand-new MD-80s every week, less than three were built each month at the close of 1994.[8]

To witness a loss of this magnitude is awesome. The last time I walked through it, Building 13 felt like a ghost town. The equivalent of a small city had simply vanished. From a human perspective, the misery of the individuals who had lost their jobs was incalculable. From an economic perspective, the impact was also enormous. The lost income represented by the 40,000 lost jobs jolted Long Beach before the effects rippled further outward to other already hard-pressed regions of California. One cannot help but wonder how such a tragedy could have occurred. Now that it has, what can be learned from Douglas's wrenching experience so that companies facing similar circumstances in the future may choose a different path?

## WHAT HAPPENED?

Depending on with whom one talks, there are numerous explanations for Douglas's failure. Joe Pirkle, a McDonnell Douglas vice president who had come from Saint Louis to help turn Douglas around, blamed the undisciplined California workforce and Douglas's permissive culture. "Maybe it's having the beach so close, or the sunshine, or maybe it's the drugs," Pirkle said. "The fact is, when you compare southern Californians to workers from Arkansas or Saint Louis, they don't begin to measure up. They just don't want to work." Vice President John Van Gels had given up on California's stringent regulations and the heavy-handed way in which they were applied. He was anxious for Douglas to reduce the size of its operations and to move manufacturing out of California to other states that would welcome a big aircraft builder. Others faulted Joel Smith, saying that his ability to communicate outweighed his ability to implement. As for John McDonnell, he continued to believe that if enough money had been available to pour into training, the company could have been turned around.

Yet somehow the company's brushes with bankruptcy had failed to penetrate the employees' consciousness. Despite the fact that manufacturing jobs in other U.S. plants were being cut in alarming numbers, at Douglas it was business as usual on the shop floor. Douglas was such an immense place that perhaps it was hard for anyone to imagine that one day it might be gone. Douglas's generosity with its managers and workers seems to have been regarded by many as a kind of entitlement—of getting something for nothing. Managers, engineers, and production workers had become complacent, and they were accustomed to having immense freedom to do what they wanted.

Working in Building 13 reminded me of being back in high school. On a typical day, just before the shift began at 6 A.M., a dozen or so younger men—blacks, whites, and Latinos—dressed in shorts or jeans, sneakers, and surfer T-shirts, milled around, joking with each other. Some wore their baseball hats backward, while others wore earrings and tattoos. Jim Keyes, a young group leader who was well regarded by both workers and managers, assembled his sixteen-person group for a brief morning meeting. His carefully coiffed hairdo and neat blue slacks and sweater set him apart from the scruffy-looking younger workers. Keyes went over a list of items for the day's installation on the two aircraft that loomed just beyond the bright lights hanging over the meeting area and workbenches. He discussed problems with absenteeism, turning to a worker who had repeatedly been absent. "How can we motivate you?" he asked matter-of-factly. "What's it going to take to get your attention? We need to eliminate the excuses." The young man did not answer but shifted uncomfortably in his chair. Another young worker, who looked like a teenager though he was already a father, started making complaining baby cries, which brought snickers from his coworkers. When he persisted, Keyes flashed him an angry look and said that housekeeping would be enforced every day. "People are going to be expected to clean their areas for twenty minutes." The young man blurted out, "Does that mean we just show up, or are we supposed to show up and clean too? You know, it's monkey see, monkey do!" He laughed wildly at his own joke. Keyes shook his head as the group disbanded and people walked over to their workbenches or to the nearby airplanes to begin the day's work.

It was not just the workers who had grown accustomed to the lax environment. Managers too had come to expect considerable freedom in their jobs. One manager called the ambiance at Douglas "a lollipop culture," adding, "People expect to be specially rewarded for doing their jobs. They're spoiled rotten." He described how employees would be awarded bonuses—which often ran into thousands of dollars beyond their salaries—for doing special projects that should have been done as part of their jobs. Extra rewards had become the norm, and there was no incentive or any sense of urgency to improve quality or control costs. Cost overruns and quality problems were routinely passed on to customers, and managers were rewarded for how well they managed crises, not for solving problems as they arose.

Even employees who were dedicated to working hard could not escape the debilitating effects of such a system. I spent an entire day with a mechanic as he searched the plant for rivets needed to join two parts that had been fabricated incorrectly. Before lunch we scoured parts bins in three hangars without luck. After lunch we talked to the Engineering Department to see if other rivets would be acceptable. None would. Later in the afternoon we discovered that the rivets' identification numbers had been transposed, and finally, as the shift ended, we located the correct rivets. The job had to wait until the next day to be completed. We had spent a total of thirteen hours locating the rivets, delaying a $30 million airplane for nearly twenty-four hours. No one seemed particularly concerned.

As legitimate waiting slowed down the pace of work, standing around and doing nothing became the accepted norm. One day in Building 13, a young mechanic who was working next to me closed his toolbox an hour before the shift ended, apparently finished for the day. As he put on a Walkman headset and began to pull his sweatshirt hood over his head, I asked him where he was going. "Roamin'," he answered. By "roaming" he was referring to the common practice of killing time by wandering aimlessly around the plant.

Managers had learned to turn a blind eye to customs like roaming, because they knew the union would be quick to react to any discipline. In an antagonistic environment, unions reap a symbolic harvest by defending their members whether they are right or wrong. The union and management each knows that drawn-out disciplinary cases are costly, and thus an unspoken standoff prevails in all but the most flagrant of cases.

As management's reluctance to impose discipline on workers deepened, so did the problems. A manager had been stabbed in the stomach by a worker in Building 13, and drugs had become a serious issue throughout the complex. The company sought to stop drugs at the front gate by testing employees before they reported for work, and four trained German shepherds kenneled outside of Building 13 periodically ran through the building to sniff out drugs and dealers. In one year alone, Douglas security employees made more than 250 undercover drug purchases to gather evidence against drug dealers within the company.

## CONCLUSIONS

Could McDonnell Douglas have done anything different to save the Long Beach plant? First, McDonnell Douglas executives waited too long to try seriously to save the huge subsidiary. They faced a paradox: How could they take control of Douglas before it was possible to do so? Though Saint Louis had tried to encourage Douglas to control its costs and quality over a period of nearly twenty-five years, every attempt had ended in failure. McDonnell Douglas executives had learned that a genuine reorganization would generate all-out conflict and that it could be achieved only with a great investment of time, energy, and money. As long as economic conditions were favorable and the parent company could continue to underwrite Douglas's losses, it was easier to look the other way. Even though costs had spiraled out of control, there was never any question about the quality or safety of Douglas planes. John McDonnell insisted that even as late as 1989 the conditions still looked manageable: "I would not call the situation at Douglas in early '89 as dire by any means. Frankly, we probably weren't aware that it was as tight as we later learned. . . . It wasn't until 1990 that it became more evident."

Second, the vision of TQMS was unclear even among the very executives who were charged with implementing it. It was, as Smith accurately described it, a "hodgepodge" of ideas that seemed reasonable on paper. But once the concepts were subjected to reality, they were quickly rendered ineffective by conflicting interests, adversarial relationships between management and labor, and mounting fear and uncertainty among workers and managers. The mounting financial pressures and immediate production needs, coupled with the program's lack of definition, offered little freedom to implement the overall strategy slowly and deliberately, correcting weaknesses as they emerged. Instead, TQMS was introduced swiftly and on a massive scale, leaving no room for learning and correction and no margin of error.

Third, the harsh way in which the reforms were introduced generated resistance from managers and production workers, who simply rejected the ideas out of hand. On learning that uncontrolled costs were threatening the entire corporation, McDonnell Douglas executives felt they had run out of time. Though they knew there would be some, perhaps considerable, negative reaction to their bold strategy, they gambled that the benefits would outweigh the costs. Though many hourly workers initially thought John McDonnell had done the right thing by essentially firing nearly half of the managers, the anxiety that swept through the company became self-defeating. Managers who might have helped save Douglas took refuge in self-protective behavior and regarded TQMS with suspicion and bitterness. When, in 1990, massive layoffs tore through the ranks of hourly workers, any remaining hopes of implementing TQMS vanished. Fearful and angry, most workers withdrew any support they might have offered as they waited to see if they would keep their jobs. Even under the best of circumstances, the union would have found it difficult to cooperate with management. But the severe layoffs drew immediate and widespread opposition, polarizing the union and management and making cooperation impossible.

Finally, the expectation that training alone could alter the powerful Douglas culture was misguided. Though the training was appreciated by many of those who attended, it had little impact on how the work of building aircraft was actually done. Still, John McDonnell continued to believe that "If someone is learning, its going to open their minds and make them more open to change, to have that learning mind-set." He was convinced that with enough time and money and some adjustments to the training, Douglas could have been turned around. "Training's key," he said. "It really is. I think training is all-important. . . . I think it could have worked if we had the time and the money to go massively and hang with it for a long period of time. In the final analysis, we didn't have the time or the money to do it."

However, in the end the effort to change Douglas failed because its production system was left virtually unaffected. As long as employees' jobs failed to require cooperation, teamwork, or trust, there was little hope of creating a "new culture" through training alone. The ingrained beliefs that had grown out of Douglas's mass production system — the adversarial relationships between management and labor, managers' authoritarianism, and complacency — proved to be intractable to change as the system of work itself remained unaltered. Aircraft continued to be built in much the same way as they had been in 1958, and the old production system continued to reinforce all of the old beliefs and behavior that had gotten Douglas into trouble in the first place. Without infusing new requirements for cooperation, teamwork, and trust into the company's core functions, there was little hope that any such human qualities could be produced.

## DISASTER OR MIRACLE?

Some observers believe that Douglas Aircraft will never recover. One researcher predicts that McDonnell Douglas will soon leave the commercial aircraft business altogether. Georgetown University researcher Loren Thompson reports that since 1990 Douglas has fallen into last place in the commercial aircraft race and that it is steadily losing market share to Airbus and Boeing.[9] Though the cash-strapped company has tried to find a partner to help share development costs for a new-generation wide-body to compete with Boeing's 777, none has yet materialized. Thompson concludes that Douglas's product line has become too narrow to enable it to regain a significant market share and that it will quit making commercial aircraft by the end of the 1990s.

But recent events point to a rosier scenario. In late 1995 Douglas landed an enormous order for eighty C-17 transport planes valued at $18 billion.[10] The air force had originally ordered forty planes at a cost of about $300 million each. Two years ago, the huge plane was plagued with technical problems and the program was more than $1 billion in the red. The company's performance had deteriorated to the point that the air force threatened to cancel the entire order. But by 1995 the C-17's span time (the days needed to build a plane) had been halved (from 1,100 days to 550 days), while the number of hours needed for final assembly and repair plunged by 80 percent. Most of the plane's technical problems had also been solved, and, according to the secretary of the air force, the plane posted "outstanding results" after rigorous flight testing.[11]

By late 1995 Douglas's commercial aircraft side had begun to boom as well. Though it had been scraping for orders through 1994, in 1995 the company sold 114 new jetliners, surpassing second-ranked Airbus.[12] In November 1995 Douglas launched its new MD-95 (a derivative of the old DC-9) to compete against the Boeing 737-600 in the potentially large hundred-seat aircraft market. Earlier in the year Douglas had been dealt a blow when SAS (Scandinavian Airlines System) gave Boeing a $1.2 billion order instead of giving it to Douglas. But just a few months later Douglas received a $1 billion order from ValuJet, a no-frills carrier located in Atlanta, for fifty MD-95s.[13] Industry analysts think that the order will give Douglas a chance to sell up to three hundred MD-95s, though it had to give ValuJet a steep (20 percent) discount to make the sale. On top of orders for the C-17 and the MD-95, Douglas split a $6 billion order from Saudi Arabia with Boeing for MD-11 wide-body jets and MD-90s.[14] And for a brief time there were high-level talks between executives of McDonnell Douglas and Boeing about a merger.[15]

The financial performance of McDonnell Douglas has also been extraordinary. *Forbes* credits John McDonnell for wielding a sharp ax, noting, "As revenues faded from $18.1 billion in 1991 to around $13.5 billion, in 1994, he succeeded in cutting costs even faster."[16] In fact, McDonnell Douglas turned a $101 million loss in 1990 into earnings of more than $570 million in 1994 and $685 million in 1995.[17] In late 1994, McDonnell Douglas stock split three for one and traded for a record high price per share of $141 on the New York Stock Exchange.[18]

How did all of this happen? According to key managers at Douglas and financial reports from industry analysts, the shake-up, the firings, and the training did make a difference. For instance, Human Resources Manager Ron Berger, who was close to the agonizing transition, believes that the layoffs gave management an opportunity to finally bare the system's problems so they could be corrected.[19] John Van Gels, now executive vice president, is credited with leading a new round of improvements. While not as bold as the TQMS initiative, the new improvements aim to alter the systems at Douglas that had eluded change. For example, up to a third of managers' salaries is now tied to the results-oriented criteria contained in the Malcolm Baldrige National Quality Award (America's premier quality award named after former Secretary of Commerce Malcolm Baldrige) — quality and productivity, waste reduction, customer satisfaction, and market share. Berger explains: "We haven't walked away from TQM. Once we got through the 'stupid period' we began to finally turn this place around. We've reduced span time to the lowest levels this company has ever seen, cut costs, and put quality back into the system. We're building better planes with half the people." Indeed, the numbers bear him out. Following the downsizing and budget-cutting, the hours to build an MD-80 decreased dramatically from 96,000 to 58,000, and the span time needed to build one fell from 150 days to 85 days, and the rejection rate of parts has been cut by 50 percent since 1992.[20]

But the appointment of Harry Stonecipher in 1994 as president and CEO of McDonnell Douglas (John McDonnell remained chairman) is regarded by most industry watchers as a watershed event. Stonecipher had attracted McDonnell Douglas executives' attention by leading Sundstrand, a failing aerospace parts maker, through a successful reorganization. He quickly announced plans for Douglas to become the lowest-cost producer of the highest-quality aircraft.[21] As Stonecipher told *Forbes*, "The financial strength of McDonnell Douglas is going to surprise the hell out of people."[22] He took full advantage of the conditions created by John McDonnell when he began to slash costs. Although Douglas Aircraft produces only a handful of aircraft today, it has cut costs so deeply that it still makes a profit and it has built up substantial cash reserves. "It has surprised everybody," said PaineWebber analyst Jack Modzelewski. "It is amazing. They didn't make a profit building one hundred and seventy planes a year, but they are making money building thirty-five a year."[23] In fact, Douglas has been profitable for twenty consecutive quarters since 1991. Next, Stonecipher hired Edward Bavaria, a former GE engine supersalesman, as Douglas's deputy president to pump up sales and to get ready for improvements in the market, a move that is clearly paying off. Even the rebellious UAW Local 148 seems to have taken note. In April 1995, under the leadership of Doug Griffith, the union signed a new five-year contract that committed it to a more cooperative relationship with the company by pledging its members to making improvements in the production process.

McDonnell Douglas seems to have finally gained control of its giant subsidiary. The costs have been extremely high, yet the experience offers significant insights for industry and labor leaders faced with similarly vexing circumstances, which we discuss in later chapters. Whether the changes at Douglas will prove to be permanent, however, remains an open question.

# PART III

# USS-POSCO

# CHAPTER SIX

# THE SHADOW OF ANDREW CARNEGIE

By THE EARLY 1980S the Pittsburg Works, located in Pittsburg, California, had become a liability to its parent company, U.S. Steel. Its antiquated rolling equipment could not produce steel and tinplate of high enough quality or low enough cost to compete in the fiercely competitive international marketplace, and U.S. Steel executives considered closing the mill altogether. But in 1986 the mill was rescued by an infusion of capital and new technology from South Korea's giant steelmaker Pohang Iron and Steel Company, Ltd., known by its acronym, POSCO. U.S. Steel and POSCO formed a joint venture called USS-POSCO Industries at the old Pittsburg Works. Over the next three years, they set about assembling some of the most sophisticated cold-rolling and finishing equipment in the world.

But in 1989, when the new mill roared to life, it was clear that the new joint venture would be hobbled by the same adversarial relationships between U.S. Steel and the United Steelworkers of America (USWA) that had been forged in the violence at Homestead a century before. Just as had happened at Douglas Aircraft, the antagonism between management and labor—a natural outgrowth of mass production—blinded both sides to the fact that they would *have* to work together if the joint venture was to survive. Steelworkers greeted each new company effort to improve product quality or cut costs as a ploy to cut their jobs or reduce their pay. Managers learned to distance themselves from their crews and behave autocratically in the belief that running the mills was their responsibility alone. Conflict was the norm.

Such rancor could be tolerated when the American steel industry was a virtual monopoly. However, as the industry was eclipsed by Japan and Korea, as well as by other foreign steelmakers, its divisive human relationships became a distinct liability. To a new company like USS-POSCO, this conflict-ridden culture would prove to be a serious handicap.

## THE STAMP OF ANDREW CARNEGIE

The lineage of USS-POSCO's adversarial culture can be traced directly to the confrontational tactics used by Andrew Carnegie as he built what would become the United States Steel Corporation.[1] Carnegie was Pittsburgh's leading steelman, with vast holdings up and down the Monongahela valley. In 1883 he bought the ninety-acre Homestead Works, which lay on the south bank of the Monongahela River seven or eight miles upstream from Pittsburgh. Carnegie invested millions of dollars in the latest technology, making Homestead one of the most advanced steel producers in the world. One man could do the work of four or five, and unskilled workers could be trained to become productive workers in a matter of weeks.[2] But, according to William Serrin, author of a recent authoritative history of Homestead, Carnegie and his partner, Henry Clay Frick, wanted what they considered to be a fair return on their investment.[3] They demanded smaller crew sizes and reductions in wages, a pattern that would be repeated many times over during the next century. The union at Homestead, the Amalgamated Association, was the last remaining union in the Monongahela valley. It was a mild-mannered craft union that counted only 800 of Homestead's 3,800 workers as members. Even though union members worked with the company in a spirit of cooperation, Carnegie demanded complete control of his business and sought to get rid of the union.[4]

The events that followed led to the infamous lockout and pitched battle between Homestead employees and Pinkerton guards described earlier. Though Carnegie ultimately succeeded in breaking the union and regaining control of the mill, the cost was enormous. The violence destroyed whatever trust existed and fostered a deep bitterness on both sides that would persist for the next hundred years.

In 1901 Carnegie sold his immense holdings to railroad millionaire J. P. Morgan for $400 million. Morgan, in turn, created the United States Steel Corporation.[5] Henry Frick served on the board of the new corporation, which continued to embrace a strict antiunion policy. A member of U.S. Steel's executive committee expressed it bluntly: "If a workman sticks up his head, hit it."[6] U.S. Steel tried to halt the spread of unionism by breaking a strike later that year, and it forced the union to give up jurisdiction over fourteen mills. With the balance of power firmly in the company's hands, U.S. Steel refused to recognize the union at all. The Amalgamated was soon banished permanently from all but a few of U.S. Steel's mills.[7]

Over the next quarter century, every attempt to organize the steel industry failed. U.S. Steel—and the other large steelmakers such as Republic, National, Weirton, Bethlehem, Youngstown, and Wheeling—were simply too powerful to challenge. But by 1934 the mood of the country had begun to change, and Congress began drafting sweeping legislation to protect industrial workers. Steel executives descended on Washington in droves to argue vehemently against federal intervention, claiming that it would destroy what they called the "friendly" relations they enjoyed with their employees.[8] A vice president of U.S. Steel testified before a Senate committee that "One of the great developments of recent years has been the progress toward complete cooperation and the abolition of conflict between the worker and his boss."[9] He likened labor relations in the steel industry to a happy marriage. "Both depend on a mutual conviction that their interests in life are largely in common, at least to the extent that they should form an alliance."[10] But Congress was unmoved, and in 1935 it passed the National Labor Relations Act, also known as the Wagner Act, which gave workers the right to organize and to bargain with their employer over wages and working conditions.[11]

Also in 1935, John L. Lewis formed the Committee for Industrial Organization (later known as the Congress of Industrial Organizations), or CIO, to organize industrial workers whose unions had been forced out of the craft-oriented American Federation of Labor (AFL). Lewis appointed former coal miner Philip Murray to head the Steel Workers Organizing Committee (SWOC).[12] The committee, which would later become the United Steelworkers of America, planned to finally establish a union at U.S. Steel, still the industry leader. Art Mullett worked for Murray as an organizer in 1936. "The steel companies were antiunion to the core, and USS led the pack," he remembered. "To them, the only good union man was a dead union man. They got ready for war to keep the union out. They had espionage systems to infiltrate the unions, and they had their own private police systems. They'd stockpiled miles of barbed wire, shotguns, pistols, ammunition, and tens of thousands of dollars worth of tear gas. It was clear what they had in mind! But the law finally brought these companies to the table."

By the end of 1937 Murray and his fellow organizers had established collective bargaining agreements with Carnegie Illinois and four other large U.S. Steel subsidiaries. Finally, after a half century of bloody conflict, steel company executives had no choice but to acknowledge the place of unions at the bargaining table. It was an uneasy alliance, however, as both sides struggled to control working conditions and wages. Antagonisms boiled over in national steel strikes in 1946, 1949, and 1952, hardening the positions of both sides. The confrontational tactics begun by Carnegie and Frick a half century earlier, and the adversarial beliefs that supported them, had taken root in an industrial culture that, despite the reforms of the New Deal, proved notoriously difficult to ameliorate.

## THE DECLINE OF AMERICAN STEEL

By the mid-1950s the steel industry was expanding on a wave of postwar prosperity. For a while, conflict was muted as both sides benefited from the growing profits. As long as both sides shared in the general prosperity, neither had a reason to upset the delicate balance.[13] Management concerned itself with controlling the workplace and keeping peace with the union, while the union rejected the notion that it had any responsibility for product quality or productivity. Indeed, prosperity began to blunt the union's zeal, and complacency became widespread.

Union leaders began to lose touch with their own members as they paid themselves ever-larger salaries and treated themselves to a large share of the industry's immense profits. One of them was David McDonald, who inherited the presidency of the union after Philip Murray's death in 1952.[14] *Business Week* writer John Hoerr has described how McDonald, who had grown up in poverty, liked his large salary, his limousines, and his bodyguards. He hobnobbed with the rich and famous and cherished the limelight. Steel executives privately considered McDonald a buffoon, but they supported him because he was able to keep the local unions under control.[15]

But the price of stability was high. To compensate for the lack of trust between management and labor, agreements were spelled out in an abundant and meticulous detail that defied common sense. For instance, according to Art Mullett, U.S. Steel once had more than 55,000 different job classifications that had accumulated over the years in long and tedious bargaining sessions.[16] An adversarial culture led each side to make extreme demands, knowing it would settle for something less. Such bargaining, Mullett said, was rooted in the constant struggle for power. With a shrug of his big shoulders, he said, "You walked away with whatever you was big enough to carry." Any added costs were simply passed along to the consumer in the form of higher prices.[17]

Perhaps the strategy seemed rational in the prosperous 1950s. Though collective bargaining offered a framework within which management and labor could negotiate, it did little to truly improve the underlying antagonism between them. The side that prevailed in the detailed language of job descriptions and wage agreements would also control the workplace, and arguing the fine points of an increasingly specialized language became the work of highly paid negotiators and labor lawyers. The formalistic, incremental style of bargaining continued to emphasize the division between the sides. That labor and management depended on each other or had anything in common was an alien concept. As long as profits continued to grow and labor and management were both assured they would get more money, there was little need to develop a trusting or respectful relationship.

By 1970, however, all this was about to change. Ominous signs were appearing on the horizon. In 1946 American steel companies produced 54.1 percent of the world's raw steel; by 1970 the amount had been more than halved, to 20.1 percent.[18] During the 1940s and 1950s steel executives had become accustomed to boom-and-bust cycles; they had learned that the boom periods would compensate handsomely for the losses incurred during the downturns. But as a vice president of Bethlehem Steel observed, "What they overlooked in the sixties was that the downturns were getting deeper and the upswings were getting less high. They couldn't get the price in a downturn because of foreign competition, and in an upswing foreign competition was skimming off the demand. So this great commandment—that volume will take care of everything—was no longer applicable."[19] Instead of investing in modern technologies in the 1960s and 1970s, steel executives clung to the traditional methods. To make matters worse, they had greatly overexpanded America's steelmaking capacity. Meanwhile, the Japanese and European producers had been forced to rebuild their steelmaking facilities, which had been destroyed in the Second World War, and had done so with state-of-the-art technology that enabled them to make higher-quality steel faster and at a lower cost. By the early 1980s foreign competitors had cut so deeply into America's markets that half of the nation's steelmaking capacity lay idle.[20] American steel executives, who had failed to read the changing environment accurately, were unprepared for this onslaught of foreign competition, and by 1984 American steelmakers accounted for less than 12 percent of the world's raw steel.[21] American steel was in a steep, seemingly irreversible decline.

But competition was coming not only from abroad but also from within. Upstart minimills—nonunion specialty producers that made steel from melted scrap—began to undercut the large integrated mills. In 1960 American minimills had only 3 percent of the domestic market; by the late 1980s their share had increased to nearly 40 percent.[22] But the growth of minimills did not make up for the loss of hundreds of thousands of jobs as the big steelmakers began closing mills to stanch their losses. Throughout the 1970s wages in the industry had risen faster than productivity had. American steelworkers had become the highest-paid industrial workers in the world, earning between $22 and $23 an hour on average—twice what Japanese steelworkers earned. Suddenly U.S. Steel was awash in red ink.

In a three-month period in 1980, it lost $562 million, the largest single-quarter industrial loss in American history. Republic Steel, one of America's largest steel producers, was also teetering on the edge of bankruptcy. Steel executives told the leadership of the United Steelworkers of America that if labor costs could not be controlled, the rest of America's steel producers would be out of business by 1990. Executives began to shut down mills and lay off steelworkers in huge numbers. By early 1982 107,900 workers, or 37 percent of the country's steelworkers, were laid off. By the end of 1982 more than one in two steelworkers was out of a job. When it was over, more than a quarter-million steelworkers would be out of work. In the mills along the Monongahela River alone the number of high-paying steel jobs shrank from 80,000 in the 1940s to fewer than 4,000 by the late 1980s.[23]

## THE PITTSBURG WORKS

One of the near victims of this massive downsizing was a U.S. Steel finishing mill that lies on the Sacramento River about forty miles north of San Francisco in Pittsburg, California. At the turn of the century it was owned by Columbia Steel and consisted of a single fifteen-ton open-hearth foundry that produced iron castings from melted scrap and pig iron. During the 1920s, however, it was greatly expanded to meet Californians' ever-increasing demand for building materials.[24] In 1930 the mill was acquired by U.S. Steel, which pumped in millions of dollars to modernize and expand its facilities. The Pittsburg Works produced a huge variety of products—cables for the Oakland Bay bridge and San Francisco's cable cars, wire for fencing and bedsprings, nails, reinforcing bars, and pipes, as well as galvanized sheet iron and tinplate.[25]

By the mid-1950s the Pittsburg Works was booming. Every day 5,200 men and women crowded through the main gate in a sea of helmets. They jostled down through the tunnel under the railroad tracks, emerging on the other side beside the enormous buildings that housed the thundering mills. Though growth had slowed somewhat since the booming postwar years, the Pittsburg Works continued to expand, adding a new tinning line and galvanized sheet facilities in 1953 and a third tinning line in 1958. Within a few years, however, most of the steelworkers would lose their jobs as Pittsburg was forced to slash its excess capacity, close its open hearths, and shut its rod, pipe, and wire mills. Also, without substantial investments in new and cleaner technologies being made, the old equipment could not meet the increasingly strict environmental regulations that proliferated in the 1960s. In 1964 U.S. Steel chose to close Pittsburg's open hearths instead of modernizing them. Little by little, the machinery in the other production facilities became worn down and obsolete. The Pittsburg Works tried desperately to survive, producing anything that might help it stay afloat. It rolled out low-quality steel products and even promised to deliver boxes of nails to customers within twenty-four hours.[26] But in the late 1970s it ran into fierce competition from Japanese producers, who began to invade its markets with superior steel at lower prices.

## THOMAS C. GRAHAM

In 1983 Thomas C. Graham became president of U.S. Steel, by then a division of USX, which was diversifying out of steel into oil and chemicals. He was determined to stem Big Steel's slide into oblivion. The year before, USX had bought Marathon Oil for $6.4 billion. Most steelworkers felt that the purchase had been an act of disloyalty—proof that the corporation was abandoning the very thing that had made it strong. Graham came to U.S. Steel from Jones and Laughlin, where he had been president since 1974. An engineer by training, he knew steelmaking in a way most steel executives, who generally rose through the ranks of finance, did not. At Jones and Laughlin he had won a reputation for being one of the best managers in business by investing in the latest technology to reduce the number of man-hours it took to produce a ton of steel. He championed labor-management participation teams (LMPTs), which worked on the principle that by harnessing production workers' detailed knowledge of steelmaking, productivity and quality could be greatly improved. With Graham's encouragement, the idea had spread at Jones and Laughlin, producing impressive savings.

   Graham, who now heads AK Steel Holding Corporation (a joint venture of Armco and Kawasaki Steel), is a tough American steelman, though he dresses like a banker in a dark suit, monogrammed shirt, bow tie, and suspenders. He is refreshingly direct. I met him in September 1992 in his

Gateway Center office in Pittsburgh, just a few blocks from where the United Steelworkers of America were holding their national convention.[27] Expecting to pass through a labyrinth of offices and secretaries to reach this man, who, despite his accomplishments—or perhaps because of them—is vilified by unemployed steelworkers up and down the Monongahela valley, I was surprised to find him sitting behind a desk in a sparsely furnished single room.

With a friendly wave, Graham motioned me to sit in a chair in front of his desk while he finished scrutinizing a paper. A moment later, he looked up and stuck out a hand as we began to talk about the problems of the steel industry. Graham has little sympathy for modern-day labor relations and lays the blame squarely at the feet of management: "We have very substantial *management* problems, and these *management* problems frequently become characterized as union problems. We have all kinds of managers who run around bemoaning unions and saying 'You know, if we were just free to run this place,' and so on. If you study situation after situation, however, you find that they *are* free, but they haven't exercised their freedom and it has atrophied. So is that the union's fault? Well, you could argue about it. In general, I'd say the gravest criticism due those of us in the integrated industry, which is essentially the unionized industry, is that we haven't exercised the contractual rights that we currently enjoy. We've got lots of critics, because we're losing money. But needless to say, human nature being what it is, we haven't focused our critics on our own flaws. We have said, 'Imported steel, union work rules, and on and on.' I believe that management wears the rose. If they succeed, they should be rewarded. If they fail, they hang!

"Managers have a fiduciary responsibility, not to the unions but to the owners of the business. They need to do what is good for the business. Ultimately they need to do that on behalf of the employees too. But there are some constraints on what they can do, because in a unionized business we have signed contracts limiting our freedom of action. As consenting adults, we have agreed to that. But within that framework you do what you can do to enhance the business, and if there is a generalized criticism that's due us, I think it's probably that we have not been vigorous enough in exercising those rights. You know, you have to become a student of the contract, and arbitration and grievances and all kinds of things, which is a long course to get down to; it's a detailed business. It does not lend itself to generalizations, but I believe strongly that an awful lot of the problem lies at the feet of the managers."

Graham does not hide his distaste for unions. He believes that "if you stand back and look at the American steel industry, we have a portion which is prospering and growing like a bad weed. And we have a segment of the industry that has been, and continues to be, in decline. The former is nonunion. The latter is union. And so, if you just take the present and the twenty-year past and extrapolate it, I guess you'd say someday the union will be irrelevant.

"I think there is a severely diminished role for unions. That's why we still revel in the Homestead strike. I mean, that era is gone. Steel plant managers today do not carry black snake whips. People don't work in steel plants stripped to the waist with their lives in jeopardy and sweat pouring off like they used to. That isn't the way it works. So it may be that somebody will devise a new model and a new product for unions. I mean, they have to have a product. I think the market is severely diminished for their historic product. If you still had unsophisticated European immigrants as a workforce, maybe that's an appropriate tactic."

Graham characterized his view as a "lone voice in the wilderness." But he is not alone. Many executives privately agree. No one doubts Graham's effectiveness as a corporate executive committed to looking out for the company's best interest, though his style and beliefs have conflicted sharply with those of the union. And most steelworkers are quick to blame Graham personally for U.S. Steel's painful shrinkage. But whatever Graham's strengths and weaknesses, the forces propelling him are forces anyone in his position would have had to grapple with. In his desire to forge a more efficient and profitable industry—even if doing so would cause the human pain of slashing jobs—he is a direct descendant of the hard-driving men who founded and built the industry a century ago.

Graham's mission was to stanch U.S. Steel's losses. When he took over U.S. Steel in 1983, it was obvious to him that the company was overextended, so he naturally welcomed feelers from the South Koreans. U.S. Steel already had the facility in Pittsburg. Simply shutting it down would open the West Coast market to the Japanese—something the company wished to avoid at any cost. "The plant as it existed was obsolete,"

Graham later recalled. "No question about that. It was going to take massive reinvestment, but we had more on our plate than we could carry. The judgment call was what can we keep and what should be retired. Some of us felt there still was the prospect of profit in the steel business, but it wasn't obvious at the time. We were the only tin producer on the West Coast, and the tinplate market is intimately tied to California's agricultural market." A joint venture, he felt, might help U.S. Steel exploit its excess capacity without its having to sell off more assets.

At the same time, the giant South Korean steelmaker POSCO had begun to produce some of the highest-quality, lowest-cost semifinished steel (called "hot bands") in the world.[28] POSCO would benefit from a joint venture with an American partner that could finish excess hot bands produced in its Pohang and Kwangyang Works and give it access to markets in the Western Hemisphere. Graham knew that POSCO "was building a massive steel capacity in South Korea. It had to be marketed around the world because there was no home market." The joint venture would also give the South Koreans a footing from which to challenge the Japanese, which they dearly wished to do.

After initial inquiries from the South Koreans in the early 1980s, USX Chairman David Roderick let it be known that he was interested. During a meeting of the International Iron and Steel Institute, Roderick mentioned that he would like to discuss the possibilities of a joint venture with Tae Joon Park, a retired South Korean Army general who was then chairman of POSCO.

## THE MARVEL OF KOREAN STEEL

Park, who has since been disgraced in a dramatic fall from power, founded POSCO in 1968.[29] Today it is the world's second largest steelmaker, producing high-quality steel at the lowest cost in the world.[30] A large part of POSCO's success is attributable not only to its state-of-the-art technology but also to its labor costs, which run just a fraction of those paid in the United States, the highest in the world.[31]

POSCO produces 70 percent of all crude steel produced in South Korea—22 million tons as of 1994.[32] Further, it exports 2.8 million tons to Japan and 1.4 million to the United States each year. In the late 1980s

POSCO's production eclipsed that of USX (which for years had been the world leader). Today POSCO produces nearly twice as much crude steel as USX does. Its two steelworks—the original works in Pohang and a newer one in Kwangyang—are built on a grand scale.

My research team and I flew to Korea in 1991 to get a better understanding of USS-POSCO's Korean parent. It was a cold, gray, rainy morning as we approached the outskirts of Pohang, leaving the serene mountains and rice paddies behind. Pohang is a hodgepodge of corrugated steel, cement, and wood buildings that, especially in the dreary rain, could be any military base or industrial town in the world.

Across the Hyung San River, which flows into the Sea of Japan, we could make out the shapes of a dozen or more red-striped chimneys that tower hundreds of feet over the steelworks. Next, the outlines of four enormous blast furnaces came into view. Huge buildings painted light blue, red, and tan enclosed the casting and rolling mills. Inside the tall chainlink fence that surrounds the 2,200-acre steelworks stood a tower that affords railroad traffic controllers a 360-degree view. A banner over the main gate proclaimed, RESOURCES ARE LIMITED. CREATIVITY IS UNLIMITED. The acrid smell of sulfuric acid hung in the air, reminding me of the Pittsburg Works.

Instead of turning left into the works, we turned right into a parklike setting. Everywhere were manicured hedges, maple forests, rocks, and pools of water—"A plant in the park," a concept created by Park, who was respectfully called "the Chairman" by everyone. According to one of our guides, the Chairman had a green thumb and knew the name of every plant by heart. As our car climbed the wooded hills, we passed apartment buildings, houses, and a futuristic sports coliseum for POSCO's professional soccer team, "the Atoms." Under Park's direction, POSCO had built a vast complex of housing, schools, shopping malls, and restaurants for its employees at both Pohang and Kwangyang to help recruit and retain a first-rate workforce in these rather remote areas. No doubt the community living also generated a sense of identity and a commonalty of purpose among the 43,000 employees, who dressed in tan uniforms and boots, lending a military air to the place.

The contrast between POSCO and U.S. Steel is striking. I had just returned from western Pennsylvania, where the remnants of U.S. Steel's once mighty industrial empire—historic mills like Duquesne, Homestead, Braddock, McKeesport, and others—lie rusting and lifeless. But here in bustling Pohang was the heart of South Korea's steel industry in the early stages of its booming development, seemingly untouched by the country's current recession. The more than 40,000 steelworkers seemed to be working in unison, even though, in other parts of Korea, violent strikes were erupting over industrial workers' demands for higher wages.

Economist Hiwhoa Moon, who heads Korea's Productivity Center and its parent organization, the Asian Productivity Organization, discussed South Korea's economic picture one morning in his Seoul office. "Though Korea had a twelve percent growth in productivity each year between 1986 and 1989," he explained, "our competitiveness has gone down the drain since then."[33] Moon, who served as assistant minister for economic policy before taking over the Productivity Center, observed that wildcat strikes had nearly crippled the country between 1988 and 1990. "Most of the strikes were violent. They were often instigated by politically motivated agitators with money from North Korea and sympathizers who live in Japan. Many of our union leaders were confused guys who bought their ideology," he claimed. He insisted that wage demands, coupled with rising imports, had upset Korea's positive balance of trade, causing the rate of productivity gains to shrink to only half that of wage increases. "Bad habits were coming to Korea from Japan indirectly through *jae-tech*, or speculative investing in stocks and real estate, rather than in wealth-producing activity."

But, Moon said, POSCO had not been affected. "POSCO's is an orderly system, and the managers behaved themselves during the strikes. So for the average worker, South Korea's labor unrest had little impact." In 1992 the typical POSCO millworker made nearly $22,000, considerably more than most other South Korean workers, and the company provides free education for two children through college. Further, POSCO pays up to a third of the financing for a house. Most important, perhaps, the company provides its employees with a guarantee of lifetime employment, though the worldwide oversupply of steel has raised the possibility of layoffs in 1996.

The man responsible for POSCO's labor relations was Executive Vice President Yoh Sang Whan.[34] When I met with Yoh in Pohang, he was managing POSCO's human resources, which include the company's technical university, modeled after the California Institute of Technology, and its research institute, where hundreds of scientists work to keep the company on the leading edge of technological and economic change. Yoh was vitally concerned with developing a corporate culture that would ensure that the company would have an influential role in the Korean economy as well as in the global one.

Yoh carries himself with a regal bearing, though he also evinces a sense for the common man. As tea was served, he spoke in his unique measured dialect, dressed impeccably but casually. A photographer ducked in unobtrusively, clicking photos of our research group as Yoh spoke of the shrinking world and the importance of person-to-person, face-to-face relationships. "This is the age of the direct experience," he said. "Up to now it has been just the upper classes who have been allowed to meet. The world is shrinking, becoming like a small town. Borders are disappearing. Our joint venture can become a vehicle for mutual understanding. This is also the time for people at the bottom, not just the upper class. The people at the bottom want to join to get the same feeling."

Yoh said that POSCO had learned the importance of continuing investment from U.S. Steel's failure. "U.S. Steel was the symbol of the industry, but there was no innovation or investment. If a company cannot make a good product or be profitable, it is the responsibility of top management, not the workers. Korea doesn't forget its old friend who stood by it in time of war." After a long pause he added, "But yours is a system problem, a *culture* problem."

According to Yoh, the joint venture in Pittsburg offered the possibility of combining the American and South Korean national cultures, blending the best of both. "Americans have a strong sense of responsibility. If I give an order, I don't have to worry because I know it will be carried out. Yours are pragmatic people who always want to 'do it best.' With such honest and good people, if a company cannot make a profit, it is management's responsibility." He added, "We Koreans have a high degree of patriotism. We are a hardworking people, with vitality and a 'can-do' spirit. If there is a will, it can be done. If we mix both together, we will succeed."

## USS-POSCO INDUSTRIES

In 1986, following discussions between USX Chairman David Roderick and POSCO Chairman Tae Joon Park, a joint venture called USS-POSCO Industries was formed. POSCO contributed $194 million to buy half of the Pittsburg plant. Together the two giant steelmakers invested $450 million to modernize its facilities. The mill's success would depend in large part on a continuous supply of high-quality hot bands from POSCO, though it would also use steel produced by U.S. Steel mills. According to the terms of the agreement, profits generated by the joint venture would first go to retire the debt incurred by the modernization. To ensure that profits would stay with the company and not be invested in other industries or sent to Korea, the agreement further stipulated that future profits were to be reinvested in the company.

How the joint venture was actually developed is a fascinating story. The old mills were forced to keep running around the clock to produce revenue while U.S. Steel and POSCO constructed the largest industrial project America's West Coast had seen in twenty years. Since then, the company has struggled to expand its foothold in a market already glutted with steel. It has weathered a continuing battle with local trade unions over who would build the project and who would unload steel from South Korean ships. Political pressures applied by the unions drew environmental regulatory agencies into the fray. For a time, USS-POSCO was branded, by the Bay area's liberal community, an antiunion, antienvironmental company. In 1993 the joint venture narrowly escaped annihilation in the wake of "dumping" charges brought by thirteen big American steelmakers against foreign steel exporters, including South Korea.

The case of USS-POSCO shows just how difficult it is to survive and prosper under such adversity. The joint venture's executives and union leaders have succeeded in building the fifth most sophisticated cold-rolling mill in the world. They have also succeeded in retraining the venture's steelworkers to run this computerized, high-tech mill in its own learning center. But the real contribution of USS-POSCO's experience is its success in altering the adversarial labor-management relationships that all but paralyzed the venture's in its early years. We now look at how the union and management were finally able to break with the past and begin to establish common ground. The joint venture is now in its tenth year of operation, and the quality of its products has improved dramatically. It has also become profitable for the first time. Whether or not the changes have permanently altered the combative relationships between management and labor, only time will tell. What is clear, however, is that unless management and the union continue to make progress toward cooperation, the company will surely be at serious risk.

# CHAPTER SEVEN

# CULTURAL PARALYSIS

THE LIGHT BLUE BUILDINGS that house USS-POSCO's modern equipment and the towering blue cranes in the river port used to unload steel from South Korean ships are visible from miles away. Like building aircraft, finishing steel requires an operation of massive proportions. Freight trains rumble through the five-hundred-acre site, and huge buildings extend a half mile to the south and three quarters of a mile to the east and west.

USS-POSCO is a downstream finishing operation for hot bands—thirty-four-ton coils of flat, semifinished steel—that are brought in from upstream works by ship from POSCO's Kwangyang Works and by rail from U.S. Steel's Gary (Indiana) and Fairfield (Alabama) Works. At USS-POSCO, the semifinished steel goes through the modernized Rolling Division—a pickling and cold-rolling process—and may be further processed into cold-rolled steel or, in the company's older Galvanized or Tin Divisions, into galvanized sheet or tinplate. This new rolling mill, one of the fastest in the world, has the capacity to produce more than 1.4 million tons of high-quality finished steel each year.

The quality of incoming steel is of critical importance to a high-tech facility like USS-POSCO's. Incoming coils are threaded onto the new line and welded together to form a continuous ribbon of steel. They then head for the bright-blue-and-yellow Pickle Line Tandem Cold Reduction Mill, or PLTCM, which extends the length of three football fields. In the first control room, known as the entry pulpit, operators manage the incoming steel coils. Their job is to make sure that the coils are properly lined up, and they are also responsible for monitoring the line's performance. More than a hundred computers collect data on line speed, temperature, and steel thickness, or "gauge." Data from the smaller computers are relayed to a large mainframe computer, which analyzes and regulates the process automatically. The information is flashed up onto a dazzling array of overhead video monitors and computer screens.

About fifty feet further down the line is the smaller welding pulpit, where the butt end of the outgoing strip is automatically welded to the leading edge of the new one. In an astonishing display of technology, accumulators—structures that tower overhead like skyscrapers—accumulate thousands of feet of steel in reserve, enabling the line to run at full speed while one section is momentarily stopped at the welding pulpit to enable the welded connection to be made.

A few hundred feet further down the line, the steel strip speeds through pickling baths, where hydrochloric acid eats away heat scales and rust and deionized water rinses the strip clean. Next it goes through five rolling-mill stands that exert enormous pressure and tension on the steel, squeezing and pulling a 4,000-foot hot band like pizza dough until it is a 40,000-foot cold-reduced strip. Each of the five stands contains six huge rolls that give the strip its shape and thickness. At the end of the line, the steel is recoiled and readied for shipment to a customer or to one of USS-POSCO's other mills, where it will be processed further into sheet products or tinplate.

Technologically speaking, when the new mill started up in 1989, the joint venture took a giant step into the future. But a tangle of economic and human problems still lay ahead.

First, it was a risky time to spend hundreds of millions of dollars on expansion since the market for steel had gone soft. Worldwide steel consumption had remained flat through the 1980s, growing less than 1 percent each year, and demand was projected to remain sluggish through the

1990s.¹ At the same time, American and foreign minimills such as Nucor and Tokyo Steel were undercutting the prices charged by big integrated producers such as USX, Nippon, NKK, and Kawasaki, thus penetrating their markets deeply.

Second, by 1989 California was becoming a questionable place in which to make a huge capital investment. Just as Douglas Aircraft's executives were chafing under the state's increasingly strict environmental regulations, U.S. Steel executives regarded the demanding regulatory climate with trepidation. To make matters worse, California's political leaders seemed indifferent to the state's economy. Tom Graham put it bluntly: "Anybody who would consciously locate a manufacturing corporation in California ought to have his head examined. I mean, you'd have to have a death wish to do that!"²

Finally, there was no way the company could survive in the intensely competitive marketplace as long as internal conflict diverted energy from producing low-cost, high-quality steel. It would require the sort of cooperation and teamwork between management and the union that was rarely seen in the steel industry. Though the relationships between management and labor at Douglas Aircraft had been bad, those inherited by USS-POSCO were among the worst of any in America. In addition, much of the leadership of USWA Local 1440 had come from mills in the Monongahela valley that U.S. Steel had already closed. These men were not only angry but bitter. Yet they had also witnessed how foreign competition had nearly destroyed the American steel industry, leaving open the possibility that some new compact between management and labor might now be fashioned.

## IN THE EYE OF A STORM

Before they could tackle these three issues, USS-POSCO's management had to fight off not only hostile unions outside the plant but also environmentalists, who had formed a powerful alliance that had vowed to stop the joint venture. Tensions with the outside unions built before the plant was actually constructed. Randy Smith, who was then USS-POSCO's vice president for industrial relations but has since retired, explained that in 1987 they had put the $350 million construction project out to bid. It had been the single largest construction project seen on the West Coast in twenty years.[3] As Smith recalled, "The union contractor's bid was $45 million higher than the nonunion contractor that we ultimately chose. We could not have gone forward with the union contractor because his cost was too high. It would have bankrupted the joint venture." But no sooner were the bids submitted than the local Building Trades Council (unionized carpenters and plumbers) began to put pressure on the company to hire the union contractor, without regard to cost.[4] Smith recounted how events had become ugly. The unions had decided to attack the company politically to try to enforce their demands. They had also wanted to make sure that any other companies contemplating expansion knew that construction work would have to be done through the union. Trying to embarrass the South Koreans and generate public support, five hundred trade unionists picketed the plant and the South Korean Consulate in San Francisco.[5] A few months later, hundreds of people jammed a Contra Costa County Board of Supervisors meeting to pressure the county to block the project on environmental grounds. The supervisors refused to stop the project. Next the unions sued the county, charging that the new mill was environmentally unsound and that the county had failed to properly regulate industrial expansion.[6] The struggle attracted a large following of influential Bay area activists and politicians, and USS-POSCO was denounced for being antilabor and antienvironment.

The environmentalists' charges were not totally without merit. U.S. Steel and POSCO had invested millions of dollars in the new mill's design, including an acid regeneration plant to recycle the hydrochloric acid used in pickling and scrubbers to clean emissions released into the air. But in a series of accidents even before the new mill opened, acid waste had been dumped into sewers, hazardous waste drums had been improperly labeled, and polluted water had been dumped into the Sacramento River. California regulatory agencies fined the company millions of dollars, providing more fuel for the angry Building Trades Council, which charged USS-POSCO with flouting environmental standards.[7]

"We were a great target!" raged Smith. "Despite the fact that this is one of the cleanest mills in the world, a steel mill projects a dirty image. People forget that this company makes a significant contribution to the surrounding community. We employ nearly one thousand people in good union jobs, and our annual payroll runs more than forty-four million dollars. The city of Pittsburg alone gets more than six million a year from us in taxes! But the building trades exploited the dirty-steel-mill image for their own ends!"

Environmentalists and unionists formed an alliance around their common opposition to the joint venture and launched an all-out assault. In the spring of 1988 ten thousand Bay area unionists, led by Jesse Jackson and other Bay area politicians and flanked by TV cameras, marched to USS-POSCO from the nearby community college to protest its antiunion practices.[8] USS-POSCO's unions could only stand by silently, caught between their own company and their brothers and sisters in other trade unions. Despite the pressure and the negative press, the construction project went forward and the modernization was completed on schedule. But as the new mill began operations and the environmental furor died down, the joint venture's image had already been badly tarnished.

Not quite two years later, on February 21, 1990, USS-POSCO again found itself at the eye of yet another storm of negative publicity. This time the ostensible conflict was over air pollution from the South Korean ships that were unloading hot bands at USS-POSCO's docks. But the real struggle was still one of jobs and union power. In question was who would unload the steel coils—USS-POSCO's own steelworkers or longshoremen?[9] Steelworkers had historically done the work, because the coils were unloaded on the company's own docks. But the International Longshoremen's and Warehousemen's Union (ILWU) demanded the jobs for its own members. In a complicated series of events, the ILWU tried to pressure the regional environmental agency to prevent South Korean ships from steaming upriver, claiming they would pollute the air.[10] The South Koreans, however, had outfitted the new ships with experimental catalytic converters, which were designed to cut the worst emissions by 90 percent.[11]

When the California authorities tested the ships, they found that the amount of emissions was negligible. Having failed to block the ships through environmental regulation, the ILWU resorted to raw power. A flotilla of picket boats surrounded USS-POSCO's docks, preventing a South Korean ship from landing. Death threats were also made against the captain and his family. Six days later, on February 27, USS-POSCO obtained a temporary restraining order from the Contra Costa County Superior Court against the ILWU. "This was environmentalism gone wild," Tom Graham complained to me at the time. "It will take California twenty years to recover. What the company had to go through to get those boats up the river. It's outlandish! Even Al Gore would not approve! *Even Al Gore!*" The press finally saw through the ILWU's ploy and blasted the union and environmental agencies for "environmental blackmail" and "abusive regulation."[12] In the end the ILWU was forced to drop its claims and withdraw all legal action.

## THE MOLD OF U.S. STEEL

But now USS-POSCO faced the thorniest of all problems: how to alter the antagonistic, uncooperative relationship between management and the union. In earlier years, when American steel had had a world monopoly, the constant warfare between labor and management had been tolerated, the costs simply passed along to the consumer. But in the new, fast-changing, competitive international steel market, any delays in raising quality and reducing costs could doom the joint venture. Speed was now of the essence.

Though Randy Smith and his managers had relatively good relations with the USWA International and with the small clerical and technical Local 2571, relationships with the larger production Local 1440 were truly adversarial. Smith knew that for the joint venture to succeed, these relationships would have to change, but he also realized that they were deeply entrenched on both sides. Managers, for instance, were socialized into a powerful belief system that journalist William Serrin characterized as "inbred, centralized, uncreative, and autocratic."[13] John Hoerr, in his book *And the Wolf Finally Came*, a harsh indictment of U.S. Steel's antagonistic labor relations, documented how the company always "seemed to go out of its way to turn unpleasantness into nasty displays of power. It fired thousands of supervisors and managers—its most loyal employees—on no more than a moment's notice: 'Clean out your desk, this is your last day,' they were told."[14]

Smith was regarded as USS-POSCO's strongman because of the close relationship he was reputed to have with Tom Graham. Graham was putting heavy pressure on the company to reduce the number of man-hours it took to produce a ton of finished steel, which was then 2.4. Graham said that number had to be reduced to 1. Smith said, "The fact is that we've got to reduce the workforce by at least a hundred and forty steel-workers to bring man-hours per ton into line. We're at about nine hundred now, and we have to get down to seven hundred sixty."

He knew the union would try to block any reductions in force as well as try to stop him from combining job classifications and cross-training crews so they could do one another's jobs. But Smith said he knew the first step would have to be taken with his own managers. "We've been working on getting an attitude change among our managers. To get them to become more participative, less directive, more supportive. It's hard to get a lot of these guys to accept the participatory concept. The trouble is that some of these old-time foremen just can't believe wage people can run teams. They just don't believe they are capable. It's going to take a long time for them to become team players. The steel industry has never been participatory, it's always been driven from the top. We're trying hard not to take sides. It can't be 'us' against 'them.' We don't have time for that now. It's got to be 'us.' We're still learning—what we're doing right and what we're doing wrong." Smith handed me a copy of Hoerr's book.[15] "Read this," he said. "It'll open your eyes!"

The belief systems that run through USS-POSCO's workforce operate unconsciously and invisibly, making it hard for either the company or the union to acknowledge its grip or break its hold. I witnessed how deep and complex these beliefs were in USS-POSCO's tin mill, a cavernous building a few hundred yards to the southeast of the newly modernized Rolling Division. The antiquated mill has not been modernized in forty years, though it still turns out high-grade tinplate. From a skylight high overhead, the sun's rays angle through a blue haze until they hit the ancient wood-block floor a hundred feet below. Atchison, Topeka and Santa Fe railroad tracks run into the west end of the mill, where shiny coils of tinplate stand wrapped in white-and-blue protective paper, waiting to be loaded onto cars for shipping. Inside the huge building the noise is thunderous. Cranes rumble high overhead, carrying fifteen-ton coils from one operation to the next, while prehistoric-looking tractors lumber from line to line with steel coils suspended on their five-foot-long snouts. Closer to the electrolytic tinning line, an acrid smell rises from the acids used to pickle the steel again before tin is applied.

The daily morning meeting of the Tin Division revealed how, even among a group of handpicked young managers, the powerful U.S. Steel belief system continued to govern managers' behavior. Seven or eight red-helmeted men filed in with coffee cups in their hands, talking and joking as they took their seats. Only Steve Frediani, the young division manager, wore a white shirt and tie, setting himself visibly apart from his managers. The meeting started after all managers had reported in. One manager (I'll call him "Ed Ford") started an exchange that revealed the gulf between the managers and the steelworkers. Ford reported, "One guy on C turn [the graveyard shift] broke his arm and can't report for work. I'm running shorthanded." The man to his side asked in apparent seriousness, "Is he right-handed or left-handed?" "Right-handed," answered Ford. "Simple," the man retorted. "Make him work with his left." Everyone burst out laughing. Later, as the men discussed whether or not to call back workers on layoff for the Number 2 line, a worker by the name of George came up. "Oh, George? Isn't he that fuckin' Communist who's always writing for the *Rank and Filer* [Local 1440's newsletter]?" one of the managers asked. "Nah, you're thinking of somebody else," said the man sitting next to him. "This guy's no Commie. He's an asshole, but he keeps his nose clean."

Though some of the managers had been friends with individual steelworkers for years, in private they talked about them in impersonal and derisive ways. As my research team and I pored over our field notes, we found only a handful of instances when managers had made complimentary comments about steelworkers in private conversation. Scornful comments made in private seemed to be part of a ritual that reinforced the "us-versus-them" belief system. New managers, eager to belong to the group, were quickly socialized into the divisive culture and learned to speak in similarly derogatory ways.

Perhaps the negative image many managers had of the steelworkers rationalized the authoritarian style of management practiced by U.S. Steel for so many years. According to one of its axioms, management reserved the right to manage the business. This belief was imprinted on all young managers—even young and progressive ones like Frediani—who knew their careers would be made or broken by their adherence to the

U.S. Steel doctrine. For instance, Tom Graham had recently toured the Tin Division and ordered that a mothballed tinning line be put into service immediately to meet the demands of the tomato-packing season. The managers were concerned about notifying the crews, who would have to forgo some vacations and work longer hours. Frediani exclaimed, "I'll take care of it! I'm here to manage the company assets. I've got to make the call."

Managers learned that in order to be promoted, they were expected to remain aloof from their crews. Those who wanted to be promoted maintained their distance by wearing ties, and until recently all the managers wore white helmets rather than the red ones worn by the steelworkers. One manager explained that USS-POSCO executives had decided to switch to red to try to downplay the differences, though some steelworkers joked that they had switched colors to blend in because white helmets made such good targets. Young managers soon learned that trying to close the gap by becoming closer to their crews could doom a promising career. The dress code, meetings that excluded workers, and the physical distance that separated managers from steelworkers translated into a rigid status difference. It also created a silent void, a kind of no-man's-land between the two sides, that made communication difficult.

Though most of the union leaders and steelworkers said they disliked this rigid, autocratic, and impersonal environment, they had resigned themselves to it. One afternoon Bill Soltis, a maintenance mechanic, joked about a recent encounter he had had with a foreman. "I worked for this fuckin' idiot for a year, and he never knew my name. Never had the decency to say anything but 'Hey, you'! One day he said to me, 'Hey, you, come here. I got something for you to do.' I said, 'Hey, buddy, my number is 3731. But you can call me "3" for short!'"

The personal distance between the two sides ensured that misunderstandings would arise. Without a regular give-and-take, familiarity and trust were hard to cultivate. One day during a break in the tin mill, three crew members sat at a table next to the Number 3 tinning line drinking from thermos bottles and talking among themselves. As a maintenance manager walked by, the conversation turned to managers. When he had passed out of earshot, one of the workers said, "You know, that's a no-good son of a bitch. He's got a poster in his office that says 'The beatings will continue until morale improves!' Can you fuckin' believe it?" The others shook their heads in dismay. In some environments, such a poster would be tolerated, much like racial jokes among people of different races who know and trust one another. But in this mistrustful environment anger flared up easily, reinforcing the negative stereotypes.

Some steelworkers hoped that their new Korean partners might make things better. In 1990 Eva Lincoln, who had been with U.S. Steel for twenty years, was working as a "classifier" on one of the tinning lines (the job has since been eliminated). Sitting in a chair, watching lighted mirrors for scratches or other surface imperfections in the tin strip that sped by, she said in a Texas twang, "I hope those Koreans come in here and get these foremen to knock off some of the bullshit! I mean, they talk to us like we was a bunch of goddamned dogs! At least the Koreans treat us like we was human. They fixed up the restrooms too. They painted them and put doors on 'em. Hell, I'd been here for twenty years, and there wasn't even no goddamned doors on the stalls!"

Kermit Coleman, a union officer and veteran steelworker, described his feelings about U.S. Steel's management style. "Like they're too good to associate with you. They treat you like you're scum," he said. Coleman said he believed there was a policy forbidding managers to fraternize with the workers. "You know, it's no accident that the doctor got shotgunned a few years ago," he said, referring to an incident in which a crazed steelworker had burst into the infirmary and murdered the company doctor. "And then the other day they caught a guy riding around the fence with a loaded gun in his car. There's a lot of anger in this mill."

## THE EVER-VIGILANT UNION

At the center of the continuing controversy was Joe Stanton, president of Local 1440. A third-generation steelworker, Stanton had been the financial secretary of the huge steelworkers' local at Homestead. When I first met him in 1988, he was in his early forties. He had a narrow mustache and wore photosensitive glasses that darkened in the light. He was wearing a T-shirt with a picture of a snarling pit bull on it, and, pointing to his chest, he joked, "That's me! I may be short, but I'm dangerous!" The more I got to know him, the more I saw that he had spoken the truth.

Against his mother's wishes, Stanton had gone to work at Homestead as a teenager "digging bottom" — rooting out the twisted red-hot metal and ash from each firing and relining the open hearth. Later he had "tapped the heat," dynamiting holes in the open hearths so the molten steel could flow into the casting machines. In time, he had become a key official in the 7,500-member local. Stanton harbors a tangible hatred for U.S. Steel because of its decision to close the mills in the Monongahela valley and to diversify into oil. "When they decided to shut down Homestead to buy Marathon Oil, it was a betrayal of the worst kind. We'd given our lives to that industry. I can't tell you how it felt. It was like cutting out my heart," Stanton said.

He transferred to USS-POSCO just after Homestead closed in 1986. Two years later, he was elected to his first term as president of Local 1440. Even as a newcomer, he seemed to know everyone in the mill by name. Stanton explained, "In the Mon valley, steel was my home and my family. Steel *was* the community. It's not like that out here. As a union guy at Homestead, you *were* somebody. You were part of a much larger community. It's not the same here. People live far away, and they don't have the same feeling for the industry."

When I met him, Stanton was furious with Randy Smith for having launched a secret drug bust without consulting the union. Stanton acknowledged that drugs were a problem among some of the workers. His objection was that Smith had planned and executed the sweep unilaterally. "What the fuck does he think he's doing? He talks about trust and then pulls some shit like this. How can you build trust like that?" he asked. Stanton said that he too hoped the South Koreans would exert more influence, adding that he had a good relationship with Yoh Sang Whan, who had come from South Korea as the joint venture's executive vice president. "But," he said, "as long as the U.S. Steel guys are walking around talking about cutting jobs, how can you progress in that environment? You hate to have this kind of attitude about working." Then he added, "You want to come to work, you want to get up in the morning and feel good, but here it's fucking impossible. You know, I've got to answer to my people. We've taken concessions year after year, but we haven't had a raise in ten years. We have to have a gain somewhere. You know, we made some big concessions here so they could build this mill, and now it's time for some payback!"

What Stanton was referring to were the concessions the USWA International had made in the 1980 national contract, as well as a 4.5 percent pay cut that both locals had agreed to in 1986 so the joint venture could go forward. The company and the union had agreed that the savings from the wage cuts would be earmarked to help finance the new learning center where the workforce would be retrained. Taking a wage reduction to help finance the new venture was a gigantic step for a union, particularly one like the USWA that had had such a long and adversarial history with U.S. Steel's management. It represented a dramatic break with the past as steelworkers and their unions claimed a financial stake in the joint venture's future. Whether or not a sense of shared ownership would help reduce the tensions between management and labor remained to be seen.

But still, in 1990, the refrain "We haven't had a raise in ten years" was often heard. At the slightest provocation, union members would pull out the thick contract they all seemed to carry in their hip pockets and point to vacation days they had given up or to the section forbidding the contracting out of work, which they claimed the company repeatedly violated.

The union was on constant guard against management's making any changes to their pay rates, which were set according to a complicated incentive scheme. Though the hourly base rate for some jobs was the same, some jobs paid more than others because of additional incentives for higher output. On balance, USS-POSCO steelworkers were well paid, even with the concessions. The average hourly rate with incentives and benefits exceeded $22 per hour, and top operators could earn upward of $80,000 in a year, counting overtime. Though a complex calculation was required to figure out whether or not a paycheck was accurate, steelworkers could do it with lightning speed, and any discrepancy was immediately blamed on management. For instance, the continuous annealing line (or "CA line") had been outfitted with new electronics that were expected to increase output. Management, well within its rights, had decided to reduce workers' incentive payments to compensate for the added output expected from the new technology. Though the managers claimed that the joint wage and rate committee had approved the change, the steelworkers said they had been caught unaware by their smaller paychecks. Steelworkers said they had been shocked to open their pay envelopes to find them short. Many of them complained to both the union and management but got no satisfaction. Steelworkers on the CA line decided to retaliate. "We talked about a strike," one man told me. "We didn't want to sabotage the equipment. Then we got it. We'd do *just* what the managers told us to do!" he said, laughing. "I mean, everyone on the line had at least twenty-five years' experience, and we knew how it ran. The managers didn't know shit. They bird-dogged our guys night and day, but they just kept doing exactly what they were told to do! That's the fastest way in the world to get things fucked up. Just do what your manager tells you!" The shift foreman recalled the incident painfully, confirming the story: "At the time the CA line was the only one that could run tin, and there was a heavy market demand for tin at the time. Everything went wrong for days. The line would shut down mysteriously, equipment would short out. The guys really had us by the balls."

In another incident the company abruptly changed the incentive rate for tractor drivers on the docks. Stanton said that Randy Smith had accused him of leading a slowdown in retaliation, an accusation he adamantly denied. Stanton said, "Then Randy threatened to fire me! I told him, *do it!* Just fucking fire me! This place has a divide-and-conquer mentality. How would you divide up a hundred dollars between five kids? You'd probably give each one twenty bucks, right? Well, here these motherfuckers would give one kid a hundred dollars and let the other four beat the shit out of him!"

How to simplify and compress the complex job classification system and the myriad jobs under its aegis continued to plague management. Smith knew, however, that reducing the number of job classifications was critical to improving flexibility and reducing costs. "In the old days it would take twelve or thirteen people to do a simple repair job—a scooter and a pickup truck and maybe four or five different classifications—electricians, pipe fitters, mechanics, and riggers," he said. "We can't afford that anymore." The question was how to convince the union to drop its opposition to combining crafts. Many traditional single-craft jobs were now obsolete in a modern mill like USS-POSCO, where computers controlled much of the work that had formerly been done by skilled journeymen. But

since the violent lockout at Homestead in 1892, union leaders have opposed combining crafts because they fear management will use the tactic
to lay people off. Joe Stanton said he did not trust Randy Smith's motives.
Late one night in a bar on a visit to Homestead, Stanton exploded when I
asked him if combining job classes wasn't inevitable. "That's a lot of bullshit!" he shouted, glaring at me across the table. "You're talking *management* talk! When you talk about combining jobs and restructuring, you're
talking layoffs! I cut my teeth here in Homestead, right across the road,
and I can tell you, these sons of bitches don't care about nothing but making money. Graham didn't give a fuck about the thousands of people who
lost their jobs. I saw hundreds of families destroyed and so many suicides
I can't count them on my hands and feet. This fucking company did it just
for money! They were making twelve percent at this mill, but they sold us
down the river because Marathon Oil looked like a better investment!" As
his anger subsided, Stanton described how the old contract had protected
steelworkers from being laid off by specifying minimum crew sizes. But,
he said, in the last round of negotiations it had been taken out. As he
talked, I thought about how the same argument had pitted Carnegie and
Frick against their workers, leading to a bloody showdown not a hundred
yards from where we sat. Stanton said, *"That* was job security! So don't
give me this shit about combining jobs and getting lean! They just want
to make more money and 'fuck the worker'!"

   The unions also opposed combining job classes on the basis of safety,
claiming that cross-training workers and cutting crew sizes to minimal
numbers would expose workers to hazards. There was also opposition on
the basis of shop tradition. Craftspeople had always enjoyed high status
among their fellow workers because of their specialized skill and knowledge. To allow new apprentices to advance without first going through a
rigorous and specialized apprenticeship was unacceptable to many journeymen, who had spent many years learning their trades.

   Combining job classifications would also require unraveling the
myriad of detail that had accumulated as a result of the bargaining
process. Randy Smith explained to me how it had all become so complex.
He pulled out the current contract and pointed to it. "This is based on
this," he said, taking out a 1972 manual. Pointing to the 1972 manual, he
said, "And this is based on this," taking out yet another manual, this one

dated 1953. Soon a pile of books spanning nearly half a century stood in front of him. "These classifications were based on work done by the War Labor Board in 1944 to make work and pay more equitable. But changing them is like moving a cemetery because they are each interrelated."

## AUTONOMOUS TEAMWORK

The same mistrust that prevented management and labor from cooperating on the streamlining of jobs also extended deeply into the plant. Though most of the managers would not admit it, they depended heavily on the steelworkers to run the mills, and some wondered who was really running the plant—the managers or the steelworkers? Randy Smith worried that the managers did not have as much control as they thought they did. Within a few months we discovered the same phenomenon we had witnessed at Douglas Aircraft: there was a remarkable degree of spontaneous teamwork among the workers. But at USS-POSCO it served a different purpose. Whereas at Douglas Aircraft teamwork had enabled workers to avoid the bureaucratic production system, at USS-POSCO teamwork allowed the steelworkers to remain autonomous from their supervisors. The steelworkers knew a great deal about the equipment and how it ran, and their informal and self-managing teamwork was one of the chief forces that kept the company running.

An incident that took place on one of the tinning lines illustrates the point. Even though the equipment is old, much of it having been installed in the late 1950s, it still turns out high-grade tinplate. Unlike the new rolling mill, which is run by computers, this equipment depends heavily on the crews' intuition and personal touch. Though a huge panel of gauges and lights displays information, many of the instruments are obscured by layers of accumulated grime. Operators tend to ignore the instruments and run the line by feel, which they have developed over many years of experience.

About a hundred feet up the line from the operators' station, the tin strip enters an acid bath for pickling. There it winds through successive baths of fuming sulfuric acid, where the ambient air temperature is close to one hundred degrees Fahrenheit. The strip snakes in and out of vats, where a thin coating of tin is applied. Finally, it heads across a roadway and past a classifier, who checks for scratches, to a finisher, who tends the recoiling equipment and readies the coil for shipping.

The crew members running the line have worked together for years. The finisher, Sal Rodriguez, told me that management tried to break them up but that they had complained to their new foreman, Larry Machado. "He's not your ordinary foreman. We ran the last guy off. He thought he was some kind of god. We have certain ways to do the work here, and when a new guy comes we have to break him in right. Machado's good to work with. He doesn't order you around like a piece of shit, he works with us."

Just as one coil was coming to the end, Rodriguez noticed streaks in the tinplate, an indication that something was wrong with one of the rolls on the line. He slipped on a pair of heavy gloves and cut a four-foot section from the strip with large metal shears, then laid it out on the wood-block floor. Over a loudspeaker he called up to the operator, "Doc" Lawson, who was standing overhead on the main platform. Lawson, a tall man in a T-shirt who wears a bandanna inside his helmet that sticks out like a tail, climbed down the stairs from the platform. He and Rodriguez measured the scratches to find out which roll was damaged so it could be identified and repaired.

As Lawson and Rodriguez tried to repair the damaged roll with a makeshift sanding block, Rodriguez's brother (who was working on the other end of the line) appeared. Failing to fix it, they decided to shut down the line and call Maintenance for help. Larry Machado walked up, his red helmet bobbing up and down and a yellow flashlight banging on his hip, and conferred with Lawson and the Rodriguez brothers about which roll seemed to be the problem. He called Maintenance on his handheld radio, and in a few minutes a lanky maintenance man in overalls with tools dangling from a heavy leather belt appeared on the platform, a stub of a cigarette protruding from a scraggly red beard. In moments, he had dismantled the equipment, pulled out the damaged roll, and swung a new one up onto a crane. While the maintenance man installed the new roll, Lawson, his assistant, Joe Garcia, and the Rodriguez brothers helped and also sanded the other exposed rolls with handmade sanders.

The line had been down for forty-five minutes when Dave Carerra, the basement man (the dirtiest job on the line), ambled up. He is a heavy-set man, and he was covered in grease from the dirty work below. Because the problem was electrical, he said, the company would pay for the downtime instead of having the production loss deducted from the workers' pay. Finally, with the new roll installed, the old steel strip was removed. One of the Rodriguez brothers made a spot weld, joining the strip in the middle. Lawson tried to instruct the brothers but they ignored him, speaking quickly and cryptically to each other in short bursts of Spanish. Carerra shook his head, laughing. He said, "There's no hope when you get those brothers together. They've been working together for so long, they don't have to talk to each other." I asked why the maintenance man wasn't working on the strip, and Carerra said, "It's a tradition. It's not in the contract, but those guys don't know the strip, so we do it."

Larry Machado was racing around to ensure that lockout procedures (safety precautions that prevent the line from being started accidentally) were being followed. Not sure of the procedures, he asked the foreman he was relieving for help, but the man just stared at Machado before turning and walking away. Carerra said, "That old fart's retiring, and he won't help Larry. He's keeping the knowledge to himself so Larry has to learn it the old way like he did."

This was what the USS-POSCO management team had to work with as they set out to convert the old Pittsburg Works into one of the most sophisticated rolling and finishing mills in the world. Most of the USS-POSCO employees were decent, hardworking people. If given the chance, most of them would do the right thing. But management and workers alike seemed trapped in the suspicious, pessimistic culture they had inherited and that conspired to thwart change at every turn. The pressures were unrelenting. The company had only five years to repay a $350 million loan that had been made to build and equip the new Rolling Division facility, which was running in the red. Somehow, management would have to find a way to neutralize the old adversarial culture's paralyzing effects if the company were to survive.

# CHAPTER EIGHT

# THE DAWNING OF A NEW ORDER

THE STEELMAKING EQUIPMENT that had been assembled in Pittsburg was the most advanced in the world. Walking through the mill in late 1989 was like taking a tour of the United Nations. Labels reading "Mannes-Mann Demag Sack," "GE," "Hyundai," and "Hitachi" identified the makers of the modern machinery. Once the cavernous new building had been constructed and the equipment installed, the challenge was to organize and train the managers and steelworkers in record time.

Technological know-how and teamwork between management and the crews were required to program and run the computerized equipment. While the technology could be learned, the teamwork necessary to coordinate management and labor was something to which both sides were unaccustomed. The thundering equipment, heat, acids, and hazardous chemicals were ever-present disaster potentials, and the operation of the mill had to be tightly controlled to ensure safety. The electric motors that produced thousands of horsepower worth of energy and the gigantic rolls that pulled and squeezed bands of steel could wreak havoc if not properly tended. Every operation, from threading and welding the steel strip to coiling it at the end, had to be precisely sequenced and coordinated. Teamwork was essential to survival. Adding to the pressure, the new company had to gain the confidence of environmental regulators, who were watching it carefully.

Such technical and human requirements were beyond the comprehension of most of the steelworkers who had run the old pickle lines and cold reduction mills. I happened to be at the company on the day the last mill was retired in late 1989. The steelworkers commemorated its final day by scrawling affectionate messages on its cast-iron sides: "GOOD-BYE," "11-30-89, LAST DAY!" They spoke of the machinery as of an old friend, aware of its every quirk. Steelworkers ran the cranky machinery by feel and by ear, listening for problems, which they could fix in the dark.[1]

Compared with the old equipment, the towering new mill represented a step into the space age. It was designed to operate with but only a fraction of the workers required to run the old one. As workers said farewell to the old, familiar machinery, they also knew that some of them would soon be saying good-bye to the Pittsburg Works. While few steelworkers trusted the motives of U.S. Steel, some knew that it was impossible to hold back the forces of change. Veteran steelworker William Perkins, a large man known as "Big Daddy," hitched his thumbs in his coveralls and said, "If it hadn't been for the Koreans, we would have been closed by now. We had to put in the new machinery. If we hadn't done it, we would have gone down the tube. But there's not enough jobs for all the people we have. We need to get ready for changes, and there's no doubt that we are going to need fewer people."

Elmer "El" Roskovensky, USS-POSCO's first president, knew it would be impossible to develop cooperation and teamwork in such a harsh environment. To reduce anxiety, he promised there would be no layoffs during the start-up. Though many steelworkers greeted his announcement with relief, others did not trust him. One young steelworker said, "It's just not practical. I like what Roskovensky's saying, but he's got to face reality. Layoffs are expected in the steel industry. I was laid off from Bethlehem, and I expect I'll get laid off here too because of my low seniority. Anybody knows that when business suffers, layoffs follow."

Nevertheless, the forty-four-year-old Roskovensky pressed ahead to expand what little common ground he could find with the union. He had already successfully started up a joint venture between U.S. Steel and Ford Motor Company. Managers talked about him admiringly as a "fast-tracker." He had a reputation of being open and accessible. His open-door policy encouraged workers to walk in and speak with him. He had promoted young men like Steve Frediani, and he had tried to blur the rigid distinction between managers and steelworkers. It was Roskovensky who had ordered the managers to turn in their white helmets for the red ones worn by the steelworkers, and he had ended preferential parking for managers.

These were important first steps that symbolized the kind of company Roskovensky wanted USS-POSCO to become. Veteran steelworkers had never seen anything like them, especially from a U.S. Steel manager. Little by little, as the steelworkers became comfortable with Roskovensky, they began to talk about him in familiar terms. Some called him "Rosko from POSCO" with a hint of pride and affection in their voices. It looked as though a breakthrough might be coming.

## THE START-UP

For the first time ever, seniority was not the prime consideration in selecting the new crews for the modernization. About 150 applicants were tested for their analytic, reading, and mechanical abilities, and 83 were ultimately selected. Not surprisingly, a feeling of pride began to develop among those who had been successful. They traveled to South Korea, where they visited POSCO's Pohang and Kwangyang Works and met their steelworker counterparts there. Some came back complaining of the change in diet—so much fish and rice—but most seemed to genuinely enjoy the experience.

Upon their return, they received months of training on the new equipment at the company's learning center, a facility that occupied a newly renovated two-story brick laboratory building that was packed full of computers and other equipment to simulate the new mill. USS-POSCO managers and the union strongly supported the idea that every steelworker should get at least forty hours of training at the learning center each year. U.S. Steel executives from the Pittsburgh, Pennsylvania, headquarters, however, were said not to be so enthusiastic. USS-POSCO managers said they were worried that if Tom Graham found out how much money the company was spending on constructing the learning center, it would surely be shut down. Amazingly, the learning center's existence was kept a secret from U.S. Steel executives, who were carefully escorted around the construction site. As it turned out, the learning center would become an important neutral meeting ground for managers and union leaders, both of whom took pride in its sparkling classrooms and advanced equipment.

The company invested heavily in its new workforce in direct monetary ways as well. Because the volunteers for the new crew positions had given up their regular jobs and the incentive pay that went with them (which frequently added as much as 50 percent to a paycheck), they were given $10,000 bonuses while they trained and learned to run the new equipment. While $10,000 may seem like a lot of money, many of the steelworkers complained that they would have earned more on their old jobs.

A conversation with a welder, Diane Goodlow, revealed how applying and training for these new jobs had seemed like a huge step to most steelworkers, especially a woman. She said proudly that she had been one of the few women chosen and that she was proud of how much she had learned during the training. Giving up her incentive pay to volunteer for the modernization had made her nervous, because she had had little confidence in her ability to pass the tests and the interviews. "I was completely intimidated by the tests," she admitted. "But I passed them, and I passed the interviews!" Goodlow described how she had traveled to Pittsburgh, Boston, and Springfield for specialized training and how difficult it had been for her to sit down with managers. "It was a first for me," she said, laughing. "I mean, sitting next to those guys was hard. We're *union*! It was really uncomfortable!" Nevertheless, she welcomed the changes: "It was long overdue—the new technology, us making decisions, some respect from the managers." As for being one of the first women in the modernization, she said, "It's still hard being one of the few women in a place like this. When I first went to work here, there wasn't even a women's restroom, and I still feel a lot of resentment from some of the men. When it comes to getting help, many of them have the attitude 'You signed up for the modernization, you figure it out.' The language is rough, and you're expected to take it. You know, this isn't your typical woman's world!"

## EAST MEETS WEST IN PITTSBURG

Even though the original partnership agreement had called for one hundred South Koreans to come from Pohang, such a large number seemed impractical, so only ten ultimately came. Despite their small numbers, however, the South Koreans' presence had been felt. Many steelworkers said they had liked how the South Koreans had treated them respectfully, calling them by name. Yoh Sang Whan, the top-ranking South Korean executive vice president, had surprised his American counterparts by taking the unusual step of personally interviewing each of the company's eight hundred steelworkers to try to establish a better relationship. It was an act that union leaders say raised eyebrows among the U.S. Steel managers, because it departed so sharply from past practice. Yoh said he had been impressed by the vast human resource the company had available but that U.S. Steel had never been able to tap, and he had quickly grasped how the antipathy between management and labor translated into a lack of trust: "Without trust you have a relationship built only on a contract where everything is spelled out. Job descriptions are prescribed, and they are too narrow and rigid to provide necessary flexibility in this new world. Human beings must operate on the basis of personal relationships, not a contract." Yoh agreed with Roskovensky that job security would have to be a top priority. He believed that such security would help trust develop and reduce anxiety among the steelworkers, allowing them to devote their full attention to the needs of the company.

Vice President of Operations C. H. Lee, the second-highest-ranking South Korean, was a quiet and friendly man even though he projected a formal first impression. "C.H.," as Lee was called, explained POSCO's interest in the joint venture: "POSCO's contribution is our experience with upstream steelmaking, and U.S. Steel's is on the downstream, or finishing, end. We are trying to establish a new model here, one in which the cultures of both parents are brought together to complement the other's strengths. It is through harmonization that we truly learn the meaning of a joint venture." He admitted, however, that U.S. Steel was the more influential of the two partners and that, for now, "We must speak in a lower voice than the American parent." But some of the union leaders said they hoped that POSCO would assume the leadership of the joint venture, because they thought the South Koreans would be more generous than U.S. Steel when it came to wages.

The steelworkers admired South Korean steel for its high quality, and many said they hoped for the day when all incoming steel would come from Pohang or Kwangyang. "Buz" Enea, a senior operator in the entry pulpit, showed me the difference one day when the steel strip tore, bringing the entire mill to a halt. As he looked down from the pulpit onto the tangled wreckage, Enea said, "The problem with the stuff that's coming in is that it's from U.S. Steel's Fairfield Works and it's garbage! It fucks up our equipment. Just look at that!" he exclaimed, pointing to the workmen below. Enea continued angrily, "This line was designed to run on the highest-quality steel. I hate to admit it, but Korean steel's the best." He shrugged his shoulders with embarrassment. "The shit U.S. Steel sends us pounds the line to death."

A seasoned operator, Harold Spahn, watched the cobbled steel being cut away. He said that he had fought in the Korean War, which had left him with some antipathy for the Korean people. He too shrugged as he said, "Maybe I should dislike the Koreans, but frankly I can't wait until they own one hundred percent of this plant. They have a different philosophy, like the Japanese. The Korean and Japanese philosophy is make the man happy on the job, make the job number one, not like here at USS-POSCO. Here management's attitude is 'Fire that son of a bitch.' Then they wonder why workers stick coils in wrong or shove stuff around carelessly." But the question of how much influence the South Koreans would actually have would be answered only with time.

## TRANSFORMING THE PRODUCTION OF STEEL

The true key to change, USS-POSCO managers discovered, lay in altering not merely the human relationships at the plant but the steelmaking process itself. They realized that changes in the technical system of steel production could in turn force changes in the traditional job classifications, descriptions, and pay systems. Slowly, the underlying beliefs and assumptions would begin to change as well.

But first the traditional crafts would have to be reconfigured into a smaller number of "supercrafts," both to make workers more flexible and to reduce costs. Managers started by combining the mechanical crafts—hydraulic repairmen, millwrights, mechanics, and pipe fitters—into one job classification called "mechanical hydraulic repairmen." Next they turned to the electrical crafts, combining electricians and instrument repairmen into systems repairmen. Then Randy Smith began aligning the complicated incentive pay systems with the new supercrafts. Though he claimed that most workers had gained several steps in their job classifications, which translated into higher pay, the unions mistrusted the company's motives and tried to block the changes at every turn.

Next USS-POSCO managers decided on a method called "statistical process control" (SPC), which is used to analyze and control variations in manufacturing and to push decision making down to the operators. After being trained in SPC, the operators would become responsible for collecting and analyzing quality data on their own operations. Though SPC promised operators new authority and freedom to monitor and adjust their own systems, some steelworkers bitterly called it "SP-Free," complaining that the company wanted them to work harder for no extra pay.

The man most responsible for promoting SPC was Bill Haley, the company's vice president for manufacturing. Haley was a metallurgical engineer, and he knew the technical side of steel in great detail. At least three times a week he would strap on a pair of steel-toed boots, jam a red helmet onto his head, and walk through the mill to see firsthand what was going on. Haley, a man in his middle fifties, was always neatly dressed in a coat and tie. His neat demeanor, short hair, and black-framed glasses projected a no-nonsense, businesslike impression, but despite his directness Haley was respected by the steelworkers for his knowledge. Not insignificantly, he also developed good relationships with Joe Stanton and with Bob Witt, the president of the smaller clerical and technical local. The fact that Haley had come up through the mill and had never lived "back east" (as the steelworkers referred to U.S. Steel headquarters in Pennsylvania) helped earn him the union leadership's trust.

Haley knew he had to find some means to convince the union that it was in everyone's interest to produce a high-quality product. But how to do it? Earlier attempts had failed. "Before the joint venture," Haley said, "we tried developing a quality management program with outside consultants, but it never got down to the wage people. The recession hit and we just couldn't afford the resources to keep it going, so it washed out." Later, U.S. Steel had embarked on a corporatewide quality drive called "quality management," but it had failed to reach the shop floor and had died out. Haley explained, "Then there was APEX (an acronym for 'all product excellence'), but I had doubts about it too. I wanted a process, not another training program. Training programs by themselves buy you nothing. Classroom training affects maybe five percent of the critical behavior we need to change. I wanted to develop a continuous process ourselves so we could really start to change attitudes."

Haley knew that whatever path the company chose, it had to be one that could be taken while it strained under the relentless pressures of production. Because of the need to become profitable to pay back the loans that had established the joint venture, the plant could not afford to stop even for a minute to allow the workers to begin the relearning process from scratch. "We settled on SPC because it promised to move us in the direction we wanted to go without disrupting production," Haley said. "We liked its emphasis on treating employees like assets, not liabilities, and we figured SPC would help us to become more competitive in the marketplace by assuring customers of on-time delivery. SPC also promised to push the quality concept down to the floor level in the plant."

Haley laughed self-consciously as he said, "You know, I'm not trying to save the world, just USS-POSCO. It's a motherhood thing with me. It's a cruel world out there, and for all of us this is a matter of survival." He was keenly aware of the tensions that existed between management and labor. But over the next six years Haley would continue to press ahead, integrating SPC and teamwork into a more comprehensive quality management system. As time went by, he rediscovered the factor that would ultimately become the key to change—the customer.

When my research team and I began working in the mills in 1989, there was little evidence that the concerns of the buyer were penetrating much deeper than the front office or the divisional managers. I cannot remember a single instance of a steelworker or a relief foreman talking about customers' needs. All of the workforce's energy seemed to be focused on ways to maximize its incentive pay, which translated into high output with little regard for quality. Haley, however, was undeterred. "We're developing a process, not a program," he said. "It's the pull from the customer that must discipline the system. Teamwork, SPC, continuous improvement—it's all got to be integrated up and down the line, or we're in a world of hurt. What I'm looking for is real commitment to continuous improvement and quality, not just compliance. It's okay to talk philosophy, but unless you've got minds that can grow and learn and a supportive culture, you'll fall flat on your face."

## WAVERING PROGRESS

In the first years of the modernization, from late 1989 until 1993, conflict raged between the union and management. Despite Roskovensky's promise about no layoffs, fewer steelworkers than were estimated agreed to take the company's offer of early retirement. In the first quarter of 1990 Roskovensky was forced to go back on his promise, and he put about sixty steelworkers on temporary layoff. This act confirmed union members' fear that the new president could not be trusted, and now the union leadership was alert for anything else Roskovensky might say. Sure enough, Roskovensky was reported to have said in a speech in Los Angeles that, at a time when USS-POSCO had about nine hundred employees, it should "run with seven hundred fifteen people like Japanese plants." The remark quickly found its way back to the plant.

Joe Stanton was outraged. He felt betrayed and worried that he might look foolish in the eyes of his members. His attempts to work cooperatively with the company had hurt him personally, he said, because some union members had already interpreted them as "cozying up with management." Stanton's worry was not misplaced: rumors were circulating that the union was being paid off by the company to resolve grievances slowly and that the union leadership had taken gifts of money from the South Koreans during their visit to POSCO. Stanton said he had had no choice but to back away from Roskovensky as the pressures from his own members grew. He said, "Rosko's saying that this plant should run leaner when we've got people already on layoff is about the most stupid fucking thing I could imagine a company president saying in public at a time like this." Despite the forward progress the company and the union had begun to make, the gulf that had temporarily been bridged reopened.

Wrangling also broke out over Smith's steps to combine job classifications, which Stanton and others interpreted as another attempt to reduce jobs. In retaliation, Stanton drew up a list of company priorities that included SPC and announced he was withdrawing the union's support. Stanton, noting that the company was applying for quality certifications from its customers, said matter-of-factly, "I won't be part of putting the company's best face forward to the public. These guys will talk to you nicely in public, but they'll fuck you in private. Maybe if the company doesn't get the certifications, they'll get the message quicker that they've got problems. Maybe they'll finally start to walk like they talk!" Bill Haley said he had been deeply saddened by Stanton's decision but remained convinced that in time the union would come back to the table.

## THE TIDE TURNS

By 1992, when we made our next visit to the plant, Haley's predictions began to come true. Many of the changes the company had set out to achieve six years earlier had finally begun to materialize. For the first time in its history, the company was making a profit. A new union contract helped relieve some of the pent-up anger and frustration that had been building among the steelworkers. The man who conducted the negotiations for the union was Bob Guadiana, western regional director of the USWA International. Though a union man to the core, Guadiana knew that without a strong economy, there was little hope for his members or for the union. USS-POSCO, he said, could become a model joint venture that could help advance his own agenda of a more just, humane workplace. "It's one of the most sophisticated mills in the world. It produces a quality product, and it's finally become profitable. If we can resolve this adversarial labor relationship, USS-POSCO can point the way to the future." Guadiana said the new five-year contract was the best in the industry. "We immediately recouped all of the money we gave up to get the joint venture started, plus increases in wages and cost of living, cash for retirees, full medical with zero deductible, profit sharing, and on and on!"[2]

In the negotiations, Guadiana had also insisted on provisions for joint decision-making groups called "labor-management participation teams," or LMPTs. LMPTs had been written into contracts for years, though they had never been widely used.[3] Although Tom Graham, who, as president of Jones and Laughlin, had become a champion of the concept in the early 1980s, only two U.S. Steel mills had ever made them work.[4] Many cynical steelworkers at USS-POSCO scoffed. "You know what 'LMPT' stands for?" one said. "*Less Men Per Turn!* That's all these fuckers want—bigger profits and fewer men." But despite the steelworkers' suspicions, the LMPT would soon become an important mechanism of bridging hostilities between the union and management.

By 1992 there was dramatic new evidence that Haley's vision of putting the customer first appeared to be taking root. The LMPT had already agreed on the need for a periodic survey of employees' feelings and attitudes and had created new union jobs called "facilitators" in each of the three operating divisions, in maintenance, and in administration. The facilitators were to be important points of contact between the mill and its customers. Haley said he had become convinced, from the experience of customer visits, that customers liked dealing with steelworkers rather than with the front office. "It also puts a good face forward for the company," he said, "showing that we're serious about responding to customer needs at the production level." He said the new positions also demonstrated the company's visible commitment to empowering the steelworkers by encouraging joint decision making on the shop floor.

Also by 1992, operators began to talk about the "customer," a word our research team had rarely heard three years earlier. In fact, the survey sponsored by the LMPT found that 85 percent of the steelworkers agreed that a customer focus would help ensure the company's future, and 80 percent said that visits to customers were important.[5] Leonard "Lenny" Chuderewicz, who had succeeded Roskovensky as president in 1990, was also credited with emphasizing the customer in a series of open-air meetings at the local fairgrounds. "It was a happening, like Woodstock!" one of the managers said gleefully. In late 1992 USS-POSCO contracted with a consulting firm, Dannemiller-Tyson, to convene four groups of about 260 workers each to discuss attitudes among the employees and to create a new vision for the company.

At the fairgrounds, where steelworkers sat side by side with managers, they all heard directly from USS-POSCO's important customers. Representatives of Campbell Soup and other canning companies told them about how late deliveries of cans were causing vegetables to rot on the docks. One steelworker admitted, "When the guy from Campbell Soup said that if we couldn't deliver the product on time they'd close the plant, it opened my eyes." "It was sort of a rebirth," said Cheryl McCarthy-Wilcox, a quality assurance manager in the sheet mill. "Finally, everyone started to see how things really are through one set of eyes. I think some managers and wage people finally began to comprehend that we're in this boat together and that if each of us doesn't pull on the oars we'll all go down."

Managers and steelworkers reported that the fairgrounds meeting had been the first time they had really been able to talk openly with each other. Al Flores, a twenty-eight-year veteran steelworker, had been shocked to hear some managers admit to being as much to blame for poor relationships as the production workers were. He said, "It surprised the hell out of me to hear them admit that they have been conditioned to be hard on the working guys and how difficult it is for them to change." A systems repairman, Rich Koza, said, "It blew me away when some of the managers stood up and said they distrusted us. I've been in this business for a long time, and I've never trusted management. But suddenly I realized they felt the same way about us." Koza described how in the meeting the managers had stuck together at first, afraid that the workers were going to pick them apart. "Man, I couldn't believe what I saw. Here after all these years, I had always thought management had the upper hand. You know, making decisions on wages and discipline. But I learned that they're just as scared of us as we are of them!"

## THE GLACIAL PACE OF CHANGE

Despite the tangible progress, the harsh, untrusting U.S. Steel culture continued to exert a powerful grip. In late 1992 emotions boiled over again—this time about vacations. The company was insisting that employees take the following year's vacation time during the Christmas holidays so it could shut down for a week and also remove hundreds of hours of vacation-time liability from its books. The announcement drew an angry response from the steelworkers and union leaders. One steelworker said, "They talk about teamwork and an open-door policy, and then they pull this kind of shit!" The company was within its contractual rights, but the steelworkers were angry because many of them wanted to keep their two weeks together for family vacations. Bob Witt, the mild-mannered president of the clerical and technical local, said that what was galling the steelworkers most was that none of them had been consulted before the decision had been made. "We were just told," he said.

Not unexpectedly, the *Rank and Filer* (Local 1440's newsletter) published an angry letter headlined BEND OVER HERE IT COMES AGAIN. The letter excoriated the company for this latest breach of teamwork.[6] "USS-POSCO management wants its employees to change and we want the old adversarial USS managerial attitude (Do it my way) to change, yet when there is an opportunity for compassion USS-POSCO acts just like USS, SAME AS IT EVER WAS!" Once again, old wounds had been reopened by the tension that lay just beneath the surface of daily life.

The relationship between U.S. Steel and POSCO became visibly strained that same year, when America's big steel producers filed unfair-trade lawsuits against foreign competitors, claiming they were "dumping steel" in the United States at prices lower than those set by the market.[7] U.S. Steel was one of the twelve plaintiffs, and POSCO was one of the targets. U.S. Steel was prepared to sacrifice the joint venture if it had to. There was little doubt that the South Koreans took a dim view of U.S. Steel's apparent belligerence. A POSCO executive warned that the South Koreans "may have to think again" about USS-POSCO's future if the trade case prevailed.[8] In the end, the International Trade Commission ruled against U.S. Steel and the other American steel producers, but considerable damage had already been done to the South Korean–American relationship.[9]

By 1993 the hope that the South Koreans might infuse the new joint venture with a spirit of cooperation had dimmed. "It's like the big bang theory," one manager joked about the South Korean influence. "The further you get from the initial impact, the dimmer the light!" There was truth in his comment. Both top-ranking South Koreans had already returned to the parent company—Yoh Sang Whan to become executive vice president and then to retire, C. H. Lee to take over as superintendent of the Pohang Works. When, in 1993, Hak Bong Ko arrived from POSCO to become USS-POSCO's new executive vice president, his charter was limited to marketing and sales. The decline in South Korean involvement came as little surprise to many in the plant. One of the finishers in the tin mill told me over the roar of the machinery that he had seen it coming: "The Koreans were always kept out of the loop by U.S. Steel!" he shouted. "Right up until Tom Graham retired, he walked through this mill every three months himself. We always knew who was in control, and it's never been the Koreans!"

The roiling union politics also slowed the pace of change. In 1993, in an unexpected turn of events, Joe Stanton narrowly lost the election for the union presidency, despite his accomplishments. He had helped negotiate a good labor contract, and he had played a pivotal role in the antidumping case. In fact, Representative William Baker, who had helped the company win the case, told rejoicing steelworkers and their families that Joe Stanton should be "proclaimed a Native Son" for making the union and the company into a family.[10]

Stanton himself was unsure what losing the election signified. He scratched his head and said, "I don't really understand it either. I didn't do much for the members when I was first elected because I was new to California. This time though, I got them the best contract in steel and I helped them win at the hearings and save the company." I asked whether he thought the antidumping suit had helped to bring the company and the union closer together. "I don't know," he replied. "It's too early to tell. Haley's okay, but most of them just use you, but I think it helped some." His final comment reminded me how deeply antipathy toward U.S. Steel is etched in veteran steelworkers. Stanton grinned as he said, "What gave me great pleasure was saving a thousand jobs for my people. But what gave me the greatest pleasure was giving U.S. Steel a good screwing in public. It really humiliated them."

## CONCLUSION

USS-POSCO appears to have survived trials that would have defeated a company with less determination. Growing evidence has attested to the fact that USS-POSCO's emphasis on interdependence and teamwork is beginning to produce results. By late 1993 steelworkers were being included in early-morning meetings that had formerly been limited to managers. McCarthy-Wilcox said, "Operators can say what's on their minds and contribute *before* decisions are made. Before, when they were excluded from the meetings, they just naturally clammed up and complained. But once they were allowed to contribute, productivity climbed and complaints dropped off." She added, "It's hard for managers in this environment to open up to the wage people and harder still to be consistent. They've got to 'unlearn' their old ways. It's like they are schizo. Deep down they feel one way, but they know they should behave differently. So they say one thing and do another. One incident undoes all of the good work. Changing this deep-seated stuff takes time and practice. You know you'll have failures and all you can do is to minimize the impact."

The results of a 1994 survey that was sponsored by the company and the union gave the first formal indications that management, the union, and the rank-and-file steelworkers had finally recognized that they would all have to pull in the same direction. A surprising 90 percent of employees agreed that improved product quality, efficiency, teamwork, and customer satisfaction were needed to ensure the company's future.[11] The bottom line began to reflect these deeper changes. I remember Randy Smith saying in 1988 that USS-POSCO would have to improve its quality so that it could compete in the more recession-proof high-quality-steel market, in which fewer producers compete.

Six years later, USS-POSCO had hit those benchmarks. In 1994 the company continued to make a profit, largely because of improved product quality and on-time delivery. At the end of the first quarter of 1994, USS-POSCO shipped 326,700 tons of steel, exceeding its business plan goal by 14,000 tons.[12] Among its finished-steel customers are a growing number of new high-quality office furniture manufacturers like Steelcase, Hon, and Reliance. The company recently won a coveted "preferred supplier" status with Campbell Soup, and it has increased its sales to other big customers, such as Del Monte and American National Can. The numbers bear out the company's success. The plant's integrated yield (the percentage of incoming steel used in the product) continues to climb, hitting nearly 88 percent in 1994.[13] Since 1989 the scrap rate (the percentage of incoming steel that cannot be used) has plummeted by 31 percent, while customer satisfaction has risen, as evidenced by increased sales. The number of rejects (steel coils that customers return) has been cut in half, while delivery performance has increased by 20 percent.[14]

Just a few years ago, in 1991, USS-POSCO received a record $500,000 fine from the state Regional Water Quality Control Board for dumping contaminated discharges into the river.[15] In a remarkable turnaround, three years later, it was chosen by the National Environmental Development Association as one of twenty environmentally conscious companies for its "unblemished record of environmental quality management."[16] The company was singled out for having reduced its discharges of chromium (a by-product that poisons waste water) by 99 percent, for having been the first steel mill in the world to use technology to reduce nitrogen oxides that pollute the air, and for having spent more than $30 million on environmental projects.

There is also evidence of deeper change. The 1994 survey showed that more than 90 percent of the company's steelworkers said they were proud to work for USS-POSCO and that they were personally committed to doing high-quality work.[17] Gary O'Brien, a seventeen-year veteran steelworker, is a good example of the changes rippling through the workforce. When I first met him in 1990, O'Brien was a tractor driver. He was angry at U.S. Steel management, and he was suspicious of nearly everything they did. Today, as one of the five new facilitators, he deals directly with USS-POSCO's customers. O'Brien said, "At first the managers didn't trust us to even drive the trucks to visit customers. Our own sales reps were uncomfortable with wage people talking to the customers." He quipped, "Maybe they thought we'd give them a discount on the price of iron!" Continuing in a serious vein, O'Brien said, "Since we've worked together with the salespeople, some of them have become our greatest allies. Customers have told me that five years ago they didn't believe the union could ever have this much participation in the company. The union's behind the change as long as conditions are safe and it doesn't reduce jobs. We've come a long way, and I've got to admit that I'm proud of my department!"

Like the heroic "little engine that could," USS-POSCO has overcome forces that would have daunted the best of managers and union leaders—a depressed market for steel, stiff international competition, battles with government regulators, warfare between unions inside and outside the company, and a suit that pitted one giant parent against the other, threatening the joint venture's very existence. As a former U.S. Steel company, it inherited one of the worst labor-management relationships in the country. A century or more of adversarial relationships hobbled the joint venture from the beginning. I witnessed the power of this culture to thwart change—even change that was required for survival. That the union was willing to scuttle the company's use of SPC to keep it from winning the certification that might expand business for everyone attests to the blindness this belief system promotes. That management would unilaterally force all employees to take one of their two annual vacation weeks at Christmas while still trying to promote teamwork seems almost beyond belief. Yet through these examples we see how the imprint of Andrew Carnegie's actions a century ago still directs what people think and do. In the recent jointly sponsored survey, fewer than a quarter (23 percent) of USS-POSCO's employees and managers said they trusted each other. And cooperation has come only slowly. Only 28 percent of all employees in the same survey said that union-management cooperation had improved in the past year.[18]

Nevertheless, this company has begun to overcome the great odds that faced it. First, it demonstrated that without a shared vision neither labor nor management could make any real progress. The agreement that steelworkers would take a pay cut to establish the joint venture in 1986 and the generous 1992 contract that included profit sharing both helped to establish the beginning of such a fresh outlook. The crisis surrounding the antidumping suit also could not help but show labor and management how much they depend on each other. Whether or not the lesson has been internalized, only time will tell.

Second, management began to transform the company at its very core by altering how steel was produced. Unlike Douglas Aircraft, which tried to train its employees in the principles of a "new culture," USS-POSCO harnessed the production system itself to bring about the changes. A critical step was creating a "pull" in the production system by systematically tying customer demand directly to the mills through facilitators. Once the new, sophisticated equipment was installed, job classifications were combined, and wage incentives were reformulated, it finally became possible to develop teamwork—because now it was necessary. Managers and steelworkers discovered for the first time just how much they had to depend on each other to get their jobs done in order to satisfy customers, without whom there would be no work for anyone.

Third, once the demands of the new production system became evident, training became useful. A well-designed production system encourages employees—if they feel even partly responsible for the company's success and reasonably well treated—to learn how to do their jobs better. And, as USS-POSCO shows, the new production system shaped the training to fit the task. USS-POSCO's experience shows how training is perhaps more useful in supporting organizational changes as they are made, rather than in leading them.

Fourth, the importance of positive human relationships between management and labor cannot be overstated. When my research team and I first started at the plant in 1989, there was virtually no common ground (or even language) between the two warring sides. The unspoken rage and mistrust were debilitating. There seemed to be no way around the paralyzing effects of this powerful, pessimistic culture. More than once, when we left the plant for the airport and home, we had trouble even talking about it. Not until we tried to drown out the gloom at the airport bar did we realize just how crippling this collective mood really was. However, as the years passed and both sides were forced to work with each other, Joe Stanton, Bob Witt, Bill Haley, and others recognized their common interest and began to build on each positive experience. As they worked together under pressure, trust slowly began to develop between them.

Have this company's struggles permanently altered the historic pattern of adversarial labor relations? Or is this only a temporary truce? No one knows. What is certain, however, is that any gains achieved today will surely be tested tomorrow as the environment continues to change. When I compare the company today with where it was in 1989, the progress is truly astonishing. The results in terms of improved profitability, integrated yield, quality, and on-time delivery speak for themselves. But even though long-standing and contentious issues such as job security, job classifications, and pay have been settled at USS-POSCO for now, conflict may break out at any time. The topsy-turvy world of union politics does not contribute much stability in an unstable world. Watching Joe Stanton lose office after he had finally begun to build a productive relationship with management is a reminder that democratically run unions will always be in a state of change. It is also a reminder that there are no cut-and-dried answers in this era of continuous change. What is needed is a process through which labor and management can solve problems as they arise. And management must take the lead through consistent, fair leadership. The lesson seems not to have been lost on USS-POSCO. The last time I saw Bill Haley, he was sitting between the new union president and Bob Witt at a conference on improving labor-management relationships.

# PART IV
# HEWLETT-
# PACKARD

# CHAPTER NINE

# REMNANTS OF MASS PRODUCTION

HEWLETT-PACKARD, voted the top U.S. corporate performer of 1995 by *Forbes*, is a giant manufacturer of computers, printers, and a vast array of sophisticated electronic instruments.[1] But it is as different from Douglas Aircraft and USS-POSCO as day from night. Though HP is a huge corporation (its 1995 revenue was $31.5 billion, and it had more than 94,000 employees in sixty worldwide divisions), it is an extremely pleasant place in which to work.[2] It is a genteel organization, heavily populated by highly educated engineers whose worlds are filled with mental abstractions. Profanity, common in aircraft factories and steel mills, would be entirely out of place here. Engineers work in open offices and talk quietly over the hum of computers and scientific equipment while sipping Amaretto-flavored coffee. The company's founders, William Hewlett and David Packard, continually reinforced the idea that HP employees were also the company's owners and were to be treated accordingly. Good salaries, stock options, profit sharing, and employment security helped to create a powerful culture that united HP's management and its employees, rather than dividing them.[3] A union has never been established there.

But even at HP one can glimpse the remnants of mass production.

The Santa Clara, California, division that became the setting for our study had been jolted by an alarming loss of sales and a massive downsizing. Its rigid organizational structure had created insulated fiefdoms, and during the 1980s, as the pace of change accelerated, speed, flexibility, and coordination among departments became all-important. Departments like R&D and marketing now had to work together and were ill equipped for the task. At the same time, Santa Clara engineers and managers had become complacent as a result of years of prosperity and had lost touch with their customers. The combination nearly doomed this onetime scientific powerhouse. In this chapter and the following ones we will see how Santa Clara was able to call on the powerful HP culture and use it to redesign the division from top to bottom. The story shows how, for an organization, culture can be a competitive advantage.

## THE "HP WAY"

The beliefs and values that guide HP employees' behavior were created by Bill Hewlett and David Packard and have been codified in a document entitled "The HP Way."[4] As David Packard explains in his recent memoir, profitability is fundamental to the HP Way: "The profit we generate from our operations is the ultimate source of the funds we need to prosper and grow. It's the foundation of future opportunity and employment security."[5] Packard's father had been a Colorado bankruptcy referee during the Great Depression, and as a young man Packard had witnessed foreclosures on companies that had mortgaged all their assets, leaving them with nothing. Back in 1938 he and Bill Hewlett had agreed they would finance their company primarily from earnings rather than from borrowed money. Another HP Way cornerstone is a commitment to innovation and contribution. Packard writes that neither he nor Hewlett wanted to create a "me-too" company. Rather, they wanted to invent new products that would make important contributions to science, industry, and human welfare.[6] This would require high standards of personal achievement and a commitment to doing a good job. "From the beginning," Packard writes, "Bill Hewlett and I have had a strong belief in people. We believe that people *want* to do a good job and that it is important for them to enjoy their work at Hewlett-Packard. . . . It has always been important to Bill and me to create an environment in which people have a chance to be their best, to recognize their potential, and to be recognized for their achievements."[7]

Packard and Hewlett had known the company they envisioned could not be structured like an autocratic military organization. "That is precisely the type of organization we at HP did not want . . . and do not want," Packard writes. "We feel that our objectives can best be achieved by people who understand and support them and who are allowed flexibility in working toward common goals in ways that they help determine are best for their operation and their organization."[8] In this way, Packard's and Hewlett's original values fostered a model of participatory management that became another cornerstone of the HP Way. Packard explains, "The net result was that each employee felt that he or she was a member of the team."[9]

Although the HP Way defines Hewlett-Packard employees with astonishing clarity, many have a hard time articulating exactly what the quality is. Lyle Hornback, a Santa Clara manager, described it as an elusive but powerful set of characteristics that had come directly from Hewlett and Packard. But he added, "I can't define exactly what it is. It's related to the concept of HP as a family. If you go into an airport in a foreign country, or to an HP office in South Africa, you find the same character: 'Can I get you a cup of coffee? Can I help you somehow?' Dave and Bill made so many people in their own image, but I can't tell you precisely what it is."[10]

Jim Collin, an engineer in Santa Clara's quartz-crystal laboratory, echoed the sentiments of many other veteran HP employees. He said that the heart of the HP way was a feeling of family that Packard himself personified.[11] Collin has been with HP since 1963, and the experience has touched his life profoundly. He whispered, "It's a *family.*" He leaned across the table and repeated softly, "A *family.* It's so simple. I've been here thirty-some years, and I used to see Bill and Dave every day. Everyone was on a first-name basis, you were expected to do your job, and you knew exactly where you stood. It wasn't any different than the family at home."

Much as Donald Douglas valued his workers, Bill Hewlett and David Packard knew their employees were their greatest asset. Collin said, "Sure, Packard wanted to make a profit. He knew that was the only way to keep the enterprise growing. But he also knew that without his people he was as good as dead! He knew that his people would make him or break him and that he sure as hell wasn't going to make it on his own! That's why he was so adamant against borrowing. You paid your own way. If you don't have it, you don't spend it. It was important to Packard to never get his ass in trouble. That way he'd never have to lay anyone off. He wanted to have some money in the bank so he could always keep people on if hard times came like they did in 1970. 'Here, you're an engineer, take this broom and sweep the floor for a while.' Or 'Here's a brush, go paint that equipment.' I mean, people did it! Pappy took care of things. You might have to shovel shit for a while, but you'd keep your job. It was never a question for any of us. We knew we were his main interest." It was this devotion that had kept HP nonunion. "I have tried to follow the basic policy that I have more reason to be interested in my employees than a union leader does," Packard once said. "As soon as the employees think that one of these union people is going to be more interested and responsive to their needs than I am, then I think they should have a union!"[12]

The value Hewlett and Packard placed on their employees was also evident in HP's "open-door" policy. Jim Collin said he had never forgotten the feeling of being able to go over his immediate superior's head when he felt he had been treated badly. Collin, one of those rare old-time engineers who had bypassed a formal engineering education, had begun at HP working on an assembly line, but he had soon realized that his engineering talents could be put to use as the company expanded. He recalled, "I'd been working as a full-fledged engineer for a couple of years, and I learned the math I needed on the job. One day I got a new boss who said I'd have to take a formal test if I wanted to continue as an engineer because I didn't have a four-year engineering degree." Collin said he had been dumbfounded because he had received nothing but outstanding performance ratings and had taught himself advanced mathematics. "I said, 'Pardon me? I've been doing engineering for years. Is there something wrong with my work?' By then I'd been out of school for some time and had forgotten most of the schoolbook math that we never used. Sure enough, I flunked the math. My boss called me in and in effect demoted me. He said, 'Too bad, but if you want to keep doing engineering work we can't call you an engineer or give you the money.' I went home furious.

After I thought about it for a few hours, I decided to go over his head because I thought I had been treated unfairly. I walked in to see one of the top managers and told him my story. His eyes opened wide as he said in astonishment, 'Pardon me? Your manager did what?' Well, needless to say I kept my pay and my title. This company's open-door policy demonstrated to me, and to lots of others who came later, that at HP you can get a fair hearing."

Though Bill Hewlett is said to have had a powerful impact inside the R&D labs, where he displayed his prodigious engineering talent, most of the employees who had worked with both of them seemed to have been more personally touched by David Packard. Said Collin, "Part of it was the difference in their personalities. Packard was a big man too, and you couldn't miss him. Damn it, you felt something when he came into a room. But he never intimidated or humiliated you. He could be rough, but after all was said and done, you respected him. You loved him. I'll never forget it. If Packard walked into a meeting with his sleeves down and buttoned, you knew that everything was all right, it was okay. But if he came in with them rolled up, that meant something was wrong. Now if he had them rolled up to his armpits, then you knew the shit was about to hit the fan!"

Stepping back to a meeting of division managers at Santa Clara in 1974, we can glimpse the core elements of the HP Way in their original form.[13] At the time the issue was a worsening profit picture. Packard opened the meeting by saying flatly that he was troubled that he had been caught off guard with the bad news. This is unfortunate in any company, but it is especially serious at HP, where managers are taught to keep on top of details so that corrective action can be taken quickly and without apportioning blame. Packard said of himself and Hewlett, "We were kind of soft about it, but I guess the most serious issue was that we didn't realize the problems were as bad as they were. So I thought it might be helpful to take a few minutes to see if we can really define what some of our management objectives in this company should be."

Here the teacher in Packard emerged as he lectured his managers about the folly of chasing market share at the expense of profit. He was direct: "For some reason, we've got this talking about one of our objectives as increasing the share of the market. I want to start right out by telling you that this is not a legitimate management objective of this company. It leads to the wrong kind of decisions. Hereafter, if I hear anybody talking about how big their share of the market is, or what they're trying to do to increase their share, I'm going to personally see that a black mark gets put in their personnel folder! Anybody can increase the share of the market by giving away their products, and that's exactly what we did in some cases over the last couple of years. We have a significant share of some markets now where we'd be just a hell of a lot better off if we hadn't ever touched that business and if our share was zero!"

Beyond market share, there was another more subtle message. One day in the not-too-distant future, Packard knew, he and Hewlett would be gone. He knew the company would have to transcend them and develop its own management team. "That is what Bill and I have been trying to do," Packard continued. "But if our results in 1973 are any indication, we've not been very successful so far. Somehow we've got to get this management team of ours on top of the job, because it is going to determine the future success or failure of this company."

Packard then became the businessman, moving effortlessly through a detailed explanation of HP's financial performance in 1973 that illuminated exactly why the managers would have to control inventory costs. Through it all was a demand for the highest levels of effort and achievement from the Santa Clara managers. Packard admonished them matter-of-factly, "Somehow you fellows didn't think this was part of your responsibility, I guess, because you didn't do anything about it. But that's your job, and we cannot run a railroad this way! If that's the way we're going to run this company, we don't need professional managers. We need a bunch of kindergarten kids. So if you fellows who are responsible for running this manufacturing area can't keep your inventories in line, we're just going to find someone who can. It's just as simple as that!"

This was not a harangue intended to intimidate the Santa Clara managers. Rather, it was a stern lecture of the kind a caring father might deliver to his errant children. It was the hard side of the HP Way. Now Packard again became the teacher as he directed the managers' attention back to the basic values upon which he and Hewlett had built the company. "By now I guess you've judged that what I'm getting at is that we return to the traditional policies of this company. That we manage it so we finance our growth from earnings and cash flow. Somehow we seem to have gotten away from that, but I see absolutely no reason why that should not still be our basic objective."

Packard then reaffirmed one of the central tenets of the HP Way—trust in the individual. "All I ask you is, let's forget about this share-of-the-market nonsense. Let's get back on the fundamental principles of management that have worked well for this company in the past. This is not anything unreasonable for Bill and me to ask of you gentlemen. You're the guys on the firing line, and you're the ones that we have to depend on to get this job done. I can't do it for you, and Bill Hewlett can't do it for you. You're the guys who've got to do it, and we want to help you in any way we can. Well, let's go back to work, and we'll see you again a little later."

As this example shows, Packard demanded the highest possible performance from his managers yet treated them respectfully as both stock-holders and owners. He trusted them to make sound decisions. Finally, there was teamwork, and there was little question that, to Packard, HP was a team to which everyone belonged.

Through the years, the HP Way has shown itself to be a valuable resource, something John Young, who became Hewlett-Packard's president in 1977, discovered as he began to move the company into the intensely competitive computer business in the early 1980s. The company's decentralized but fragmented organization and its well-mannered decision-making style, which had evolved from the R&D labs, were ill suited to the fast-moving, rapacious world of computers. The autonomous divisions were hard to coordinate and manage, and they had few incentives to co-operate.[14] The sales managers reported solely to the executive committee, causing the sales representatives to lose touch with the engineers who designed the products. Furthermore, the executive committee took an inordinately long time to make important decisions—a luxury that could not be tolerated in the fast-changing world of computers. By the late 1980s HP had become, according to *The Wall Street Journal*, a "bureaucratic morass."[15]

At this point morale at HP was at an all-time low, and even though the company had been profitable every year since its founding, some industry observers wondered if it would survive.[16] Young knew that the management structure was failing and he would have to act quickly to stop the fall of earnings and stock prices. He turned to Chairman Packard, who until then had left the day-to-day operations in Young's hands. With the seventy-eight-year-old Packard at his side, Young began a massive reorganization. Layers of management were removed, and strong leaders who could cut through red tape were charged with bringing new products to market quickly. Investors responded to the aggressive cost cutting and streamlining as HP's earnings and stock prices rebounded.[17]

The company's steady double-digit growth in earnings, which carried well into the 1980s, stood as silent testimony to the wisdom of Hewlett's and Packard's ways. Between 1970 and 1980, HP's net revenue exploded from $365 million to $4.3 billion.[18] During the same time HP's employees grew in number from 16,000 to 57,000.[19] The company's generous benefits plan ensured that employees would share in its wealth, and even in the troubled nineties, HP was rated one of the top companies in America to work for, in large part because of its pay and benefits.[20] HP's wages were equivalent to those of similar companies, but employees were also encouraged to share in the company's gains through a discounted stock purchase plan, a matching savings plan, and profit sharing. Keith Ferguson, a veteran HP engineer, recalled how the original profit-sharing plan (which had once accounted for 25 to 30 percent of his yearly income) had brought with it a strong sense of ownership. He said, "I remember guys standing around in the halls talking, and someone would say, 'Hey, Joe, get back to work. That's my profit you're wasting!' Most of the assembly lines had visuals showing quality defects. This was real profit sharing. It wasn't some management tool to control us."[21]

The powerful culture had proved its value in the computer side of the business. But as 1992 began to draw to a close, a new question emerged: Would the HP Way be able to guide the company's venerable twenty test and measurement divisions out of their deepening tailspin and propel them toward new opportunities?

## SANTA CLARA

To find out, my research team and I went to work at Santa Clara in early 1993. The third oldest division in the company, HP's Santa Clara production facilities lie in the middle of California's Silicon Valley, a few miles south of HP's international headquarters in Palo Alto. Throughout the 1970s and 1980s, Santa Clara had become accustomed to double-digit annual growth, generated by its high-tech test and measurement equipment—frequency counters, atomic clocks, and laser interferometers (electronic instruments that measure frequency, time, and motion with scientific precision).

At one time, Santa Clara alone had provided 10 percent of Hewlett-Packard's revenue from sales of its scientific instruments. However, beginning in 1986 its revenue had started to drop. For several reasons, over the next several years sales had plummeted, and 1,000 of Santa Clara's 1,600 employees had left in a deep and painful downsizing. Because of the company practice of guaranteeing employment, many employees had transferred to other HP divisions, though some had quit the company altogether.

Marty Neil, a twenty-year HP marketing veteran who took over the division in 1991 to try to restore its economic vitality, remembered, "In eighty-five and eighty-six the test and measurement business had changed irrevocably. The business had left us, but it took us five years to see it." The problems were complex. Technology had always reigned at Santa Clara, and no competitors could match the scientific breakthroughs or the high technology that sprang from its R&D labs. Customers knew that, although they paid premium prices, they were getting the highest-quality technology available in the world. Santa Clara's atomic clocks set world standards for measuring time, as did its lasers and counters for measuring distance and frequency. Especially during the Cold War, when the extent of the Soviets' technology development was unknown, defense agencies preferred HP's products over others because of their advanced designs.

In a growing economy, when defense budgets seemed without limit, HP's strategy of building premium products at premium prices made sense. It was profitable as well. However, in the mid-1980s, when defense spending was sharply curtailed, HP's engineers' love of science and their pursuit of perfection at any cost quickly became a liability. The years of designing products without specific customers in mind proved to be costly.

HP was further hurt in the mid-1980s, when Congress abolished sole-source contracting—the practice of awarding government contracts without competitive bidding. Since the 1950s HP had garnered vast

amounts of business from defense agencies, as well as from defense contractors like Hughes, McDonnell Douglas, and Westinghouse, as sole suppliers of sophisticated general-purpose test equipment. Marty Neil said
candidly, "These lucrative contracts were like the wind in HP's sails." In
his twenty years with HP, Neil had seen the dependency on sole-source
contracting grow. He said, "Aerospace defense was our lifeblood. And we
began to equate high performance with high-priced boxes decked out
with all the bells and whistles."

The test and measurement market was also changing. Customers
were shifting from analog to digital equipment, and computer-aided engineering was proliferating. Both changes portended the decline of the
stand-alone, off-the-shelf test and measurement equipment that had made
Santa Clara famous. Computer-aided engineering could now produce
designs of such high quality that they never required testing. Also, renewed customer demands for quality forced HP's manufacturing customers and their suppliers to improve their production techniques. As
their quality improved, they realized that testing added unnecessary costs
to production and that much of it could be eliminated.

The technology began to change too. Neil said, "The handwriting
was on the wall for some time. We were just slow to read it. The customer
base we'd always counted on began to disappear, but we continued like
nothing had changed. Among the test and measurement divisions, we
were getting the lowest returns on our investments in R&D, because all of
our effort was aimed at our traditional markets, not at the new growth
areas." Neil knew that the division would have to change. He said, "Our
challenge was to change from being an inward-looking box supplier to a
customer-focused supplier of solutions. We needed a new business charter outside of traditional test and measurement, where we could find half-
billion-dollar opportunities and unlimited growth."

According to Neil, though Santa Clara had become successful by
making general-purpose equipment, the market was becoming increasingly specialized: "We were introverted, absorbed in science and technology, which overshadowed everything else. Santa Clara was derisively
called the 'Science Fair' division." He described how in earlier years Santa
Clara had benefited from being its own best customer. Its engineers had
used Santa Clara's products—frequency counters and signal generators,

for instance—in their daily work, so market information had easily been found at the "next bench." Neil said, "The 'next-bench paradigm' worked well in the early days, when the market was predictable and growing and engineers worked in close proximity to each other. But when the market began to change and the new divisional structure put physical distance between designers and the next bench, we created the 'virtual' next bench in our minds. We didn't have to ask customers what they wanted, because we could imagine their needs!" This introversion caused the division to lose its ability to communicate both internally and with the outside world. Neil said that management had responded by creating teams that cut across departments but that it had not trusted the teams to make business decisions. Neil said, "It led to an endless 'do loop' where nobody could make the hard decisions that were needed. Products were often late, and optimistic sales forecasts were rarely realized. Not only were we in the wrong businesses, but we had the wrong organization."

Although the warning signs were unmistakable, no one could figure out what the root problem was. Neil said that, as a result, "we blamed everything for our failure. We blamed field sales for not paying enough attention to our products. After all, we had the poor business results to prove it!" Blaming others was a convenient ploy that continued to mask the larger environmental change.

The problem was that one of the HP Way's central tenets—the expectation of high levels of achievement and contribution—had undergone a subtle but profound transformation. To many of the senior engineers who had been hired in the 1950s and 1960s, high achievement and contribution meant *scientific* achievement and *scientific* contribution, something for which they had always been generously rewarded. Most Santa Clara engineers were passionate about their work, and the instruments they designed took on human qualities. Retirement parties were thrown for old instruments, and engineers sang ballads that testified to their endearing features. But the environment had changed. For the first time in the company's history, new products could not be designed simply according to the advice of fellow engineers. Instead, their design would have to be determined by customers.

Keith Ferguson, who went to work for HP in 1958 after graduating from MIT, described how the meaning of achievement and contribution had shifted. His eight-by-ten-foot cubicle was crowded with computers and instruments that hummed and blinked as he talked. "I'm an R&D engineer," he said, leaning back in his gray steel chair. "I'm interested in how it sells, but I am most interested in the contribution it makes to society. I want to do something like no one has done before. To do it better. I'm not sure Packard would agree, but I've always thought of profit as a tool—as a means, not an end. I always figured that with the contribution, profit would come.

"By contribution, I mean measuring time more accurately, or producing more accurate frequency signals. When we flew one of our cesium clocks around the world, we found out how much time variation there was between Boulder and Paris, for instance—in billionths of seconds. That didn't matter much then, but it sure does now. It also helped shed some light on Einstein's theory of relativity. That's contribution to me.

"When I came to work here, I wanted to be proud of my work. To make it the best quality possible. Quality came at a high price, but then we had the money. We were good at what we did, but that also meant that we were insular. We were just like the customer, because every engineer used voltmeters and oscilloscopes like the ones I have here," Ferguson said, patting the instruments on his bench. "Market research was right here."

Ferguson said he thought it was natural in a scientific company for engineers to be more interested in technology than in the customer. Many engineers are more comfortable inside the familiar laboratory than they are in the marketplace. Ferguson spoke candidly of his own fears: "Often I don't understand the customer's environment, and I'm afraid of looking dumb. Also, we're so open here in the way we talk. There are no secrets. But I worry about divulging information in casual conversations with customers. I also worry that I may get committed to something I don't want to. It's like calling up someone you don't know for a date!"

Ferguson said the schism between engineering and marketing had existed for years. He asked with a grin if I'd heard of his "ten-instrument-shelf theory." He explained, "We wanted more market information early in the product development cycle, but many times we didn't get it until the end because marketing guys were off doing other things. My theory was that to get Marketing's attention early in the product definition phase, we'd build nine instruments and put them up on a shelf. When we put the tenth one up, the first would fall off and hit a marketing guy on the head and wake him up. He'd rub his head and finally ask, 'I wonder what this is and what features our customers want?' " But by 1993 such division and independence could no longer be treated as a laughing matter.

The cherished HP "family feeling" had also begun to change in an ominous way. Like the employees at Douglas Aircraft, who felt the company owed them something for nothing, employees at Santa Clara had begun to take the company's generosity for granted. The company generosity and its "family feeling" had gradually eased into a form of entitlement that was no longer connected to achievement or results. Marty Neil called it the "doughnut culture." He explained, "We slipped into this paternalism, and doughnuts became the visible symbol of the problem. It was a tradition that employees were served doughnuts and coffee every day at every HP site. It became a ritual. We had a full-time guy who did nothing but *doughnuts*," he said incredulously. "Then there were endless debates about whether or not doughnuts were healthy, so we'd have *fruit* and doughnuts. Then in the lean years in 1984 or 1985 there was a corporate decision to put a stop to it because it cost too much. You'd think the world was coming to an end. People complained that they'd *earned* their doughnuts. To many, the loss of doughnuts became the embodiment of how the HP Way was changing."

Next, the "family feeling" began to transform into a set of beliefs that insiders derisively called "terminal niceness."[22] This means that employees are expected to be nice to one another to preserve corporate harmony. Above all, they must avoid conflict. The term also has a deeper meaning — that a lack of creative conflict may be fatal. Lyle Hornback explained the lack of conflict as an unhealthy outgrowth of the enduring HP family feeling. "When you come to HP, the expectation is that you'll stay forever, and part of that family feeling is denial," he said, raising his hand to blind his eyes. "Whether it's conflict, alcohol abuse, or anything else that's hard to deal with, I guess in any close relationship we naturally try to deny it. We'll try everything to find a niche for someone who isn't working out. The external conditions have changed, but no one wants to acknowledge it. At some level, the HP family doesn't want to accept the change, and they're reluctant to discuss it."

Hornback described how the security that employees had always taken for granted had begun to give way in the face of change, and that, while the company was continuing to observe an unspoken practice of employment security, few felt very secure. "We were *HP*," he said. "No one had to charge too hard—there were no hoops to jump through. But now even the hardware engineers at the top of the pecking order have begun to feel it. They were always secure in their positions, but it's not the case today. There are no more safe havens."

David Dills, Santa Clara division's personnel manager, amplified Hornback's observations. He said, "Until very recently, the management style was to never overreact. It was modeled for you, and to behave otherwise was to risk your job. New people were quickly socialized by the group, and if you didn't conform you were shunned. We always had pockets in the organization where employees who didn't fit in could be put, so we never had to face some of the tough personnel decisions we have to make today. But those days are over."

Without correction, Santa Clara's indulgent and self-protective attitude would surely be fatal. The turnaround in HP's computer business, however, had demonstrated that the paternalistic culture could change. Now it was up to Neil and his managers to see if Santa Clara could develop a customer focus and drive a renewed sense of urgency and accountability deep into the organization. Such a transformation would be monumental: not only would the division have to develop a new organizational form, but its managers and engineers would have to learn to survive in an unpredictable and unforgiving environment. They would have to learn how to take risks, how to resolve conflicts, how to forge new relationships with customers. By 1993 Neil and his managers knew that the journey that lay ahead would be difficult. But they also knew that without radical and painful surgery to restore earnings, the division would surely be dissolved.

# CHAPTER TEN

# ALTERING THE SYSTEM OF WORK

MARTY NEIL WAS STAGGERED by the Herculean tasks that faced him in the first months of 1992. First, Santa Clara would have to be weaned from the illusion of security in the stagnant test and measurement market. Second—and more important—its employees would have to be led into new and uncharted businesses that had barely begun to acquire form. Although a worldwide revolution in communications was clearly taking place, much of the underlying science and technology had yet to be invented. Third, the venerated HP Way would have to be reexamined and brought into line with the new demands.

Neil knew he had little choice but to step off the once secure business platform that had supported Santa Clara. A new line of business would have to be found quickly. Neil's boss, Tom Vos, general manager of the Test and Measurement Division's Electronic Instruments Group, wanted fast results.[1] Vos, a rough-hewn man, looked more as though he had come off the football field than out of the mannerly world of HP. Regarded as a hard driver, he was responsible for turning around HP's San Diego division and spawning some of the company's most successful products, including ink-jet printers and plotters. Vos knew it would take enormous pressure to turn a division like Santa Clara around. Though Vos gave Neil the freedom he wanted, he also made it clear that financially Santa Clara was on its own. Any new investments it chose to make in products would have to come from earnings from its existing line. Vos himself was under pressure, as all ten test and measurement divisions had been rocked by the turbulent marketplace, but, as Neil said, "Santa Clara was the problem child. You didn't have to be a genius to read the writing on the wall. Unless we could turn things around, we would be consolidated."

Naturally, designing precision instruments for a technology that was only then coming into existence was risky, since no one knew exactly what would be needed. "How do I lead an organization into a brand-new area that is barely taking form?" Neil wondered. "How can I understand the customer's needs if I have never been there myself? Can I lead this division, never having been the customer?"

To try to answer these questions, Neil established a three-step process. First, he and his management team would identify the business sectors with the most promise, ones that Santa Clara could enter from a position of strength given its experience and resources. Second, they would create a new organization that could rapidly and efficiently develop products for these new businesses. Third, they would do a careful analysis of the HP Way to ensure that its underlying values and beliefs would drive the new organization in a productive direction. Each of these risky steps would have to be taken in record time. Neil and his managers had already researched the emerging communications market and delineated its broad outlines: The demand for data transmission had mushroomed, pushing existing communications systems' capacity to their limits. Adding to the congestion, the explosion of multimedia transmission — still and live video images — demanded millions of times the transmission capacity that existed. Banks and other financial institutions also needed to be able to synchronize their electronic transactions to ensure that coding and decoding were precisely sequenced so that they could avoid losing data, which was the same as losing dollars. Furthermore, a new world of wireless telecommunications was opening multibillion-dollar markets for manufacturers such as AT&T, Motorola, Northern Telecom, Alcatel, and Nokia. Neil was convinced that a vast new market lay in combining existing technologies to synchronize the flow of data in the communications and electric power industries. These new products would be like stop-lights that control the flow of traffic, but instead of regulating cars they would regulate the flow of data. By synchronizing the transmission of data, this new technology would ensure its integrity and help customers maximize their networks' capacity. The prospects looked endless.

If Neil and his managers had judged it correctly, the idea of a timing infrastructure would prove to be of great strategic significance. It would be a growth marketplace of gigantic proportions—$500 million annually or more. But it was also a colossal gamble: the market was not yet clear, and the products that would probably be needed lay well outside Santa Clara's established product lines. Could Santa Clara's engineers—who had grown so insular—go out and find customers for these new product ideas? Could the products actually be designed and produced as Neil hoped they could?

Murli Thirumale, one of Santa Clara's best marketing managers, had confidence that it could be done. He shared Neil's vision of a timing infrastructure that would synchronize data flow. Thirumale, who had worked for HP for twelve years, had risen quickly at Santa Clara, causing some engineers to grumble, though most gave him credit for his ability to grasp complex ideas easily. He certainly understood what was going on in Santa Clara. "We'd been tooling around in the Bay area's 'back roads' [a reference to a popular television program that takes viewers into San Francisco's back country, where time seems to have stopped]. We got away with it because the environment was static," he said. "New-product development around here has been about as exciting as watching grass grow! But the pace is changing. We've come out of the quiet back roads onto the crazy freeways, where everyone's driving seventy miles an hour. Now we have to learn defensive driving. We have to learn to race and dodge. We have to be always at the edge of control!"

Thirumale was convinced that the world was moving rapidly toward developing a timing utility. "It will be like that power outlet," he said, pointing down to the outlet on the baseboard. "But instead of power coming out of it, you'll have precise timing. And it will be the same anywhere, anytime in the world, and it will be cheap. Power was the utility of the industrial age, and timing will be the utility of the information age." He expanded on the need: "Where we're going as a society is being able to provide information anytime, anyplace. But we've been trapped in the past. We're fighting its decline. It's like paddling upstream when you're about to be swept over Niagara Falls." Thirumale continued, "Imagine that you're managing a pension portfolio and that you're trading with the Tokyo Stock Exchange in the middle of the night. Prices are changing every thirty seconds, and your databases have to be updated, synchronized, and time-stamped. It means, 'At this precise time, the exact price was this much.' As more people enter into these transactions, each of the points has to be synchronized."

Thirumale acknowledged that HP's atomic clocks, which had for many years set the world standard for precise time, could be used for such a purpose but that at $60,000 each they were prohibitively expensive. The market for the *generation* of precise time is relatively small, as is the market for its *transmission* (perhaps $15 million each). But Thirumale's eyes opened wide as he described the market for the *recovery and distribution* of time. "It's huge, enormous! It's the equivalent of bringing power into your house. And there will be endless applications—telecommunications, data communications, and wireless communications."

Another reason for the growing need for synchronization is the explosion in the amount of data being transmitted around the world. Transmitting data in the form of voices does not require a lot of capacity. However, when video images and data are transmitted, the requirements for volume and speed increase geometrically. The clarity of the transmission is also critical, because noise distorts the signal, producing errors, and errors cost money. Australian Telecom had studied data transmission failures and found that 80 percent of them had stemmed from poor synchronization. Other problems occur in wireless communication, when signals are handed off from one grid to another. When voice communication is poorly synchronized and handed off, it is accompanied by annoying snapping sounds. The problem is worse for data because the snap and crackle of poor synchronization can cause it to be lost altogether. There are other applications for synchronization technology as well. In sophisticated factories, such as USS-POSCO, where speeding coils of steel must be cut exactly, operations must be synchronized precisely. Thirumale imagined the day when home computers and other smart devices would proliferate into every corner of life. He said, "There's nothing new about timing synchronization. But a timing utility *is* new. It's revolutionary."

Designing such equipment was one thing, but how could HP's engineers be motivated to leave their insular world to find new customers for these products? Could HP tap these markets before its competitors did? Neil's answer was the establishment of technology partnerships with large customers who were certain to be leaders. Mike Cunningham, a seasoned HP marketing manager, explained the theory. He said, "HP can leverage its engineering know-how into the design of new products. In this business, the pioneer prevails, so we've got to learn how to get in early on the R-and-D phase. The pioneer can ride the wave for twenty years. But the one who gets in late can never break the stranglehold of the guy who gets there first." Cunningham continued, "We've got to swallow our pride and become more like Burger King! You want onions, you get onions! We have been too self-sufficient for too many years without thinking of the customer. We shoveled sand in the back door and shoveled products out the front door. We'd tell customers, 'Look at this great new product we have for you.' It was take it or leave it. We can't do that anymore. These telecommunications companies have tremendous purchasing power. If they want our equipment on every one of their ten thousand trucks with custom functions, then we need to learn how to design and deliver."

Changing this mind-set would be a massive task. Neil exclaimed, "Ever since I've been here, it has been science for science's sake, technology for technology's sake! That's got to change and change fast. We've got to learn how to live with our customers. Once we learn to do that successfully, we'll discover hidden markets. This isn't a dating game. We've got to figure out how to move in together."

## REVERSING MASS PRODUCTION

To help chart the path, Neil adopted a concept called "Sell, Design, Build, Support," otherwise known as "SdbS." SdbS attempted to change mass production's push-the-product-out-the-door philosophy by reversing the process—first selling the product idea, then designing it into the customer's prototypes, and finally building large quantities and providing follow-up support. Jerry Purmal, Santa Clara's Precision Motion Control Group (informally called "Lasers") manager, had pioneered the concept on a smaller scale when he found that his leading transducer customers had nearly been drawn away by competitors. By working closely with customers such as Nikon and Seagate as they designed new products, Santa Clara's laser engineers learned how to respond to their customers' needs better and faster than their competitors could. Neil was convinced the same strategy could work for all of Santa Clara's products. Neil intended to promote the SdbS philosophy as a way of linking Santa Clara's engineers with their customers early in the design phase of new products. Santa Clara marketing and R&D engineers would help their customers design prototype components, which could be integrated into end products. "Then," said Neil, "We can move in and support new customers like crazy."

The last part of Neil's plan was a restructuring of the entire Santa Clara division, from its R&D labs to its production facilities. Late in 1992 he gathered a cross section of his managers into an organizational design team. After analyzing the new business plan, the team made sweeping recommendations about the kind of organization needed to make it a reality. Santa Clara had to become a bottom-up, customer-driven organization. First, so that critical decisions could be made faster, decision making would be pushed down to the individual businesses, where teams would be held accountable for results. Second, the managers in charge of R&D, marketing, and other functions who reported to Neil would be replaced with what the design team called "customer segment managers." These new managers would take the lead in developing alliances with customers from which an SdbS strategy would be fashioned. It would become Santa Clara's version of a "pull" system. The managers would also coordinate teams drawn from volunteers from the Marketing, Engineering and Design, and Production Departments. Managers would give up their traditional authority and become more like coaches and mentors.

Neil hoped for nothing less than a restoration of the original HP Way by redefinition of individual contribution and achievement in the light of contemporary business requirements. Neil said, "For empowerment to work, it takes common values, beliefs, and operating principles. I have great faith that we've got the foundation to build on. But creating a renewed sense of accountability has got to become the backbone of our operation."

Neil knew that his neck was on the chopping block. Tom Vos had described his plan as a "you-bet-your-career" kind of decision, and Neil had tried before to change direction at HP and failed. "When I took over the division in 1991," he recalled, "we decided to carve out a market in disc-testing equipment, but it was a big mistake. It looked perfect. It met all of my requirements. It had a customer focus, and it promised to move the division away from its sole preoccupation with technology. But I failed to appreciate the complexity and the competitiveness of the new market. I didn't ask the hard questions *before* we moved—and we failed. But I learned an important lesson from the failure: there's nothing more dangerous than an idea—when it's the only one you have! I know that everyone is not thrilled about the new course," he admitted. "It's a lonely path, and I've got to admit I feel greatly exposed. But there isn't any other sensible way to go."

## THE "REDESIGN" CONCEPT

The method that Neil and his management team decided to use to restructure the division was called "sociotechnical systems [STS] design," or "work redesign."[2] STS originated a half century ago in England's gritty coal mines, when psychologist Eric Trist and former miner Kenneth Bamforth discovered that as small, self-governing work groups were formed in the mines, greater performance followed.[3] These self-governing work groups were, in fact, throwbacks to the nineteenth and early twentieth centuries, when coal mining had been done by small groups in dark and dangerous conditions. But the natural teamwork had been lost when new technology had been introduced to increase coal production. Soon miners had begun working like their counterparts in factories above ground, doing repetitive tasks under close supervision. However, the companies discovered they still needed small, autonomous teams of miners to extract coal from smaller veins that could not be reached by the heavy equipment. The work of these teams was designed jointly by the managers and miners, a breakthrough in management-labor relations, which like those in the United States had become nasty and adversarial. As Trist and Bamforth observed these early self-managing teams, they noted that productivity, quality of work life, and job satisfaction generally improved because employees could control their working conditions. Fred Emery, an Australian disciple of social scientist Kurt Lewin, who had pioneered worker participation, later joined Trist and elaborated the theories that now underlie sociotechnical systems design.[4]

The STS model spelled out by Trist and Emery years ago is guided by a simple set of principles.[5] Its aim is to create organizations that can learn from their environments and adapt rapidly to changing conditions. Organizations are systems, and all of their parts are interrelated. The goal is to optimize the functioning of each of the subsystems—the technical system (how the work actually gets done) and the social system (employees' values and beliefs)—and to avoid conflicts between them. Companies that ignore this principle may end up pursuing short-term profit at the expense of long-term growth or investing in technology without considering its impact on people. Another principle derived from Trist's and Bamforth's original observations is that individuals from all levels of the organization should take part in the development of a redesign—especially in the areas about which they know most. A third is that everyone must be committed to searching out "variances" (unexpected errors) in the flow of work or information, which can then be corrected at the source. In theory, by creating a new work system through such close collaboration, those who share in its design also share in its ownership.

There is a period of intense anxiety in the moment between an old organization's being rendered useless and a new organization's birth. Leaders of a redesign must have faith in the process—like trapeze artists, who must release their grip on one bar before reaching for the next—in order to make the transition from the old organization to the new one before the latter is fully functional. Work redesign is an irreversible process, because once employees take the power to make decisions and share in the organization's management, they resist giving it up.[6] Unlike TQM, which, as we saw at Douglas Aircraft, can be implemented without touching the organization's core, redesign works only when leaders are willing to pull an organization up by its roots and start over. It is an anxiety-producing process, one that is perhaps done best only when executives know that doors have closed behind them, leaving no other way out. Neil agreed, saying "I didn't begin this redesign to tinker with the organization. I went into it out of desperation, and it scares the hell out of me!"

But Neil was not as alone as he had first imagined. In fact, Santa Clara was one of a growing number of HP divisions that were attempting to redesign themselves. In the late 1980s Hewlett-Packard executives had begun to realize that, as the economic environment became more uncertain, the company's divisions would have to become more nimble and adaptable. In 1988 Stuart Winby had come from the American Productivity and Quality Center in Houston to head an HP corporate consulting group called "The Factory of the Future." Winby's charge had been to help HP's divisions make the transition into the new and turbulent environment, and it was no accident that he had decided on redesign as a strategy. Redesign, Winby had realized, was philosophically in tune with the sort of teamwork and initiative spelled out by the HP Way. Between 1988 and 1992 he had worked with more than twenty divisions, and his efforts had produced lasting results: five-to-one returns on the divisions' investments, saving the company many millions of dollars.[7] The divisions that had redesigned themselves had also developed greater flexibility, enabling them to respond quickly to future changes in the environment.

So far, Winby's work had been restricted to redesigns in manufacturing, but he had correctly anticipated that as the environment became increasingly unstable, work redesign would be required further up the chain of product production, where the greatest value is added: at the boundary between R&D engineers and large commercial customers. This was precisely the opportunity Santa Clara now offered. These "nonlinear," or "value chain," redesigns carried greater risks than did the more visible and linear factory floor redesigns, because knowledge-adding functions like R&D and marketing are abstract.[8] Work is done invisibly inside employees' heads, where thoughts and information flow in unpredictable, nonlinear ways that sometimes appear to be almost random. Patterning new customer-driven behavior from such seeming chaos would be difficult and would test the limits of the process. Though Champion Paper and a few other companies had successfully done nonlinear redesigns, none had done them under the pressure that now confronted Santa Clara.

## REDESIGNING SANTA CLARA

As Neil would soon discover, however, starting down the path of redesign requires more than a good theory—it also requires a powerful motivator. "At first I figured I could do it myself," said Neil. "I thought I could drive the change and keep the pulse of the organization, but I soon realized I could never do it alone."[9]

In May 1992 Neil's organizational design team, with Jenny Brandemuehl (Neil's new transition manager) as its leader, went to work to come up with a winning strategy in just a few months. To accelerate the process, the design team shortcut many of the traditional steps (such as doing separate business, social, and technical analyses) to rapidly craft new businesses and a new organization.[10]

For ten weeks the design team met feverishly, trying to find ways to shorten the traditional STS analyses. Team members mapped how products were conceived, designed, and brought to market, and they documented the division's organizational strengths and weaknesses. Neil and his managers favored keeping only two of the division's three businesses—the small but profitable Precision Motion Control Group ("Lasers") and a new group called Timing Solutions for Communications, which would bring the existing frequency counters, modulation domain analyzers (MDAs), monitoring and timing equipment, cesium clocks, and synchronization equipment into a single organization. Synchronization, Neil was certain, represented the future of the division. First, however, he had to win approval from his superiors.

Though Ned Barnholt (the senior vice president of HP's $3 billion test and measurement organization) and Tom Vos had given Neil the authority to take the steps he thought were necessary, they remained skeptical. In a mid-1992 meeting they cautioned Neil about straying far from Santa Clara's traditional charter. Barnholt told Neil, "Stick with what you've got. Don't venture too far outside of T and M [test and measurement]. Don't do a 'bet your division' and then come to us for money. There's lots of opportunity. You've shown us exciting market trends. But what we didn't hear about is how you're gonna *win*. Our competitors won't roll over and play dead. We need to either find a discontinuity in the technology or a significant competitive advantage."

Neil rejoiced after the meeting, "It was a watershed. No one said, 'Don't do it.' Sure, we could have taken the safe way and stayed in the traditional T and M, but we didn't see how we could make a real contribution or survive. Going outside of T and M was risky, but we decided to push ahead."

To foster a new customer focus and accountability, the new organization would be formed as a matrix. Unlike HP's experiments with matrix organizations in the late 1980s—which had failed because of their centralized, bureaucratic structures—Santa Clara would be designed as a flat, flexible matrix organization.

Such a structure would free managers of the seemingly endless paperwork so they could work with customers. It would also foster teamwork, principally between marketing and R&D. The vertical dimensions would reflect the new "customer segment" businesses. The horizontal functions—new-product development, manufacturing, personnel, and finance—would provide services as needed. Accountability would be ensured by allowing the individual businesses to purchase these services elsewhere if their needs could not be met internally.

Neil was convinced that some core elements of the HP Way would have to be restored before much progress could be made.[11] Most important, employees' commitment to high levels of contribution and initiative now had to be redefined as "adding value to customers." Employees also had to become accountable for their decisions in a new way. Neil believed that "the backbone of accountability will lie in having clear measures that will cascade down through the organization. For the first time ever, teams will understand how they will be measured, and they will come to expect it every quarter. There will be no surprises. If teams are not going to make their targets, they'll have to explain what they're going to do about it. Accountability will become the means for empowerment!"

## THE HEART OF THE MATTER

In the course of its grueling analysis, the design team had found that Santa Clara was getting an unusually low rate of return on its investments in new-product development. No one knew exactly why, but it was clear that before the division could go much further its internal processes would have to be understood and corrected. Because there was so little time to do everything, a special product development team was appointed to discover the root causes of the low rate of return. The team's findings confirmed what many had thought were the root causes of Santa Clara's problems.

The team (led by Mark Allen, an R&D manager who had been a member of the original design team) analyzed twenty-five recent projects and mapped how each one had progressed from an idea to a product. Much to everyone's dismay, Allen's team found that, on average, each project had cost twice as much as the original estimate and sales had reached only half of the original estimates. Also, the projects had almost always been finished late. Allen and his team started to work backward in the process to understand why it worked so poorly.

Allen's team documented how, despite declining sales, many engineers were simply continuing to design products according to their own scientific passion, not market demand. New projects were often poorly defined because there were no incentives to provide accurate sales and cost information, and forecasts were almost always wrong. Managers also knew that promotions came faster to those who were able to minimize conflict. So, rather than subjecting poorly defined products to analysis, which would surely generate conflict, managers frequently defaulted and simply rubber-stamped them.

Without the capacity to decide among new products and with few means of holding employees accountable, engineers and managers had learned to navigate according to the pressures of the day. When asked for improved performance—higher sales forecasts, a shorter time to market, or reduced costs—they would simply produce optimistic reports, safe in the knowledge that there would be no consequences. It was the division's worst-kept secret. One engineer said, "I learned that you told management what they wanted to hear. You told them you'd meet the schedule, even though you knew there was no way to do it. You just learn to hope that someone else's schedule slipped more than yours. That way, even though you're late, it's soon forgotten. But on the other hand, if you give a realistic schedule, you stand out. I did that once when I was young and foolish, but I'll never do it again!"

The lack of accountability produced low morale. One engineer complained, "It's not a healthy situation. No one ever gets anything done on time, and everyone's always behind schedule. Ultimately, people give up and stop worrying about it." He paused as though to focus his thoughts. "I think that it's hopeless. I've begun to feel like I'm playing for the New

York Mets—every game I play, I lose. How can you be motivated when you lose every time you're up at bat?"

When upper management became frustrated with Santa Clara's inability to meet its commitments and applied pressure, Santa Clara managers would often react defensively by pulling back the resources allocated to new products. They had developed "choke points" in the system at which they could intervene if they had to. But this arbitrary decision making demoralized engineers even further. Some complained that when their projects had been terminated with no warning or explanation, they had felt powerless and resentful. One R&D engineer said, "Your project gets canceled, and you wonder why. You've never had any criticism or feedback. It kills my commitment, but the guys in management don't seem to realize it. They just yank the resources right out from under you. To add insult to injury, then we get a bad rap for not coming through on our commitments. How can you guarantee to meet any target when you don't have any control over the resources?"

The behavior encouraged crisis management, or "fire fighting," as it is called at HP. An engineer commented, "One of the bizarre things around here is that if you do a good job and you're under control, you're not noticed. But if you are out there fighting fires every ten minutes, it looks like you're the shining star who just saved the company! You're a *hero*! You pulled them out of another one, *and* you get a big raise! What's wrong with that picture?"

Santa Clara had always been known for its high-tech but risky products—its frequency counters, lasers, and atomic clocks, which had set world standards. Going for the "grand slam" had become part of Santa Clara's culture, rather than growing more slowly but steadily with smaller "base hits." Now, with Santa Clara's very future on the line, the value of the grand slam had intensified. One home run could save the division. Keith Ferguson put it plainly: "There are a lot of costs to getting into new markets. We've chosen good ones, but the question is whether we will be able to generate the funds needed to sustain us while we work our way in. The grand-slam mentality still exists here. It's present. We're still expecting to be able to go out and jump into timing solutions for communications, for example, and within a year to be reaping great profits. It won't happen that fast. It will take a long, painful period of time to get there. My question is, will the people who control the funding have the patience to give us the time to get there?"

Before Ferguson's question could be answered, Santa Clara would have to get the way it developed new products under control. Allen's team's analysis showed that it was possible to standardize new-product development and that products could be brought out on time and within budget. This idea, however met with immediate objections from some R&D engineers, who claimed that R&D was an unpredictable, creative process that defied standardization. "You can't invent on a schedule!" one engineer scoffed. But Allen's team showed that, while research was hard to standardize, the development phase could be made predictable. One engineer agreed, saying "Sure, things can go wrong in development. That's why it's called 'development,' not 'production.' But we lump R&D together and resist standardization. Mark's team showed that it is predictable. On average it takes twice as long as planned to get a product to market. So we've just been using the wrong multiplication factor! The bigger problem is that the culture doesn't support setting targets and striving for them. Because many fear failing, they won't take the risk. How do you manage that?"

## FINE-TUNING THE REDESIGN

Now, with the evidence laid out before them, Neil and his design team began to act. As planned, they left Precision Motion Control Group ("Lasers") intact. Most of the division's new resources would be targeted on developing and supporting the new and larger group, Timing Solutions for Communications, upon which the division's future would rest. It would operate according to all the principles laid out by the design team and become a bottom-up, customer-focused organization like the lasers group.

Next, a transition team, headed by Jenny Brandemuehl, was formed to do the microredesign of Timing Solutions for Communications. This group included about sixty engineers, and Brandemuehl had to push a vast amount of learning and change into a six-month window. To ensure a broad representation of skills and experience on the transition team, Neil opened it to volunteers. Fliers showing a sixteenth-century map of

California asked for "Pioneers to chart a new map for Santa Clara." Though a few members were specially invited because of their backgrounds, most of the twelve members of the team were chosen by a surprisingly open process.

Despite its democratic beginnings, full empowerment of this new transition team was not automatic. Even in a trusting, participative environment like Hewlett-Packard's, few of the original design team members would give up control voluntarily. Some worried that the new transition team might ignore some of their pet recommendations. Half of the group favored taking a hard line—simply telling the members what they had to do. One manager said, "I think that our recommendations should be followed closely. I think we should simply tell them." Another manager suggested passing the ideas by the transition team members for their reactions. Someone asked, "What if they say no?" Another manager said, "Tell them we're doing it anyway!"

Neil himself was worried about whether the transition team members could understand the complicated issues that were involved quickly enough to be of value. As frustration grew, it became clear that nearly half of Neil's staff had serious reservations about giving the team much power. In fact, a smaller—but vocal—subgroup wanted to retain all of the power so it would not necessarily have to heed the transition team's final recommendations. But the redesign had now run too far to turn back. Jenny Brandemuehl and Peter Gaarn, a consultant from the Factory of the Future, urged Neil and his managers to follow their instincts and to trust that the team would produce results.

Neil saw the contradiction: he had talked about empowerment and accountability, but when the moment came to give up control, he became unsure. At the kickoff lunch, however, he repressed his instincts to hold on to control. He told the transition team members that he expected them to develop a new organization built on personal leadership, accountability, initiative, teamwork, and continuous learning. He said that he wanted this new organization to be flat, with fewer layers of management, and that he wanted it to work on the "pull" principle, by which teams would take full responsibility. Whatever reservations he still held, he kept to himself. But morale hit an all-time low as engineers grumbled loudly about changes that were rumored to be coming.

## I'M A LAB MAN, AN R&D MAN

To lift employees' spirits in this last phase of the redesign, Neil threw a dinner in Santa Clara's well-appointed cafeteria. The events that transpired revealed an unusual glimpse into how HP's capacity for introspection could help employees prepare for the changes. The building's ceiling-to-floor windows open onto a campuslike setting, with lawns, volleyball courts, and a redwood pergola, beyond which lies Silicon Valley. Earlier in the afternoon, the halls had been abuzz with rumors about the identity of a mysterious dinner speaker. Some said that they had heard that David Packard himself was coming. Others thought it would be HP's new CEO, Lew Platt. The truth was that Marty Neil and Fran Groat, a veteran HP skit creator, had fashioned an evening of comedy to relieve the accumulated stress. The ritual dates back to the company's early days (and outsiders are rarely invited); the skits are intended for fun, but they also diffuse aggression and help employees and managers rediscover and strengthen their bonds. That night the humor served to bring to the surface issues that were tension-filled and undiscussable—budget cuts, job security, the new business plan, and the engineers' introversion and fear of customer contact.

After dessert, Neil took the podium as if to introduce the guest speaker. Instead, a man dressed like a 1960s hippie popped out from behind a curtain on the makeshift stage, startling the unsuspecting audience. He wore long hair, a beard, a jean jacket, and sunglasses. As he began strumming a guitar while simultaneously playing a harmonica braced in front of his mouth, people recognized the old Bob Dylan favorite "The Times They Are A-Changin'." The singer began with lyrics that had been tailored for Santa Clara:

> Come gather round, Santa Clara,
> Wherever you roam,
> And admit the changes around you have grown,
> Now that every damn budget's been cut to the bone,
> And only the ants are the ones with a home!
> Oh, the times they are a-changin'!

Nervous laughter tittered through the crowd as some employees began to realize this was a spoof. Except for Neil and the small group who had planned the event, who were doubled up with laughter at a nearby table, everyone had been caught completely off guard. The singer continued:

*Once we had Sandblaster [a reference to a failed project],*
*Oh, boy was it chic.*
*Then it went south, and we were up shit creek,*
*Now we've got a new business, that's really unique,*
*Since they came up with* SYNCHRONIZATION,
*And if we're really lucky, it might last a week!*
*Oh, the times are a-changin'!*

By now the guests had recovered from the initial shock, and they were laughing hysterically, clapping, and singing. As the evening went on, there were more skits and roasts. At the end of the evening, a nerdlike engineer appeared on stage, dressed in plaid pants and sneakers, grinning intermittently to expose exaggerated buckteeth. He began the final song of the evening by tapping out the beat: "One, two, three point five." The audience howled as he began thrusting his hips awkwardly to the loud music.

*I was born in on-line mode,*
*When it comes to brains, I've got a truck* load,
*Was educated at MIT*
*And graduated with a* Double E!

*I'm a lab man, R&D man,*
*I'm a lab man, R&D man.*

*Promise plenty, deliver less,*
*What you'll get is anybody's guess.*
*Dress me up, take me out, and then*
*I'll see customers, but*
JUST DON'T MAKE ME TALK TO THEM!

*I'm a lab man, R&D man,*
*I'm a lab man, hardware man!*

As the guests got up from their chairs at the end of the program, some still wiping tears of laughter from their eyes, I got a more positive glimpse of the HP "family feeling" as interpersonal bonds that had become strained during the months of the downsizing and redesign were renewed. Despite the raucous humor, it had been a long, painful trip for the Santa Clara survivors, who were now looking to their common culture for direction and support. Most knew that the journey had just begun, and there was little doubt that everyone was in it together.

# CHAPTER ELEVEN

# A PAINFUL
# TRANSFORMATION

IN MID-1993, after four months of grueling work, the new organization was finally unveiled.[1] Timing Solutions for Communications (TSC) would comprise four businesses of related products—frequency counters, modulation domain analyzers (MDAs), cesium systems, and synchronization equipment. It would be headed by Murli Thirumale, who would concentrate on strategic issues—finding new opportunities in the newly forming global market—while four program leaders would head the individual businesses. While these program leaders would be evaluated on profits and losses, they would also, for the first time ever, have full control over their resources. The new organization would operate like a free market of talent in which project leaders and engineers would work together by mutual choice. Engineers would report to a home base, but they could work on multiple projects and bill for the hours worked on each project, much as lawyers in law firms do. Empowering engineers to choose their projects freely was intended not only to drive accountability down into the organization but also to expose unpopular projects quickly. The free market of talent would also serve to identify any engineers who had difficulty adjusting to the new conditions and, it was hoped, cut engineers' dead time to zero.

These were enormous changes, especially for a once venerated, conservative division like Santa Clara, and resistance soon began to surface as the clash of values and beliefs became apparent. Some engineers liked the free-market concept but feared that they might be evaluated by nonengineers or by managers who did not know their work at first hand. Other engineers complained that they were being treated unfairly because they had to shoulder most of the changes themselves. Still others worried about the engineers who could not fit in. Would they try to derail the changes? Could they be transferred?

Not surprisingly, the strongest resistance came from the engineers in R&D. They had always commanded the highest status at HP, especially at Santa Clara, and they were certain that the new customer focus would be achieved at the expense of science and technology. They warned that profitable short-term projects would be favored over long-term investments in science. One engineer commented, "If we had an engineer who was the world's expert in frequency analysis, I wouldn't care if he knew *anything* about the market. It's the scientific knowledge that's important. If we can't stay ahead of technology, we're going to lose. We'll be out of business."

A survey we did in mid-1993 revealed how widespread these worries were.[2] Although 90 percent of Santa Clara employees agreed that the new customer focus was vital to the division's survival, more than half of them said that it threatened the division's historic commitment to science and technology. The negative results were especially pronounced in the R&D labs. Neil was not surprised. He said, "I know that many of them don't trust the customer focus. R&D is directly in the line of fire. I suspect that, even though I came out of Bell Labs, some worry that I lack an appreciation for technology because of my marketing background."

Within a few weeks even stronger resistance from the R&D engineers began to surface. Electronic messages began circulating on HP's internal network, making fun of the redesign, and there was growing grumbling in the hallways. One engineer explained, "The R&D design engineers have always been the kings of the hill. It's been part of our culture. They were paid the most, and they were the most highly regarded employees here. Now they see that marketing is going to drive the division. It's a radical change for them, and R&D is going to be the toughest nut to crack." Fears were partly confirmed as marketing was given greater precedence in the new organization. Another engineer complained bitterly, "Hewlett-Packard is turning to a business orientation. Ever since Bill and Dave stepped down and John Young took over, things began to shift to an MBA attitude. Nothing was more important than the bottom line. Accounting and finance have gained tremendous power over how we do things. Now it's marketing. Young and his guys didn't care about technology. Many of us are getting the feeling that top executives have no idea how important R&D is to a company like this. I can just picture them saying 'Let's see, these engineers in R&D, what do they do? How much are they costing us? Do we really need them? Maybe we should just contract out the R&D to a job shop!'"

Managers, however, had only limited sympathy for these criticisms. They knew that unless these engineers could learn to work with their customers, the division would not survive. One manager commented sarcastically, "All they want to do is to design products. They whine, 'We want to be designers. We don't want to go out on customer visits, we don't want to follow production problems, we want to design. That's why we didn't take VSI [voluntary severance], that's why we haven't transferred. We like our jobs, we like what we're doing.' They'll sit over there until someone moves them to some other desk! They're not going to move themselves into marketing or to manufacturing. I think the only way this could happen is if we said, 'Look, there is nothing for you to do. If you want to stay in this division, you gotta go into marketing and figure out what our customers want, or else you don't have a job.' It will have come down to that."

Privately, many engineers agreed but hadn't wanted to face the conflict that out-and-out dismissals would have created. So, as one engineer commented, "The redesign was the only way to do it. It was like getting canned the HP Way. It was rational. It was built on analysis and group process. If you get a group together and they say, 'This is the answer,' HP employees will go along."

But would they? This was the question that worried Marty Neil and his managers as they began to implement the recommendations.

## TESTING THE NEW ORGANIZATIONAL PRINCIPLES

Within the first few months there were encouraging signs. The first group to try out the new customer focus was a self-managing SdbS team of seven engineers. The engineers, who had been drawn together from marketing and R&D, were committed to developing new software that would enable Santa Clara to customize its general-purpose MDAs. The MDA is an instrument that enables manufacturers like Seagate, IBM, and Northern Telecom to isolate and remove the underlying causes of unwanted signal variation (called "jitter"), from electronic products in the design stage.[3] Before the advent of the MDA, HP's customers had used oscilloscopes, which helped to estimate the amount and whereabouts of jitter but, because of scientific limitations, could not identify the exact source of jitter or remove it.[4] But, as disc drives, compact disc players, and telecommunications equipment became more technologically advanced, jitter became a more serious problem that had to be removed. Though MDAs could now help equipment designers remove jitter, it was a new idea and the information was displayed in unfamiliar formats. The customized software written by the SdbS team members was designed to make MDAs more user-friendly by displaying data in more customary ways. The idea was to use the software to increase sales of the much more expensive and profitable hardware, the sales of which had slowed in recent years.

By itself, this little team was expected to have only a limited financial impact on the division. Its real significance was as a test case of Santa Clara's new organizational principles. By the time we started working with the team in the fall of 1994, it had been in existence for two months. Its revenue targets had been negotiated with Neil, and team members were working feverishly to bring the first software to market. Two other related software products would follow in rapid succession. Then there would be a lull while the engineers wrote three final software products, which would be brought out later in the year. By the midwinter of 1994, the team had settled into a comfortable working pattern. It soon became clear that these men were in the middle of learning how to balance their natural love of science with the new customer requirements. As we watched them struggle, we began to appreciate how difficult this transition really was. A glimpse into one of the team's weekly morning meetings reveals how these engineers were learning to integrate science and marketing.

A few minutes before the meeting was scheduled to start, Errol Shanklin, a youthful, energetic sales engineer who had emerged as the informal team leader, scurried around to locate the others. "Oh, we're still missing Luiz. He must be in the bathroom," said Shanklin as he flopped into his chair at the round table. (Luiz Peregrino and David Chu, another team member, bear the title of "senior scientist," the highest professional accolade an HP engineer can win.) A few moments later, Peregrino appeared, announcing his apologies in a heavy Brazilian accent. Smoothing his gray hair into place with his fingers, he pulled up a chair to an empty spot. After the engineers had reviewed the agenda, they suddenly switched to a scientific shorthand punctuated with grunts and mumbles that was nearly incoherent to an outsider.

David Chu, peering through his glasses at the group, announced, "SONET" [a reference to a new product].

PEREGRINO: Fix the bug.

ANOTHER ENGINEER: The testing panel will do it.

PEREGRINO: The D bug.

CHU: [Something unintelligible.]

PEREGRINO: No, it has to be fixed.

SHANKLIN: Is it test time?

CHU: Not relative to bugs. Test time.

SHANKLIN: What?

ANOTHER ENGINEER: Sounds right to me.

CHU: [Something unintelligible.]

This incomprehensible conversation continued for a few more minutes. Then, equally abruptly, the topic shifted back to the customer and to marketing. The near-seamless change in the conversation from scientific thought to marketing strategy was evidence that the new principles were taking root.

I was also struck by the unusually wide intellectual and emotional span these engineers had been forced to develop to enable them to integrate the two worlds. Shanklin passed around a bulletin the team had written about their products' features in order to communicate better with HP field engineers and customers. The single page contained three vignettes titled "Wonderful Stories." The group was in high spirits, and members clamored for someone to read a description aloud. Bob Perdriau, a veteran HP engineer, picked up one of the sheets and cleared his throat self-consciously. He grinned as he began to read like a door-to-door salesman making a pitch.

"Hey, *Pete*," he began dramatically, his face reddening. "I just learned about a new HP product for measuring *token ring jitter*. Sounds like it was made just for *you*. It does all the interoperability jitter tests you need." Perdriau read a few more sentences before closing "You can even see cycle-to-cycle jitter. Can we set a time to *talk* more about it?" Enthusiastic approval came from the other engineers around the table, who laughed and joked with Perdriau about his theatrical delivery. Here was compelling evidence that the HP Way was still very much alive, though it was going through a reinterpretation. These men were not concerned with coffee and doughnuts or other entitlements—they were seriously focused on their own and the division's very survival.

However, even among a group of self-selected, highly motivated engineers like these, fully adopting the culture of marketing and sales was not easy. Bruce Greenwood, an engineer from the MDA group who had become the SdbS team's program leader, had changed a sign on his desk that originally had read PRIORITIZE, FOCUS, AND WIN to JUST WIN! It was a reflection of the harsh new reality. Greenwood said that the biggest hurdle was helping team members learn to tolerate the uncertainty and ambiguity of the human relationships that are a natural part of marketing and to take more risks. He added, "At HP, the business decisions were always left to the business teams, and most individual contributors [HP terminology for "employees"] have typically been shielded from risk. The business part isn't rocket science, but it requires engineers to really expand, to take on more responsibility, to go out and talk to customers. Selling product ideas in the changing marketplace is like panning for gold, but we haven't become really good prospectors yet."

Greenwood explained that recent experience had taught him that the hardest part of getting engineers to change was helping them get over their fears. "Many of them are not comfortable with the culture of selling," he explained. "I try to encourage them to relax and be themselves. To those of us that have done it, it's no big deal." He described how they role-played customer visits and then analyzed each role to demystify the process of selling. "I try to get them to see that everyone's there for a purpose. The customer wants a certain product at a certain price, and we want to sell it," he said. "But engineers have never been used to thinking in those terms, so it requires a new perspective." He said that many engineers worry that customers will reject them or that they will intrude on other people's privacy. "Most of all, it's a matter of confidence and developing a tolerance for rejection," he said. "These guys have to learn that they *can* solve customers' problems. But seven out of ten times sales calls are dead ends, so they've got to develop thick skins."

I asked Greenwood if he thought whether this diffidence about business was inherent or learned. He said he thought that for some it was "hard-wired" and very hard to change but that most could learn. "Sure, engineers tend to be more introverted than marketing people," he said, "but people can learn to do both. That's what's important about this SdbS concept. We're not following it to the letter at all, but it's a kind of touchstone for us to fall back on, to help us keep focused on the customer."

David Chu, a thoughtful, unassuming man who is highly regarded for his scientific contributions, explained that the new concept had to be truly internalized to work. He said that unless the customer focus concept became part of everyday life, engineers could agree intellectually but their behavior would remain unchanged. "In the past, this division has been big on slogans," he said. "There were charts on the walls and clever sayings. Last time it was the 'User Focus' and before that, 'Knowledge of the User,' or something like that. It has been done so often that people have begun to view changes with a grain of salt." Chu explained that internalizing new concepts is especially important when they are risky or difficult. He said, "As we take on responsibility for marketing, engineers now face the risk of looking foolish or being rejected. Naturally, it would be less risky to stay in the office. So if I have not internalized the idea that I must work with customers to survive, I could think up valid reasons to stay in the office and avoid the risk. You see, that way I subscribe to the new principle intellectually, but I continue in my old behavior." As we observed the SdbS team develop, it became increasingly clear that Chu was right. It was the new work system that truly began to drive these new ideas home.

For most, internalizing the change was difficult and the lessons were learned only on the job, where the consequences were real. "The engineers can't appreciate it until they sweat it," Bruce Greenwood said. "It's not in their natural makeup to go out selling, and, furthermore, there's no security in it. There's only risk. There were expectations by upper management that this conversion would simply happen, but I've become convinced that you can learn it only through experience, from the school of hard knocks. This is a long-term change we're after. We want all of our people to think of this team as their own small business and to run it that way."

Despite the pains of the transformation, this little group was challenged and learning continuously. Keith Ferguson, who had joined the group when it was formed, said that he was enjoying the new latitude and had noticed that unexpected benefits grew out of an expanded customer focus. "In the past R&D and marketing pointed fingers at each other to assign guilt or blame," he explained. "But now we're learning as a team—both R&D and marketing—and there's a shared responsibility and understanding of what's going on."

## ACCOUNTABILITY AND EMPOWERMENT

By late 1994 there was growing evidence that the redesign had begun to pay off—new products were being brought out on schedule and within budget. "I wouldn't say we are a self-directed team that sets its own goals yet," said team member Atul Tambe, "but we are a self-managing team. We're moving in that direction." Greenwood said he was surprised at the amount of work the team had been able to produce. "The old R&D manager used to talk about product velocity, but we're doing something we've never done before by birthing four products at once. And we're doing it with fewer people." Greenwood turned in his chair, pointing behind him. "Two years ago we had two aisles of people back there," he said. "Now we have half of one aisle!"

Most of the team members were enthusiastic about working as a team. Teamwork, in fact, may be especially well suited to the R&D environment. David Chu, for instance, said that he placed a high value on working as a self-managing team. "In a project like this," he said, "you are evaluated by your peers, rather than by a manager. A manager is interested in getting revenue or getting projects completed. He or she doesn't really care who does the work, as long as it gets done. But when the group is run by peers, we care that the work gets done, but also that it gets done well and that we all succeed. Everything is open, and we are accountable to each other. Everyone wants to appear efficient in the eyes of his peers. We like not having a manager because there is less nonconstructive competition than there is when you have a boss. We all share responsibility in this group. There is no nebulous person, no boss, who is supposed to know all. If I don't know something, then the others probably don't either. It's shared. We are all concerned." Chu laughed. "We bite our nails together!"

Shanklin shared Chu's enthusiasm, but he was frustrated and sometimes depressed by the overload of decisions and work. He said, "I look forward to coming to work in the morning as long as I feel in control. We're pretty well organized, but we've got a million things to do and I get pleasure from going down the list and checking things off. I feel like I'm in fairly good control and that I'm accomplishing things. Then it's great! I come to work and I'm enthused, and away we go. But when things get overwhelming, like where we are right now, I feel like I lose control. I say to myself, 'Okay, we have five top priorities. They all need to be done by Monday.' I can't get them all done, so which ones am I going to drop off the list? How do I make that trade-off? That's not fun! I just go around and talk to others on the team to get their opinions. It's tough, and it's no fun."

Shanklin complained that, although the team now has responsibility for the budget, the antiquated information system had failed to keep pace. In the past such information had been unimportant at his level, but now it was critical. "We've always had a department budget, but I've never been held accountable for exactly how much I spend," he explained. "I've never paid close attention to it. But I've got to be honest with you. I really don't know just what the budget is. We don't have a system yet to tell us, so I can only guess. It doesn't make me too comfortable." But the new process as a whole was praised. "Before the redesign," Bruce Greenwood said, "when engineers would want to buy something, upper management would simply increase the spending limit. But now we'll be judged on whether or not we stay within our budget and revenue projections. That's the definition of empowerment."

Greenwood brushed aside the idea of failure, "If we fail, we'll all wind up in résumé-writing class." But he added how he really felt: "I may be naïve, but I believe I have a soft place to fall. My assumption is that there will be someplace for me to go in the company. It's not something I like to think about, because it takes away from my productive time. I like to focus on solving problems, not on the 'what if we fail' question." But Greenwood left little doubt that feeling secure, or at least expecting to be treated fairly, was a prerequisite for paying full attention to the new world that was unfolding in front of him.

## THE SMART CLOCK

Within the new Timing Solutions for Communications group, the development of synchronization equipment was led by Murli Thirumale. Thirumale had embraced the concept of self-managing teams out of necessity. He said, "It was a business imperative. Engineers have to be in the field, and they have to be able to make decisions on the spot. That translates into the need for a flexible organization built on a strong culture of shared values. In times of slow change, we needed managers who could keep the ship sailing on a straight course. In the old world, managers who could manage the bottom line got promoted. But in this chaotic new world, we need leadership. To me, leadership means having a vision and acting on the basis of data, instinct, and conviction. It also means empowering others to act."

The ingredients for the "smart clock" that Thirumale's group hoped to develop already existed within Santa Clara but, like many inventions, needed the right impetus to come together. That impetus came in the form of an inquiry from a well-known company that specialized in wireless technology. This potential customer asked for bids on designing a prototype clock to install in a new wireless communications system. An engineer said, "They want a clock that will emit a one-second pulse that is rock steady and works for years. They also want it to be cheap and to run forever even if the power goes off."

This was the moment Santa Clara had been waiting for: It was the first true SdbS project that had emanated from the outside. It could open a door to the new communication information systems marketplace and fit neatly within the division's new strategic map. And it could be the first large step toward the larger vision of a ubiquitous global timing utility.

Within hours, Santa Clara's engineers were on the phone with the customer in a self-imposed race to see if they could develop a paper prototype within a month's time. If the customer was persuaded, HP and a small number of competitors would be chosen in the next round to build real prototypes from which a winner would be selected. An eight-person team was promptly assembled and went to work to figure out how to give the customer what it wanted. Thirumale handpicked some engineers for this critical project, though the rest volunteered after reading an announcement posted on the hallway bulletin board.

Once the prototype was fully developed, some engineers said they felt a new wind was beginning to blow through the division. One said excitedly, "Our projects have typically been three-year projects, but we popped this one out in *three hundred hours*! There's no way the old organization could have worked this quickly." Lyle Hornback, the group's sales support manager, was equally excited. He said, "The team pulled together and decided it was something they wanted to go after. It met every day, working toward a common goal. It was the first project that fit right into our new direction, and everyone on the team could stand up and be counted. I'm sure that if this opportunity had come last year, we could have never responded without the organizational changes that we've been through." Another veteran engineer said it reminded him of the old days, when individual contributions had had more of a direct impact. He said, "There are eight people on the team, and one person out of eight can make a huge difference. If we win it, it will produce a lot of new business for us."

For his part, Thirumale was thrilled by the prospects offered by the new project. He said, "It's not accidental that we're now calling projects by the customer's name. Not 'Frisbee' or 'Sandblaster' but by the customer's name. It's just another sign of the customer's impact. Now we've put the customer at the beginning of the process rather than at the end."

HP was selected as a finalist, and a few months later Santa Clara got the contract to start building the product. Marty Neil was ecstatic. "It's a marriage of technology that we had already developed," he said. "It's an elegant solution. It's cheaper and more reliable than anything else available." He laughed. "It's a dumb oscillator with a smart clock. Its heart is a quartz oscillator that converts electrical energy to mechanical and vice versa." He continued, "The irony is that I tried to kill the quartz oscillator business last year to make life simpler. I thought it was a distraction more than anything else." Neil gave credit to Jim Collin, who had formed a team to analyze the quartz oscillator business, for persuading him to keep it. Now quartz oscillators were at the heart of the division's potential turn-around.

Tom Vos was watching Neil's progress closely. He agreed that a timing utility held great promise. He told me, "This new project is a great way to get going, and it may provide the nucleation point. We can provide value to our customers that they can't provide on their own. Plus we've got a global omnipresence, financial backing, and a reputation for first-rate technology. Those are important attributes when you're dealing with big international customers who don't want to take chances on whether or not you'll be there tomorrow."[5]

Vos supported Neil's efforts to restore a sense of accountability. "Marty's getting results," he said. "But there's no recipe for this kind of change. You've got to have good leaders. To me, the organization comes second. I think that with good people you can make any organizational structure work. At first I was skeptical about Marty's customer segment teams. But he's using the structure to help people embrace a new vision and to tie it all together."

I asked Vos if he worried about Santa Clara when he went home at night. He laughed and said, "Yeah! It scares the crap out of me! But they've caught on to the new paradigm, and they are learning how to stay close to the customer. I have faith in the process as long as they go step by step. The trouble is that I'm impatient!"

## A PAINFUL TRANSITION

There is little doubt that Marty Neil was about as far out on a limb as he could go. He had a strong conviction that the investment in synchroniza-tion, though risky, made sense. "Anybody who thinks there is safety in test and measurement is suffering from an illusion. We're in the middle of a revolution, and there are no safe havens anywhere." Fortunately, Santa

Clara had inherited the adaptable HP Way, the value of which is abundantly clear. First it was at the heart of the Computer Division's turnaround in the 1980s.[6] Now the same beliefs and values had begun to reinvigorate the Test and Measurement Divisions. Integrity, respect, and trust for the individual provided hospitable conditions in which this radical, high-speed redesign could develop. Also, HP's belief in teamwork had enabled employees to look beyond their individual needs to work for a collective good. The new customer segment teams were beginning to learn what empowerment meant as they became accountable for results. R&D and marketing were learning how to work with each other in cross-functional teams. Neil said, "Teamwork used to mean that you were expected to help out, and it was always part of the HP Way. But now the meaning of teamwork has changed, and teams are making big decisions—it's been a huge cultural shift." Santa Clara's experience reinforces one of Hewlett's and Packard's original beliefs—that if people are given tools and resources, they will do the right thing.

Starting down this new path has not been without cost. In fact, the division's success has exacted a huge price, paid most prominently by the thousand men and women who had to leave Santa Clara. Many had left against their wishes. No doubt most of them had loved their jobs and had been loyal to the company. But HP had run into the dilemma that has become so familiar to many other American companies that have been forced to downsize. Although from all accounts the company had stood by the HP Way and treated its employees fairly and with dignity, the hard truth was that 60 percent of them had had to go. While, in the strict sense of the word, no one had been fired, because employees who found themselves without jobs could transfer to other HP divisions, in the end the company had had to protect its own core to survive.

By late 1994 there was evidence that Santa Clara was beginning to turn the corner as the worst of the pain of its transformation receded. Its new businesses were showing results, and there were indications that the new principles were taking root, though morale continued to be low.[7] Earlier in 1994, forty more employees had been transferred to other divisions from manufacturing and custodial services as more "nonessential" jobs were contracted out.

But when I last talked to Neil in early 1996, I could not miss the combination of relief and pride in his voice.[8] "We're not out of the woods yet," he said. "Our business in 1995 was a lot healthier than what we'd projected, and the division's revenue grew by about twenty percent. Our operating profits were a hundred fifty percent greater than our estimates, and most of that came from the new timing and synchronization products." Neil said that the SdbS team of software engineers had met its revenue projections and that Santa Clara was now producing the "smart clock" in large quantities. Other large telecommunications customers were being lined up as well. Neil said that steps to introduce the "smart clock" to potential utility customers in New Zealand for synchronizing power transmission had been well received and that he expected to have some more orders by the end of the year. "A year ago," he said, "we didn't know what to work on. Eighty-five percent of our engineers were working on old stuff. But today eighty-five percent our engineers are working on new timing and synchronization products and there is more business than we can handle! For the first time in years we're beginning to hire new people."

Neil said he thought the new organizational principles were being internalized and that new meaning had been injected into the HP Way. He took comfort from a recent survey that had showed that 81 percent of all Santa Clara employees said they understood the division's vision and its mission and that they agreed with the need for high levels of individual contribution. Nearly three quarters (74 percent) of the employees had been favorable about reaffirming the HP Way—and Santa Clara was significantly above the HP average.[9]

## CONCLUSIONS

What can be learned from Santa Clara's experience? What does it add to our observations of Douglas Aircraft and USS-POSCO? Can any of the lessons be transferred to other organizations that are forced to undergo the same kind of change? I think there are at least four key lessons that warrant discussion. First, there is little doubt in my mind that without the strong feeling that everyone was in the same boat, and without the expectation of employment security or at least fair treatment, little progress would have been made. Nor would it have if these bonds had not existed or if engineers had been consumed by worry that they were going to be fired. Here we can see the powerful advantage Hewlett-Packard had over both Douglas Aircraft and USS-POSCO, whose cultures all but paralyzed them as they tried to break out of the grip of traditional mass production.

Second, the existence of these strong bonds was not accidental. The company had benefited from the lucky draw of two unusual founders, but from the beginning HP's culture had been consciously recognized as an asset, and it had been carefully managed over the years. I am not trying to gloss over the painful experiences endured by so many of the employees who had to leave. Even within this striking success there is a hard side. But for the survivors it was the HP Way that helped them navigate through the pain and uncertainty of the radical transformation.

Third, Marty Neil and Jenny Brandemuehl used the redesign to bring the engineers themselves into the decision making. By enlisting the engineers — the very ones who had the most to lose as well as to gain — they could truly begin to correct the root causes of the division's problems. The engineers themselves went through a powerful learning experience as they took ownership for the division's future and the accountability that went with it.

Finally, Neil and his managers, like Bill Haley and his colleagues at USS-POSCO, recognized the importance of linking the division with its customers through a "pull" system. Such connections are important so that changing demands can be interpreted quickly and the organization can adapt rapidly to ever-changing conditions.

Marty Neil is pleased with the progress the division has made. However, he said, "We will never be comfortable again. Our success so far has only given us a reprieve. It's eased some of the pressure that has allowed us to focus and to go after the things we're good at doing." But everyone agrees that at HP — and in the new economy — the need for restructuring will not only continue but intensify.

# PART V
# NUMMI

# CHAPTER TWELVE

# THE DISINTEGRATION OF MASS PRODUCTION

OUR EXAMINATIONS OF Douglas Aircraft, USS-POSCO, and Hewlett-Packard have revealed the vital importance of establishing trusting relationships between managers and employees—and the impossibility of change in their absence. At Hewlett-Packard especially, we saw proof, despite the pain of transition, that such trust is of inestimable value. But is Hewlett-Packard the rarest of exceptions, or can other companies successfully transform themselves?

We find the answer at NUMMI, a joint venture formed by General Motors and Toyota in 1984. NUMMI—the acronym for New United Motor Manufacturing, Inc.—is located in a huge plant in Fremont, California, on the edge of the San Francisco Bay. The plant had once belonged to GM but had been closed in 1982, a victim of Japan's economic prowess. But in an amazing turn of events, GM and Toyota reopened the plant just two years later. The joint venture's managers were a mix of Japanese and Americans, but its production workers were drawn chiefly from the pool of angry GM-Fremont workers who had lost their jobs when the plant closed. Skeptics claimed it would never produce a single car.

Today the skeptics' voices have been silenced, and NUMMI is

widely acclaimed as an unqualified success. In 1994 it produced more than 350,000 Geo Prizms, Toyota Corollas, and Toyota compact pickup trucks. It produces the same number of vehicles in the same plant with only 65 percent of the pre-NUMMI workforce.[1] More important, its quality is among the highest in the world. In 1993 J. D. Power and Associates rated NUMMI's pickup truck the highest-quality compact pickup truck available. In 1994 NUMMI won J. D. Power and Associates' "Silver Quality Award" for its Geo Prizm, which scored higher than any other American-built car ever rated. The Toyota truck and Corolla received high ratings as well, even exceeding the quality produced by NUMMI's Japanese sister plants.[2] NUMMI has also become a substantial exporter. In 1993 its exports exceeded $400 million, including 26,000 Corollas to Taiwan and $78 million in parts to Japan.[3] NUMMI has been expanded three times and today represents an investment of more than $1.8 billion. It employs 4,400 men and women in high-paying union jobs. It has also created a revolutionary model of industrial relations that have exchanged adversarial relationships for cooperative, productive ones. NUMMI has also proven to be a powerful economic magnet as parts suppliers have clustered around the plant to take advantage of the new business and to learn Toyota's "lean production" techniques. Together, NUMMI and its suppliers have pumped more than 20,000 jobs and $1 billion into the California economy each year.[4] It has also proven to be a significant gateway for American automakers to learn from Toyota.

The lessons drawn from NUMMI's success have not been lost on GM. In 1989, when my research team and I began working on the assembly line, we got the impression that the joint venture was of greater importance to Toyota than it was to GM. Everyone seemed convinced that Toyota would buy out GM in 1996. But when John F. "Jack" Smith took over as president and CEO of GM in 1992, he sent out a directive that GM would have to develop a production system similar to NUMMI's, thus indicating a renewal of the huge corporation's interest in what it could learn from the joint venture. Smith had also headed GM's side of the negotiations that had established the joint venture, so he had an insider's view of what had transpired. "We had huge issues ahead of us," he explained. "GM and Toyota were different cultures, and we had our own federal government set against us. It looked impossible at times. But with the quality and efficiency that NUMMI has achieved, it is the Mecca of the auto industry in North America."[5] NUMMI's stunning success has not been lost on Tatsuro Toyoda, either. Toyoda, who in 1994 was president of Toyota Motor Corporation (today he is vice chairman) but who also served as NUMMI's first president, remarked, "I have a special place in my heart for this company. It is an excellent example of the benefits of cooperation between two great companies. NUMMI's success proves that labor and management can work toward mutually beneficial goals that serve the best interests of all employees. Especially given the doubts of many when this company was first opened, it is a shining example for the world of what people working together can achieve."[6] But were NUMMI's achievements repeatable? Can the lessons learned there be transferred to other manufacturers as they try to exchange their outdated mass production methods and adversarial labor relations for new ones?

## THE DISINTEGRATION OF MASS PRODUCTION

When you approach the NUMMI plant by the freeway, it rises up like a huge apparition from the surrounding fields and wetlands. Eighty-four football fields can fit under its four-million-square-foot roof. The plant was built by GM back in 1962, when Japanese companies accounted for only 5 percent of the U.S. auto market. But this onetime state-of-the-art facility had degenerated greatly over time. It had been dubbed "the battleship" by angry workers, partly because of its drab, greenish tan military bearing but also because of the undying conflict that churned within it. The plant had suffered wildcat strikes, sick-outs, and numerous slowdowns during its twenty-year history. A bomb had exploded in the administrative building (no one was killed), and prostitutes, alcohol, and drugs were easily available on the premises. One executive described Fremont as a "scary place." One GM worker said, "There was shit all over the place. The parking lot was covered with broken glass. It looked like a diamond field in the morning sunlight. Busted beer and whiskey bottles all over the place! It looked like pigs lived here. People would sit wherever they wanted and read books, eat, and play radios. I remember working on a car that was full of chicken bones left over from a guy's lunch. Nobody cared."

Evidence of the lack of pride and discipline was everywhere. An autoworker recalled, "Lunch was a big flea market in the parking lot. You could buy booze, women, leather goods, steaks, and seafood. Employees did all the buying and selling."

Alcohol and drug use was rampant. An autoworker said, "You could buy any kind of a drink you wanted upstairs for two bucks—rum and coke, whiskey, you name it. I would chug four beers in front of the guards and then go back to my boring job on the line installing tires. Drugs were sold openly. Guys would ride up on bikes and try to sell you pot, hash, 'ludes, heroin, and crack." Another added, "You could buy *anything*! There'd be hookers right outside the door. You didn't even have to buy pot—the plant was so full of smoke you'd get high just walking through it!"

Not surprisingly, Fremont had the worst disciplinary record of any GM plant. Absenteeism ran 20 percent each day. Quality suffered as well. "It was 'lick 'em and stick 'em,' " recalled one autoworker. "Do a lick of work and stick the customer with the shoddy product. We didn't care about nothing else but getting them out the door. I saw a car come through that had one blue side and one green side! I saw some with different-color hoods and tops!" The only thing people dreamed about was working less. As another put it, "We used to have a lot of time off. Whenever a new model was introduced, the plant would shut down for weeks or even months and we'd still get paid! It was like a vacation! And when the line would be shut down for half an hour, they'd send us home! There were wildcat strikes too. When you added up pay from the plant and the union, you'd end up earning more when you were on strike than when you were working!"

At the root of the problem was the mass production system and its outdated beliefs. Years of bitter experience had taught generations of managers and autoworkers the futility of trying to work together. The gulf that separated them was huge. Like the managers at Douglas Aircraft and USS-POSCO, GM-Fremont managers did not fraternize with the hourly workers. Instead, they kept their distance, separated by ties and white shirts, private parking spaces, separate dining rooms, and enclosed offices. The harsh and adversarial bargaining between the company and the union, coupled with the autocratic GM management style, only fueled the mistrust on both sides. A former GM employee who later became a manager at NUMMI said the production system at the old Fremont plant had somehow run by itself. "Management basically abdicated," he said. "They had no control over what went on inside the plant. Take inventory, for example. Stockmen would pile parts up to the ceiling, enough for a week. They'd work for three hours and play cards for the rest of the shift. The stacks were so tall that they would fall over. Broken parts would be all over the place. Managers would scream and yell, and the workers would clean up the mess with shovels. It was unbelievable! I wanted to go into management at GM, but I didn't because it was a horrible situation. There was no way management and the union could work together cooperatively. The only thing management thought about was to how to produce, produce, produce. It was 'Get the cars out the door at any price' and worry about the quality later. The union spent all of its time screwing around with management."

While the employees had eventually resigned themselves to the system, many of the former GM workers said they had felt bad about the low-quality cars and trucks they had produced and their lack of pride in their work. A union leader said the workers had known how to improve the system but had kept their ideas to themselves. But the deeper problems had lain well beyond their control. An autoworker said, "I'd be talking to people, and they'd find out I was from GM. Man, I'd be embarrassed. But you know, they made us build cars that way. One day I found a bolt missing. I called the supe over, and he said, 'What's the matter with you, boy, you going to buy it? Move it!' Then, when the plant failed, they blamed us." Instead of taking pride in the vehicles they produced, the autoworkers had taken pleasure in their reputation as militants, challenging GM at every opportunity. It would take a powerful antidote to alter the system of work as well as the confrontational behavior and its underlying complex of antagonistic beliefs. Surprisingly, the answer would come from the Japanese, who introduced a new way of working cooperatively, and a production system that would replace GM's mass production system, which, by 1982, had proved to be unworkable.

## A WIND FROM THE EAST

Unknown to most Americans, Japanese industrial and government leaders had been watching America carefully for years. Japan's near destruction in World War II had left it with no alternative short of a complete industrial rebirth. As its leaders scanned the world for ideas on how to re-

build their industrial base, they borrowed—as discussed in Chapter 2—
from such seemingly disparate sources as Frederick Taylor, Elton Mayo,
and Kurt Lewin. They also discovered the pioneering work on quality
management that was being done by American quality experts W. Edwards Deming and Joseph Juran.[7] Blending these ideas with teamwork
and some concepts transferable from mass production, Japanese manufacturers created a hybrid, a new system that was well adapted to their
small country. When Deming visited Japan in 1950, he was shocked at
what he found. He was so impressed with the Japanese production methods that he predicted that Japanese products would penetrate international markets within five years. Though most Japanese managers
themselves would not believe it, Deming's predictions would soon be realized.[8]

About the same time Deming was discovering the effects of his
teachings in Japan, young Eiji Toyoda landed in Detroit to learn what he
could about American auto manufacturing. His family had become
wealthy as a result of his uncle's textile power loom–manufacturing company. In 1937 Toyoda Spinning and Weaving spun off Toyota Motor Company to build trucks for Japan's war in China.[9] Later, in 1947, the company
began manufacturing passenger cars for a market already dominated by
the large American and European automakers. For three months in 1950,
young Toyoda examined Ford's huge River Rouge and Highland Park
plants, toured a Chrysler plant, and visited suppliers. He was surprised to
find that Japan was not as far behind as he had imagined. In his autobiography, Toyoda remembers thinking, "Detroit isn't doing anything Toyota doesn't already know. At the same time I was certainly not
presumptuously downplaying Ford's tremendous lead. After all, their daily
output was 8,000 units; ours was a piddling 40. You might as well compare
a pebble with a boulder."[10]

The lessons Eiji Toyoda took from America and applied to his own
country were the genesis of what would ultimately become known as
"lean production."[11] It was clear to him that pure mass manufacturing
would not work for his small island nation.[12] Japan lacked capital, and it
was facing stiff domestic and international competition from American
and European automakers. Furthermore, Toyota was burdened with a
large permanent workforce. In 1946, as a result of having to downsize to

reduce costs after the war, Toyota had reached a settlement with its unions that it would provide lifetime employment if the unions would agree to flexible work assignments.

Toyota then took the lead in pioneering the new production system in Japan. Years earlier, in 1929, Eiji Toyoda's uncle, Kiichiro Toyoda, had begun thinking about how to synchronize the production line with the flow of parts.[13] The idea was to produce flexibly and in small batches without making a huge capital investment. For postwar Japanese companies, this was the next logical step. And of great significance to our story, the system Toyota invented rests on a radically different set of human assumptions than mass production does.[14] The power of this production system lies in the simple, parsimonious way it arranges work and human effort.

Simply put, the aim of "lean production" is to shorten the time between taking a customer's order and delivering the product by relentlessly removing waste—or *muda*, as the Japanese call it—from the process.[15] The system was created by reorganizing some seemingly disparate ideas worked out by Taiichi Ohno, Toyota's lead engineer, who had started out in the 1930s at Toyoda Spinning and Weaving. One idea Ohno had taken from Ford was the practice of having parts delivered to the assembly line in small quantities only as they are needed. At Ford, this "just-in-time" concept had kept inventory costs low, but Ohno had also used lean inventories to expose and correct weaknesses in the system. When a defect is discovered in a part, the small number of that part on hand is quickly removed and the problem is worked back to its source.[16] Another idea Ohno borrowed from Toyoda Spinning and Weaving was a foolproof defect prevention scheme that caused a loom to halt automatically if a thread broke. This idea, which Ohno coupled with an *andon* board, which signals how the line is running, and an *andon* cord that workers can pull to stop the line in case of problems, formed what came to be called *jidoka*. *Jidoka* is a self-regulating production principle that ensures higher quality because defects are caught at their source. Every employee assumes responsibility for doing his or her job correctly the first time and not passing defects along to the next worker. This employee responsibility is the cornerstone of the Toyota system. Workers are considered important assets, and they are expected to contribute ideas about how their jobs can best be done. In Japanese plants engineers are indistinguishable from production workers because, out of the conviction that workers' knowledge is valuable, they too work on the assembly line.

Because the Toyota system depends on workers' knowledge and experience, it requires fewer inspectors (and fewer workers) than mass production does.[17] In early experiments at Toyota, Ohno demonstrated how workers—who had been trained to run more than one machine at a time—could standardize their work so that their jobs could be done by others in precisely the same way at the same pace. Later, managers and workers could balance jobs so that everyone was working at about the same level of difficulty and speed.

One principle that is central to Toyota's lean system is known as *kaizen*, or continuous improvement, which also means continuous change. Because it is a dynamic system, the Toyota system requires that workers be flexible and that they be able to do a variety of jobs. The demarcation between jobs is frequently blurred, and workers are paid on the basis of seniority rather than on the basis of what job they do.

These are the key elements of the Toyota production system, an arrangement of men and machines that is beautiful in its simplicity and precision. Through experimentation, Ohno found that by standardizing work and removing all waste, including excess inventory and human motion, problems can be laid bare. When these problems were worked back to their root causes and corrected, the system could be made to produce higher quality at lower cost. Because production was regulated by customer demand (in contrast to mass manufacturing, in which production levels are set by engineers' forecasts), it became known as a "pull" (as opposed to a "push") system of production.[18]

But could it work in the United States? By 1980 Toyota executives were searching for a way to make further inroads into the huge North American market. They also wanted to determine if Toyota's "lean production" system could be adapted to a unionized American environment. General Motors seemed a likely partner, since it wanted to add a new small car to its line and its executives wanted to learn about Toyota's production system. After initial discussions between top executives of both companies, GM and Toyota began their negotiations.

## THE CREATION OF NUMMI

Despite this initial common ground, there were still enormous problems that had to be overcome. Each partner spoke a different language and had different customs. Could they work cooperatively with each other? Could the joint venture work within the confines of U.S. trade regulations? Would Toyota agree to recognize a militant union like the UAW? If it did, would the union be flexible, or would it bog the joint venture down with restrictive work rules and red tape? Who would manage the plant, GM or Toyota—or would they share the management? Even if the UAW International could be persuaded to support the formation of the joint venture, would the local union agree? Each question represented a serious problem, and each had to be solved.

The GM team was led by Jack Smith, who was then GM's director of internal and joint venture programs. The Toyota team was led by Kan Higashi, then a Toyota purchasing executive. Dennis Cuneo, Toyota's antitrust lawyer at the time, recalled that when the negotiations between GM and Toyota were first announced, "a shock wave rumbled through the industry. Here was GM, which for six decades had been our largest and most successful industrial enterprise, saying that it had lost the ability to produce competitive small cars and had to turn to the Japanese. The media interest was intense. Ford and Chrysler immediately announced their opposition. Iacocca was particularly vocal. He made all kinds of outrageous claims, saying that 'this was a bad deal for America' and that the venture would 'set off a chain reaction that would result in the loss of a hundred thousand jobs.' Antitrust experts expected the FTC to veto the deal, because it involved two of the largest automakers in the world. The UAW made it known that it intended to represent the workforce of the venture and would not tolerate another nonunion plant. Editorials and op-ed pieces praising and criticizing the venture appeared in *The Washington Post*, *The New York Times*, and *The Wall Street Journal*."

The Federal Trade Commission (FTC), wary of a partnership between these two giant auto companies, opened a highly visible antitrust investigation, to which it assigned some twenty-five lawyers and economists. Meanwhile, GM and Toyota each retained top law firms to help them navigate through the thicket of American antitrust law (which, written in

the late nineteenth and early twentieth centuries, virtually outlawed partnerships between competitors).[19] Toyota's legal team included Earl Kintner, who had headed the FTC under President Dwight D. Eisenhower,
and Cuneo. Cuneo was chosen partly because of the good relationships
he had established with Toyota executives during earlier negotiations between Toyota and Ford but also because of his knowledge of antitrust law.
A curious blend of conservative and liberal, Cuneo says he is a registered
Democrat but votes Republican. He started his legal career as a prosecu-
tor in the Antitrust Division of the U.S. Department of Justice, but he soon
became disillusioned with the job. "I went into Justice bent upon doing
good and breaking up the likes of GM," he said. "I soon learned the bu-
reaucrats—including me—who were supposed to be working in the public interest were on their own power trips and behaving just like the guys
they were supposed to regulate! My experience at Justice taught me that
government intervention was usually a poor substitute for the free market." Cuneo knew that NUMMI's formation would be a watershed antitrust event. "Just a few years ago, the FTC and the courts would have
never allowed this joint venture, despite all of its positive benefits. This
was a chance to advance a more rational and contemporary interpretation
of the antitrust laws, and I was thrilled to be part of it."

At the same time as Ford and Chrysler were petitioning the FTC to
halt the joint venture, Toyota and GM were faced with the question of
what to do with the former GM-Fremont workforce and how to handle the
UAW. When word leaked out that Toyota was considering hiring a new
nonunion workforce, near hysteria broke out among the 5,000 former GM
workers who were then out of work. They marched around the plant with
anti-Japanese placards warning REMEMBER PEARL HARBOR! To them, the
prospects of a joint venture with a Japanese company offered only a beach-
head for a larger invasion of America's flagging economy.

GM and Toyota were in a quandary about how to handle the complicated labor relations. According to Cuneo, Toyota preferred that GM
take the lead, since its own executives had no experience in dealing with
an American labor union. But GM was in even a worse position because
of its long history of labor antagonism. What was needed was a skillful negotiator, someone who knew the issues and who was trusted by all sides.
At the suggestion of Earl Kintner, Toyota retained William J. Usery, Jr., to
serve as a mediator to handle these delicate negotiations.

Usery, a former secretary of labor under President Gerald Ford and head of the National Mediation and Conciliation Service under President Richard Nixon, is not an ordinary negotiator. He is a large man with flying white hair who reminds me of Mark Twain. He speaks with the passion of a Southern Baptist preacher, fixing you through his glasses with watery blue eyes and periodically drawling "Ya unda-stand?" to make sure you get his point. Usery is also a master of his trade. He has settled more deadlocked strikes than any man in American history—in the post office, the railroads, the steel and auto industries, and professional football. He also mediated the recent baseball strike. Usery draws on logic, conviction, and homespun Georgia humor to bring antagonists to a common understanding. He insists that people respect each other's rights—a conviction he said was instilled in him by his parents in rural Georgia, where he had grown up and where he once taught men's Bible classes. To Usery, his work is a mixture of politics and religion. He said, "To me, representing people is a *calling*, an honor that carries great responsibility."[20]

Ten thousand miles away at Toyota's headquarters in Toyota City, Japan, Bill Usery took the first steps to start a productive discussion between Toyota and GM. From the outset, Usery recalled, some of the GM executives had been extremely defensive, doubting there was little if anything they could learn from Toyota. "The tension was so thick you could cut it with a knife," Usery said. "The GM people sat on one side of the room silently with their arms crossed, staring straight ahead at the Japanese. They were fuming, thinking, 'You think *you're* going to tell *us* how to build cars, do you?'" He said that the differences in American and Japanese negotiating practices and the languages had made things particularly difficult. He had had to negotiate through two translators—one for him and one for Toyota chairman Eiji Toyoda—and he had quickly become exasperated as he had frequently had the same conversation three times with different groups of Toyota executives. Despite the fact that they had been negotiating about grand principles and vast sums of money, Usery said it had been the human exchange that had made it difficult, even for an experienced negotiator like himself. He admitted, "It was very, very frustrating. You were never sure you were communicating accurately, because someone else was doing the translating. It would bother me to no end. Something would get translated, and they'd start laughing! I didn't know what they were laughing about. They'd be doubled up laughing. I'd think, 'What the hell did I say that they're laughing about?' It would drive me up the wall." Usery said that American slang had been especially problematic for the Japanese. He recalled having told a Toyota official that something he wanted to do was like "putting a fox in the henhouse." Usery said, "The translator looked at me, and said, 'Fox?' 'Henhouse?' 'Fox?' He said it about three times while he was trying to translate it, to get it across to the Toyota executives. But it just wouldn't translate. He just broke down. It took me about three seconds to get that fox into that henhouse. But it stopped the meeting cold, and it took all of us thirty minutes to get that damned fox out!" But as they had worked together, Usery said, these human problems had begun to diminish.

Next, however, a serious obstacle had emerged—one that could have derailed the joint venture. Toyota executives had refused to recognize the UAW or to hire any of the laid-off workers because of their militant reputation. It had naturally been hard for Toyota's executives to fully grasp the contrast between Japanese company unions and American trade unions. Furthermore, the union militance in the old GM plant was legendary. Toyota executives, who had heard the horror stories, could imagine that a majority of the workforce in their new plant would be drawn from what they perceived as lazy, undisciplined workers.

Usery had sought help from his old, respected friend Doug Fraser, who was about to retire from the UAW presidency. He had met with Fraser in Detroit and told him in confidence, "I need to know how you feel about this deal with the Japanese, because we've got the biggest bluewater ocean in the world between us. We speak a different language. We have a different culture. We don't have any working experience with the Japanese like we do with the Europeans. There are also some strong negative feelings by the UAW about Japanese cars. Do you think we can make this fly with the union?"

Fraser had told him that with some responsible commitments from both sides and some luck it could work. The rash of plant closures in the early 1980s had cost the union's members hundreds of thousands of jobs, and Fraser had wanted the joint venture because it would put thousands of union members back to work. Usery said he had believed there was a chance that a joint venture could work despite Toyota's reluctance to hire the former GM workers because of their militance and because the Japanese privately considered them lazy. He explained that it had been an emotionally charged message to deliver to the top UAW officers and he had worded it as diplomatically as he could. Usery recalled how a silence had settled over the room as the UAW leaders digested what he had just said. Suddenly, one official had jumped to his feet and shouted, "Goddamn you, Usery, I'll punch you in the face if you call our guys lazy bastards again!" Usery had explained that he was only reporting Toyota's impressions of the American workers. The official had exploded, shouting, "Okay, you son of a bitch, but they're *our* lazy bastards!" Usery said the official's outburst had brought howls of laughter from the others, helping to soften the union's opposition. Ultimately the union leadership had agreed to continue to negotiate with Toyota to try to arrive at an agreement that included the UAW.

On the other side, Toyota executives had begun to realize that the chances of a joint venture without the UAW were dimming, and they had asked for more discussion. After a series of meetings, Toyota had finally agreed to hire a majority of the workers for the new joint venture from the ranks of the unemployed GM-Fremont workers and to recognize the UAW as their bargaining agent.

Despite assurances from the UAW, Toyota's management had remained skeptical. But human relationships would prove to bridge the differences. One of the most important people involved in creating these personal bonds was Bruce Lee, the UAW's western regional director, who was among the first senior UAW officials to meet with the Toyota board of directors. Lee is a big, white-bearded man whose presence fills a room. He is a crafty negotiator, adept at arguing fine points of logic, but who is also known to resort to physical force when he has to. Lee recalled, "Toyota wanted to see if I was all right. If I was okay. They wanted assurances I wasn't going to bomb their plant or something." After Lee had met with the Toyota board of directors, there had been a reception for the American visitors. He had sat next to Eiji Toyoda. Lee said, "We were all enjoying the drinks, talking about the sumo-wrestling championships, and the chairman was right in there with us. I'm talking to the chairman, and we're laughing. But all of a sudden his face got stern, real serious. He looked me straight in the face, and said, 'You don't look like Bruce Lee.' I decided to give it a shot. I said to the chairman, 'Well, I am Bruce Lee, goddamn it. I died, you know, and now I've come back as a sumo wrassler!'" Lee recalled how Toyoda had burst out laughing, instantly forging a connection between them. "Right away I knew two things about the man then," Lee said. "He liked to drink, and he had a sense of humor. He was all right. And that's when we started opening up with each other. He became very open and friendly, and it made me realize that there was really something in this for the union."[21]

Even though Lee had recognized the value of the joint venture, many of his more traditionally minded colleagues in the International had not. The traditionalists had argued that Toyota should be forced to hire back workers by seniority and that any new contract should include the language from the old master agreement that specified work rules in tiny detail. Don Ephlin, head of the UAW's GM Department, could have given in to them and killed the project in its infancy, but Ephlin had seen the promise in NUMMI and had stood firm in the face of opposition. Bruce Lee had gone to Owen Bieber, who had replaced Fraser as president of the union, and told him that if the traditionalists won out the project would die. Lee recalled, "I told Owen, the people from the GM Department can assist, but they can't drive it. If they get their way, they'll insist on language from the master agreement. They'll put things in there that are of absolutely no value to the people. Some of our people are so tunnel-visioned they'd insist on a goddamned mountain of stuff to climb over. And it wouldn't make one bit of sense to the working person." Lee said Bieber had seen his logic and cleared the way for him to take charge. "I've always appreciated Owen for that one," Lee said. "He bit the bullet, and there were some people who weren't too happy."

Finally, the local that had represented the GM workers had had to be disbanded so a new one could be formed to represent the NUMMI workers. Somehow, the leadership of the old local had to be convinced that disbanding would be in their best interest. Lee said the UAW local had hated GM and had no intention of changing. "They didn't have a plan. They couldn't imagine they might have a real role to play in this new venture, so all they planned to do was to get in the way!" The leadership of the Fremont local had actually filed suit to block the joint venture, prompting Lee to intervene in the growing conflict. Usery recalled, "Bruce had the hardest job of all. He had to go face a group of people who were fighting mad now. They had lost their jobs, and now he had got to get rid of that local."

Lee's next step had been both surprising and unprecedented—he had invited the leadership of the old local to become the leadership of the new one. As Lee admitted, "These guys were as tough as nails! They'd strike GM as fast as you could snap your fingers." But he had also known that they had great leadership potential, so he had carefully kept the group intact during the two years since the plant had closed, employing them as job developers and organizers under his jurisdiction. Lee had begun to meet regularly with the old committee and talked with them about how the joint venture was offering a new lease on life. "I really worked them," he admitted. But he had also told them they'd have to get around the old local, which had been an important union rallying point against GM for so many years. Naturally, the idea had not been popular. Lee said, "I spelled out the facts of life for them. I said, 'If we get the opportunity to go back to work and I get you in there in places of responsibility and you fuck this thing up, you're not going to have to worry about the company firing you, I'll fire you! I'll fire your ass in a hot second! What I want you to do is give it a fair hearing. If you go in and you give it a fair hearing and then come back and say this is a bunch of bullshit and it just don't work, then I'll say, 'Fine! I'll get you out of there and we'll try something else.' " Lee sat back and said in a mock whisper, "But the truth is that nobody knew what they were going into. We just had to go in and find out for ourselves!" With the leadership finally committed to the new undertaking, Lee had persuaded the local to drop its lawsuit opposing the joint venture. He and other officers of the International had taken it over and issued a new charter, thus clearing away one more roadblock to reopening the plant.

Lee said he had taken a gamble to work with the Japanese: "I didn't know if Toyota was going to come in with a system that nobody could live with. I just didn't know. But I had a feeling in my guts that they didn't know either." The stakes had been high. If the union had cooperated and given away some of its traditional job protections to provide the flexibility demanded by Toyota and the workers had then found the conditions intolerable, Lee would quickly have become the target of union opposition.

Still no final agreement could be reached. Despite the progress Usery had made, Toyota had remained skeptical about working with the

UAW, and the traditionalists within the UAW had opposed giving up the traditional work rules and accepting Toyota's production system. The 120 days originally allotted to forming the joint venture had been about to expire. On the basis of a letter of understanding, GM had also gambled and invested $45 million in building a new stamping plant and outfitting the assembly operation at Fremont. But, because of the company's mounting liabilities, GM executives had balked at giving Toyota a time extension. Usery had known that stopping then—as GM wanted to do—would doom the joint venture, so he had decided to call on Roger Smith to try to break the deadlock. Smith had already pledged his support for the joint venture, and he had told Usery that he knew that his executives were good at obstructing change but that no one would stand in his way. Usery now had to test the depth of Smith's commitment. Smith was in Germany, and his secretary had arranged a phone date for 7:30 the next morning. Usery recalled that after having a few drinks and dinner he had gone home late. He had had trouble sleeping because he had kept thinking about the phone call. He had been convinced that without Smith's personal approval, the project would surely founder.

At exactly 7:30 A.M., Bill Usery had been put through to Roger Smith in Germany. "Hello, Bill," Smith had said, "what's the problem?" Usery said he had explained the situation to Smith. "Roger, we're spending a lot of GM's money," he had said. "We're just about to put this joint venture to bed, but now your people have gotten in the way. They've said to stop. They won't let us go any further." Usery said that Smith had taken a breath and replied, "Bill, you have my authority to do whatever you have to do to make this project go. You forget my people and do whatever is needed!" Usery said the conversation had lasted fewer than three minutes. Usery had been elated as he hung up the telephone. Now, for the first time, it appeared as though the joint venture might become a reality.

# CHAPTER THIRTEEN

# THE REVOLUTION
# OF LEAN
# PRODUCTION

FINALLY, IN EARLY 1984, everything began to fall into place. After months of arduous negotiations, the agreements that Bill Usery had so carefully crafted with General Motors, Toyota, and the UAW were signed. Toyota agreed to hire the majority of workers from the pool of unemployed GM-Fremont workers, to recognize the UAW as the bargaining unit for the new venture, and to pay union-scale wages and benefits. The UAW agreed to accept the Toyota production system, to greatly increase the flexibility of its work rules, and to simplify the myriad job classifications. The union also agreed to give up its traditional right to strike in exchange for a promise from the company not to lock the union out. Finally, GM agreed that Toyota would manage the plant. Usery was jubilant.

A passage from the first page of the letter signaled that the new venture planned to blaze a new trail and break the destructive hold of America's industrial culture. It read:

> Both parties are undertaking this new proposed relationship with the full intention of fostering an innovative labor relations structure, minimizing the traditional adversarial roles and emphasizing mutual trust and good faith.[1]

But both sides would have to wait for FTC approval before anything else could happen. According to Dennis Cuneo, the Reagan appointees, led by Chairman James Miller, argued that the venture would enhance competition by making GM more efficient and serving as a demonstration project for a new model of labor relations.[2] The Carter appointees, led by Michael Pertschuck, feared that the venture would confer monopoly power on GM and that it would be the first step in the abdication of the American auto industry to the Japanese. Pertschuck claimed, "Battalions of neo-classical economists standing on the head of a pin cannot obscure the threat that this marriage of competitors poses to the American consumer, nor the fact that this venture is a plain and unambiguous violation of the antitrust laws."[3] On December 22, 1983, the Federal Trade Commission, after one of the most intensive investigations in the history of antitrust law, voted three to two to give NUMMI the preliminary go-ahead.

Cuneo remembers his reaction when he first heard Dan Rather announce the FTC's decision as the lead story on the CBS *Evening News*. "At first I was ecstatic. I had spent more than two years working on the project, and we defied the conventional wisdom by winning approval. But I also knew that our task wasn't over. The FTC approval was only preliminary, and Lee Iacocca said he would use the courts and Congress to overturn the decision." Nevertheless, the FTC decision held up to congressional hearings, a lawsuit by Chrysler (joined by Ralph Nader), and intense media scrutiny, and NUMMI finally received FTC approval in mid-April 1984, albeit with a number of conditions attached—including a requirement that the venture be dissolved by 1996 to reduce the chances that these two giant automakers could monopolize the market. But with no major obstacles left, everyone's attention turned to the Fremont plant. It was there that the work of creating an entirely new industrial model would begin.

## BREAKING THE MOLD

It seemed odd that a company of the size and stature of Toyota would send a senior member of the founding family to guide the development of a single assembly plant eight thousand miles from Japan. But to Toyota, NUMMI represented both a great opportunity and a great risk. It would be a test of whether its "lean production" system could be adapted to a unionized American setting. In addition, if the system could be operated under these new conditions, Toyota could likely establish a significant foothold in the North American market.

NUMMI's first president, Tatsuro Toyoda, was familiar with America, having received an MBA degree from New York University in the 1950s. At Toyota, he had spent much of his career in international operations and had been a member of the company's board since 1974. At NUMMI, Toyoda quickly developed a rapport with the Americans. I heard numerous stories about how he regularly walked through the plant, stopping to talk with team members about their jobs and families. When I first met Toyoda in 1994 at NUMMI's tenth-anniversary celebration, the warmth and affection people held for him were obvious as he walked through the plant, greeting workers and managers as old friends.

Toyoda relied heavily on Kan Higashi, who had been Toyota's lead negotiator in the joint venture and had become NUMMI's executive vice president. Higashi told me that from the beginning he and Toyoda had known they would have to go slowly and learn how to adapt their production system to the foreign conditions.[4] Higashi had known that the Japanese would have to work closely with the Americans to avoid the risk of polarization. He said, "We knew that it would take strong and consistent leadership from the top of the organization and we would have to stand behind our American managers."[5] In addition to Toyoda and Higashi, a number of other Toyota executives took key management positions. For instance, Kosuke "Ike" Ikebuchi, a NUMMI vice president, took responsibility for teaching the Americans how to run the Toyota production system. Significantly, GM also had a number of executives strategically placed at NUMMI, including Facilities Manager Jim Peters, who had actually built the original Fremont plant back in 1962. Bob Hendry (who had also been part of the negotiations) had come from GM's Finance Department to become NUMMI's first manager of general affairs and comptroller. Other GM managers were placed in the stamping plant, the paint shop, Quality Control, Purchasing, and Production Control. Rounding out the team, three Americans were hired for key posts: Dennis Cuneo took over NUMMI's legal affairs; Gary Convis, who had managed a Ford plant in Cleveland, was put in charge of manufacturing; and Bill Childs was hired from General Dynamics to head human resources. Despite assurances from Bruce Lee, Childs had been advised by the former GM management to keep the old UAW leadership out. Childs explained, "The old GM management couldn't see that we had something brand new in mind. I figured that bringing the old bargaining committee back *might* work, and I knew it would help cement relationships with Bruce. To be truthful, we couldn't keep them out anyway—sooner or later we'd have to deal with them." So, according to plan, the new UAW Local 2244, headed by leaders of the old local (Tony DeJesus as president and George Nano as chairman of the bargaining committee) formed an alliance with the new management team, and together they went to work.

The first task was to select frontline supervisors and to hire the hourly workforce. In an unusual turn of events, managers and union leaders worked together in a space in the plant that had been hastily set up in a large conference room. Everyone—the Japanese and American managers, as well as the union leaders—sat side by side on folding chairs and did everything from stuffing applications into envelopes to conducting interviews with job applicants. "I remember how overwhelming it seemed," Cuneo recalled. "We had to select and train twenty-five hundred people from a workforce that was known for poor workmanship, high absenteeism, and union militancy!"[6] But despite the challenges—or perhaps because of them—everyone seemed dedicated to what lay ahead. "It was truly a partnership right from the get-go," said Bruce Lee. "Everyone was in it together."[7]

In March 1984 about five thousand applications were mailed to former GM workers with a letter that explained that NUMMI employees would be expected to contribute to an atmosphere of trust and cooperation and that poor-quality workmanship and absenteeism would not be tolerated. About three thousand applications were returned. It had been two years since the shutdown, and many former GM workers had found other jobs. Others knew they would not fit into the new company and never replied. Once the applicant pool had been established, UAW officers and NUMMI managers personally screened and tested each applicant. Some applicants took themselves out of the running after going through the interview process, where they were told they would be expected to work cooperatively and treat one another (and management) with respect. Most who applied and completed the interviews, however, were hired. Bill Childs said that 80 percent of the first 2,200 people hired for the new venture had originally worked in the old GM plant. He added that only about 300 applicants had been rejected outright—usually because they had had outstandingly poor work histories or drug or alcohol problems. He commented, "To be honest, we didn't look all that hard at their records, and we took a lot of people back whom we would not have hired off the street."

Managers, on the other hand, were screened especially carefully to make sure they were committed to the new management principles. Applicants like Mike Mulleague, a former GM manager, received close scrutiny, and few with his background were hired. Mulleague laughed, "They looked me over real carefully to make sure I wasn't carrying any GM baggage. T. Toyoda personally interviewed me," he added proudly.

Many of the more traditional managers and union leaders were thrown off balance by the new collegial relationships. They had never seen anything like it before. Tony DeJesus, president of Local 2244, said that he had had trouble adjusting to the blurry lines between management and labor. DeJesus had been shocked when he had been asked to interview applicants for managers' jobs. He recalled, "Hey, I spent most of my life fighting these guys, and now they wanted me to *hire* them? It didn't make sense." He had gone home after work and tried to explain to his wife that the company wanted union members to participate in hiring managers. "My wife said to me. 'Tony, you've been bitching about these managers all your life and now you get a chance to hire them and you refuse. What's the matter with you? You can't have it both ways!' " DeJesus said with a smile, "At that moment a lightbulb went on in my head. Toyota wanted to hire managers we could work with. That *was* something new!"

But giving up traditional union authority, even in exchange for job security and a healthy work environment, was a huge step for the union leaders, and to make this new human relationship work they had to give up beliefs that had been deeply etched into their psyches from years of bitter experience with management. To expect these feelings to disappear overnight would be naïve. They would have to be broken down in the same way they had originally been formed—by trial and error. Tony DeJesus recalled an incident that reveals in microdetail how slowly culture changes. He had been put in charge of collecting completed job applications as they were returned, organizing them into files so the applicants could be matched with job openings and telephoned for interviews. Unknown to anyone else, he had further organized the application files by job classification and seniority, thus replicating the very system the union had just agreed to abolish. "They had no idea what I was doing," he said with a laugh. "But goddamn it, I didn't want these managers to forget there was a union they had to deal with! We weren't just going to roll over and play dead!" DeJesus explained that Gary Convis, the new manager of manufacturing, had interviewed an applicant and promised him a job. DeJesus had been angered because Convis had ignored the applicant's lack of seniority, and he had decided to test the company's commitment to trust and mutual respect. DeJesus said, "It really pissed me off when I found out. The guy had only four years of seniority, and I had others in my file who had more. I talked to my guys about it, and we agreed that if we didn't march over there and take a stand, we'd never have any real input." DeJesus recalled a meeting with Convis: "I said, 'We've got a procedure, and I don't appreciate your ignoring it.' Convis read me the letter of intent about how seniority wasn't going to count. I said to him, 'Look, you want to come in here and do what the fuck you want, you're not going to build a single goddamned car!' " According to DeJesus, they had both stormed out. A few hours later, Convis had called him on the phone and apologized. DeJesus said, "I was astounded. Gary agreed that he would go through me from then on. I'd never had a manager apologize to me in twenty years. And I've got to admit, it made me feel good."[8] So, for a time, new hires were informally hired partly on the basis of seniority.

While DeJesus felt good for the moment, cooperation of this kind between the union and management created confusion, especially among the union leaders, whose reputations were on the line. After all, just a few years before these men had led one of the most rebellious and militant locals in the country. DeJesus himself had led a wildcat strike at GM in 1977. Now they were expected to lead the disbelieving workforce in the opposite direction—to cooperate with the company! To some, cooperating with management was an act of extreme disloyalty. To DeJesus it felt like moral suicide, as voices from within organized labor warned Local 2244's leadership about the dire consequences of cooperating with management.[9]

But economic conditions in the San Francisco Bay area were bad in 1984. GM had of course closed, and Ford's big plant in nearby Milpitas had also been shut down. Jobs in manufacturing were disappearing at an alarming rate, and local political action to stem the rising unemployment rate had proved futile.[10] George Nano, chairman of the bargaining committee, knew it would be difficult to establish a new identity for the militant local, but he also knew there was no alternative. "We still had some power," Nano said. "I mean, we weren't down and out. Everybody knew that if we had refused to accept the Toyota production system, there would have been no joint venture at all. And we showed them in the first negotiation when we walked out that we weren't going to be no fucking company union!"

But, he explained, "We felt alone. We didn't want to be fucking assholes—the Judas goats of the trade-union movement. There was no one to ask whether we were right or wrong to cooperate with the company. There was no blueprint, and we were apprehensive. We had no intention of being used by the company, and we knew we'd be accused of being backsliders."

Nevertheless, the union set aside its misgivings long enough to give the new arrangement a chance. Little by little, both sides made tangible progress in learning to work respectfully with each other, and people began to look at NUMMI in a new, curious, and hopeful way. *Fortune* observed:

> As a cooperative endeavor between a symbol of Japanese efficiency and a powerful U.S. union, New United Motors is the most important labor relations experiment in the U.S. today. If Toyota can succeed in producing a car to Japanese quality standards at near-Japanese costs using unionized U.S. workers, the venture could force profound changes on the rest of the U.S. auto industry—and perhaps on other industries as well.[11]

NUMMI made a massive up-front investment to get these relationships off to a productive start. First, the company spent more than $3 million to send six hundred of its new employees to Toyota for training.[12] At first, DeJesus declined the invitations to go to Japan. He told me he had been skeptical about whether the experiment in cooperation would work, so he had excused himself, saying the trip to Japan was too long. Finally, however, in late 1984, he had relented after realizing that his presence in Japan was symbolically important to Toyota. DeJesus said he had been surprised to see how important NUMMI was to the Japanese. He said he had been treated like royalty. He and other leaders of the local had been interviewed on TV news programs, and Japan's prime minister had even made a surprise appearance at Toyota to speak about the significance of NUMMI and global cooperation. The Americans had worked on Toyota's assembly line to learn the system and had later gone out to Nagoya nightspots, eating and drinking with their Japanese counterparts. He said, "We learned how close-knit the managers and workers are on the floor. They have to be to work that hard! American workers always bitch when things don't go right. But the Japanese have a respect for authority. It's not a dictatorship, it's not forced, it's just part of their culture."

After the Americans returned, Toyota sent four hundred Japanese coordinators to Fremont to teach the principles of the production system. DeJesus laughed, recalling how the Japanese and Americans had been forced to communicate in sign language. He said, "We found out that at first we could understand each other with very few words. We worked hard, and on the weekends we took the Japanese to our homes, and—some other places I won't discuss!" Little by little, the Japanese and Americans had begun to establish friendships and mutual understandings that would prove to be of immense value later on.

## A NEW EMPLOYEE COMPACT

But it would take even more to alter the traditionally adversarial relationship between management and labor. Something had to precipitate a break with the traditional "us-against-them" mentality that had kept the two sides polarized for generations. I first detected signs of this change in 1989, when my research team and I went to meet with the UAW local. We sat at a large conference table across from DeJesus, Nano, and seven or eight UAW officers. Until then, NUMMI had routinely denied requests from academics to study the plant, and we needed the union's approval. They were skeptical of academics, but they listened, evaluating us warily as we described what we hoped to do. Suddenly Nano exploded, jabbing his finger into the air and yelling, "I don't have much use for you academics! I don't want you coming in here and fucking this thing up for us!" Then he said something that astounded me because I had never heard a union person say anything like it before: "This company is the goose that laid the golden egg!" Nano exclaimed. "If this plant goes down, we go down. Our families and our children go down. It's their future too!"

Beneath this intimidating greeting, Nano conveyed a message of profound significance: both sides had finally recognized their interdependence—both would have to survive and prosper if there was to be a future. What made the message especially memorable was hearing it from the lips of a union leader who had spent most of his life shoving GM up against the wall. Nano's point haunted me for the next five years. It was so simple yet so elusive. Why had the message failed to penetrate Douglas Aircraft or USS-POSCO in the same way? Were a total shutdown and mass layoffs like NUMMI's required to drive the point home?

The answer can be found in NUMMI's serious commitment to regarding its employees as assets and treating them fairly. NUMMI's no-layoffs policy was probably the single most important instrument of creating this new philosophy. The idea had originally come from the Americans: Dennis Cuneo and Bill Childs had suggested it to Kan Higashi as a symbol of the new company's intent. Cuneo said it had been clear from the very first labor negotiations that NUMMI wanted to break the traditional mold. Layoffs had always been a sore point—autoworkers had always felt they were treated no differently than pieces of machinery: at the first sign of a downturn, they were the first to be let go. Though the unions had responded with rigid work rules and income protection, Cuneo and Childs felt that the Japanese concept of job security would be more appealing and would set the right tone for the joint venture. Higashi and Toyoda endorsed the idea, and it was quickly embraced by both the management team and the union. The policy was revolutionary in American industry. It said the company would lay off no one unless it was compelled to do so.[13] It stipulated that before anyone was laid off all contract work would be dropped and executives would take substantial pay cuts. Bill Childs said the policy was more symbolic of the company's commitment to treating its employees fairly than anything else. "The language is so vague you could drive a truck through it. But it expresses the intent of this company without a doubt."

Cuneo said that workers naturally distrusted the policy at first, because no one had ever seen anything like it. But it has since been seriously tested several times, and the company has honored its promise every time. For instance, in March 1988 NUMMI was forced to reduce production 40 percent because of a slump in sales. Most American auto companies would have followed tradition and laid off the second shift, but NUMMI demonstrated its commitment by standing behind its policy. Nobody was laid off. Team members who were not needed on the line were trained or retrained in the basics of the new production system—standardized work, problem solving, and so forth.

The value employees derive from feeling secure, especially in the face of rising unemployment, and fairly treated cannot be understated. First, the policy is a visible, tangible reminder of the company's commitment to fairness. It has also brought forth a willingness on the part of team members to invest themselves more fully in their jobs. A 1993 company survey revealed that 88 percent of the hourly employees deem job security to be *the* most important aspect of working at NUMMI. The policy also began to establish a new philosophy that was critical to gaining employees' voluntary participation—that employees be regarded as assets rather than as costs that can be trimmed at management's discretion. Bill Childs said, "You can see it in the suggestion program. We get about ten thousand a year, and about eight thousand are adopted. Two thirds of the team members participate. At GM, maybe you'd get a handful." Most important, team members are instrumental in sharing their ideas about how to improve the production system, even if it means working themselves out of a job—because they know they will be reassigned to a similar job somewhere else in the plant.

NUMMI's employment security policy further reinforced a new set of human relationships as managers began to learn to respect their employees. Gary Convis said this was a "last horizon" that managers had to overcome. He added, "The Japanese know that to make things more waste-free and streamlined, they have to work with the people on the line. They have to work with their people, to listen to them for their ideas, and to work with them to support theirs." Convis explained that when something goes wrong on the line, most American managers go looking for a culprit—someone who is slacking off or doing something wrong. In contrast, he said, "Japanese managers go looking for the problem. They trust their team members are doing their best. When something breaks down, managers feel it's their responsibility and they're apologetic out of respect for their team members. It's that mind-set that the Japanese have helped teach us."

Kan Higashi explained that he had used every means available to establish the concept of cooperation and fairness. He had striven for a general leveling—fewer levels of management, no executive perks, and a blurring of lines between Japanese and Americans, managers and team members. Higashi admitted that after a fifteen-hour day there would be nothing he wanted more than to sit with his Japanese colleagues to drink and speak Japanese, but he had resisted because "I knew we would be misunderstood if we ate separately, so we all ate together. The things we did at NUMMI, like creating open offices and a communal cafeteria and getting rid of reserved parking spaces, we did out of necessity." Higashi joked, "Your academic friends say we imported 'Japanese management techniques,' but what we did at NUMMI was not found in Japan!" He added, "These were not gimmicks. Rather they were symbols of our concept and of our intent."[14]

As Toyota's production system was introduced, the management team and the union compressed job classifications, balanced jobs, and created a flat wage structure. GM's former eighty job classifications were collapsed into just three—one production class and two higher-paid skilled trades classes—all of which fell into the same $19-to-$21 hourly wage rate.

NUMMI's flat wage structure also helped reinforce the new philosophy that the company's fortunes would rise or fall on everyone's effort and that everyone would share equally in the company's success. A flat wage rate is a hard concept for many American managers to grasp because most are taught that employees will work harder only if they are paid more. But Convis was convinced that "Our team members are ready and willing to change as long as they feel they are being treated fairly. We've tried to avoid favoritism and to level out the harder jobs. A single pay level is as fundamental to the success of this company as is the security of employment policy. We have learned from the Japanese the importance of tying the company's success, and the success of the individual, to things they can control."

## ALTERING THE SYSTEM OF WORK

As we worked on the assembly line, it became clear that the Toyota production system was the driving force behind NUMMI's conversion. Without doubt, the GM shutdown had driven home the message that employees were going to have to change their deep-seated beliefs to survive, and provisions for job security and fairness had gone a long way to demonstrate the company's goodwill. But without an effective system to harness and direct workers' energy, little progress could have been made. That kind of system—the Toyota system—and the principles behind it are evident at every step along the assembly line, from the stamping plant, where hoods, fenders, and other parts are stamped, through the body shop, the Paint Department, and down the 1.2-mile assembly line. Every ingredient—standardized work, *jidoka, andon, kaizen,* and just-in-time planning—plays its own part in continuous improvement of the production process.

The Paint Department is a perfect example of how the Toyota production system underscored a new set of principles. "Paint," as the department is called, is a complex operation in which specially formulated chemicals are applied in ways that meet some of the strictest environmental requirements in the country. Preparation of surfaces has to be done to near perfection, paints and solvents must be mixed correctly, coats have to be sprayed with a knowing hand, and heat has to be carefully controlled. Not only does the fickle paint technology have to be managed, but the car's paint job is the first thing a customer sees. Thus, NUMMI's continual inspection for "fit and finish" makes it a high-visibility operation.

On the brightly lit sealer deck, team members apply a white sealer around the inside of the doors of Prizms and Corollas. About four hundred men and women work in Paint. They are organized into teams of about six hourly workers each. Each team has a leader (also an hourly employee, who is paid a fifty-cent-per-hour premium for coordinating the work). Above the team leader is a group leader, the first level of management.

Watching a team member at work makes it obvious that it takes dexterity and control to get the sealer exactly where it is supposed to go without leaving an excess. Any excess is "skived," or scraped off, with a flat-edged plastic tool in the few seconds the car is at the station. Time is of the essence, for a worker has only fifty-five seconds to do the job before the car automatically moves to the next station. The length of time the car is at the workstation is known as "*takt* time," for the German word meaning "meter" or "musical rhythm." *Takt* time—the speed at which the assembly line operates—can be varied to match fluctuations in sales. Such precise timing keeps the entire plant running on a common rhythm and produces a tension that requires team members and managers to be alert. Each job has been broken down, studied, and standardized by team members themselves to make sure the operations are done exactly the same way time and time again. The jobs have also been balanced among the team members to even out the difficulty. Team members rotate to other jobs within the team every two and a half hours to avoid injuries from repetition and to help distribute the workload evenly.

On this day the new batch of sealer was too runny, and it started to ooze down the doors as the car bodies moved down the line. A team member spotted the problem, reached overhead, and pulled the *andon* cord. The moment she pulled the cord, amber lights at the station—and also high overhead on the *andon* board—lighted up, revealing the exact location of the problem. The tune "Greensleeves" was piped over the area's loudspeakers, and the line stopped when the car reached the next yellow marker a few seconds later.

When the line actually stopped, the *andon* board light changed from amber to red, signifying the line was down. The team leader hurried over and listened to the team member's complaint. He quickly realized that the sealer had been mixed incorrectly and called on his radio for some to be brought to the line immediately. Because NUMMI's just-in-time system allows only a limited amount of material to be on hand at any time, the small batch of bad sealer could be quickly removed and replaced with a correct mix. But the problem solving did not stop with putting the right sealer into the team member's hands, as it would have in a conventional plant. Instead, the group leader traced the problem back to its root, which turned out to be a new team member on the second shift who had not been properly trained to mix sealer according to the standardized procedure. When the team member came back to work on the next shift, he was retrained, and the issue was discussed at a group meeting the following day to determine if any other corrective action was needed.

This example reveals how stopping the line acts like a trigger, forcing problems to the surface, where they can be solved. A serious commitment by the company is required, since each minute the line is down represents about $10,000 in lost revenue. Even though expecting team members to stop the line seems like common sense, under mass production they had never been given such authority. Gus Billy, a wiry man who has many years of seniority and serves on the local's bargaining team, commented, "At GM you just didn't stop the line. The superintendent would have your ass. *No one* had that authority except him. You were just arms and legs. Your mouth was to say 'Yes, sir' and 'No, sir,' and that was it!" But giving workers authority to stop the line required them to take responsibility for ensuring quality at every step of the operation—a cornerstone of the Toyota system.

In truth, however, some NUMMI team members try to avoid stopping the line because they fear they will be scrutinized or that their supervisor will get in trouble. Other team members pull the cord just long enough to activate the light and music to get the team leader's attention, then pull it again to shut the signal off without actually stopping the line. Managers, however, *want* to see the line stopped occasionally, because it indicates that the team members are alert and that the system is being improved. All line stoppages are recorded by "Oscar," a huge electronic board that provides management with a continuous, up-to-date flow of information on stoppages and production time, and managers actually worry when there is no downtime. As one group leader put it, "When there's no downtime, I know that my people are sending junk through or they're trying to be superstars." This group leader's philosophy—which is at the heart of the production system—is that the group should be generating a few minutes of downtime each day, because the pursuit of perfection is an ideal, not an end state.

But NUMMI is not perfect, and managing such a dynamic system is hard for managers too. In 1989 internal audits at NUMMI revealed a significant rise in defects. Kan Higashi decided to take corrective action with a "back-to-basics" movement to reaffirm the system's fundamental principles. He called the new emphasis on the basics a "spiritual revival" and intended it to break employees' complacency and to refocus on putting quality first.

Gary Convis called the assistant managers and group leaders together to announce the back-to-basics initiative. The session was held in a room called "the church" because religious services are held there, but this was no spiritual event. When he walked in, Convis looked angry and tired. He was dressed in jeans and a blue V-neck sweater. Like an angry hawk, he towered over the thirty blue-shirted group leaders and assistant managers who were seated around a large table. He did not smile.

"Ladies and gentlemen," he began, "we've got serious problems. Quality is our number one priority, and the amount of time the line's been down should be ample evidence to anyone that we mean it. Somehow we've lost sight of the *jidoka* principle and replaced it with 'quality through inspection.' We can't have it." A silence fell over the room as everyone looked blankly at Convis. He continued, "This doesn't make sense. We're all human and make mistakes. But I can't hide my feelings about how I want this place run. We must lead by example. 'Seek, inspect, and repair' is not the way we run NUMMI. There's no guarantee that NUMMI will continue. You have an obligation to your teams to see that their job security is assured. We have slipped badly." As the tension built, the managers shifted uneasily in their chairs. Convis continued, "Some people in this company don't care about job security. They should go. They should be terminated. It's like a cancer. I'm talking about a small number of people, but like cancer, it's got to be corrected before it spreads. I'm not on a witch-hunt, but cancer spreads. We've disciplined only four or five people in the past five years for workmanship. People can be counseled and turned around."

The tension in the room rose. "But it's only you and the team leaders," he continued. "There's no one else out there." The room was silent. "I want you to think about what you are going to say to your people. I want you to be a model. Practice talking with your groups. Become a leader. Work with your team leaders. Use them as extensions of yourself. That's what you are, leaders." The meeting ended and everyone filed out silently, one by one.

On the way back to the line, two group leaders were griping. "They've been after productivity, productivity, productivity, and now the chickens have come home to roost," said one. "It's about time someone did something." The other said, "Come on, Frank, we've been coasting. You know that. We just sat back on our laurels, and now we've found out they had thorns!" I asked Mike Mulleague what he thought. He said, "We just got too goddamned complacent. We've rolled along for a year, knowing we had problems. It's like 'Nobody robbed my house for the past year, so today I won't lock the door.'" But Mulleague said that he was confident that the renewed focus would restore NUMMI's quality. He added, "To the Japanese, failure's not all bad. It's an opportunity."

In the following months, a flurry of new *kaizen* projects was launched as management pressed groups and teams to rethink how jobs had been standardized and balanced and how quality could be improved. Each afternoon between shifts, groups of managers toured the plant, looking for ways to improve things and checking parts bins to make sure they were properly labeled. Some team members resisted the back-to-basics movement, complaining, "Management doesn't know what the hell's going on down here" or "When things get screwed up, it's the worker who catches hell. They want us to use this new system, but most of the managers haven't changed a bit!" Others, however, welcomed the renewal. One team member said, "It's about time. There are a lot of intelligent people down here on the line who want to keep increasing their responsibility, to keep learning. You need to set and reset your goals." Though some team members continued to grumble, the back-to-basics movement had the desired effect as defects fell to an acceptable level.

A similar cycle occurred a year later, in 1991. Osamu Kimura, who had been executive vice president, had taken over as NUMMI's third president when Kan Higashi returned to Japan. To Kimura there was a constant need to "renew the company's spirit" by finding problems and accelerating improvements. Kimura launched the "J-1 program" (a reference to the J. D. Power and Associates number one rating, to the attainment of which Kimura had committed the company). He said, "We made it a campaign with buttons and banners, so that employees could see our commitment each day." By reinforcing the basics, the J-1 program refocused the employees' energies and broke the downward cycle, leading NUMMI to win the highest J. D. Power and Associates rankings for U.S.-built compacts and number one for compact trucks.

It is part of Toyota's philosophy that frank, open discussions about problems are an opportunity to improve the system and to maximize learning. Such direct discussions sometimes create bad feelings, but conflict is forced out into the open, where it can be managed and defused. For instance, NUMMI inspectors routinely tear down vehicles to find defects. Four days each week, managers and team leaders congregate under the rumbling assembly line in an open forum to discuss defects that have been found by the inspectors. It is a form of accountability rarely seen in other companies. Jesse Wingard, NUMMI's plant manager, is convinced that this form of visual control is a key not only to producing high-quality vehicles but to creating a healthy human environment.

The following example gives a feeling of the dynamics of this form of public accountability. One day in 1993, three Corollas and three Prizms stood under bright lights, covered with yellow tags. About sixty assistant managers, group leaders, and team leaders gathered around an area that had been cordoned off. A manager from Quality Control began the meeting by taking the microphone and pointing to the charts showing the defects per vehicle (or "DPVs") for each area—stamping, paint, and assembly—and for major problems—"squeak and rattle," "fit and finish," "water leaks," and "mutilation." An ascending red line on one chart showed that defects had been rising dramatically. Picking the first defect—an ill-fitting left front door—for discussion, he called on the responsible group leader to come up and explain the defect to the group and the countermeasures he proposed to take. A middle-aged man wearing a shop apron came forward and took the mike. He looked nervous, especially when he saw Wingard working his way through the crowd at the back of the room. He haltingly explained the defect as a body design problem, another way of saying it had not been his group's fault. Failing to acknowledge one's own errors and trying to place blame elsewhere is taboo at NUMMI, and this group leader soon suffered the consequences. Wingard moved up to the front and took the mike from the group leader, who was glaring out at the crowd. He said slowly, "It's *no* body problem.

It's an *operator* problem! Your group has got to work this out with the team!" He continued, "This car went through ninety-five percent of the process after the error was made. No one caught it. Everyone has to check these cars. No one saw it? That's unbelievable!" No one was smiling, and the side chatter had hushed. Wingard now had everyone's attention. He continued, "Our target is 1.7 [defects per vehicle]. We'll need a god-damned big board if the numbers keep going up. You're not paying atten-tion. You can't *inspect* in quality." After more presentations, the group disbanded for the day. Afterward, Mike Payne, an assistant manager, ex-plained, "These meetings can be hard, but they keep us aware of what's going on in the plant. They also give us the chance to teach our team lead-ers to see where the problems are." Payne acknowledged the pressure of being exposed publicly. "Yeah," he joked, "you can run but you can't hide! You don't want to be seen there too often."

While NUMMI's openness can be bruising, employees know where they stand. The underlying philosophy stems from Toyota's consensus form of decision making. Everyone involved is brought into the process with the knowledge that a group decision, which includes all points of view, is stronger than a decision imposed by a single individual. To be sure, as Dennis Cuneo warned me, NUMMI was not as much of an in-dustrial democracy as some might think. "Some of your uninformed col-leagues think we vote on everything here," he joked. "But we don't take votes, and the majority doesn't necessarily rule. What we do is try to hear different points of view to learn from the team members and to make sure that everyone's voice is heard."

I learned about the process firsthand when I began working on the assembly line. I was installing battery straps under the hoods of Corollas and Prizms when the group leader, Roger Gallet, began to implement a new idea—a *kaizen*—that was intended to reduce the group's size by one. The details had been worked out by the group weeks earlier. Ed Gonza-les, a team leader who was working next to me, joked, "*Kaizen*'s like throw-ing a cherry bomb into a chicken coop! Feathers fly," he continued, making floating motions with his hands, "but then they settle." The plan required exchanging some jobs—installation of batteries, grilles, and windshield washers—up and down the line. After moving parts to the new locations and showing the team members how to do their new jobs, Gallet stood back and watched. One team member complained loudly about his new job installing batteries: "This isn't in standardized work!" Gallet pulled out his stopwatch and said calmly, "It soon will be. If this works, we'll just add it in." Gallet timed him through three trials and seemed satisfied. As Gallet walked away from the line, he explained, "This fellow's been in the group for two years. He tries to torpedo any new idea: 'It can't be done.' Mr. Negative!" he joked. "It doesn't hurt for him to have his say. You know, it takes both positive and negative to make a current!" He added philosophically, "He's not a bad guy. He just had to be heard. Walk over tomorrow and watch. He'll be doing fine." True to his word, the next day "Mr. Negative" was conscientiously installing batteries.

NUMMI's is a powerful form of decision making because everyone who contributes claims ownership for the ultimate decision. Tony Fisher, who once worked for GM and now heads NUMMI's Environmental Affairs Department, described the power of consensual decision making. "The Japanese ask questions and seem to talk endlessly about solutions," he said. "It may take a long time to make a decision, but once it's made, that's it. Pity the person who tries to undermine the decision once it's made." He described how an American manager had once tried to intervene when a decision had already been made. "The Japanese sat the guy down and straightened him out. 'That's *our* decision,' they said, 'and we're going to put our heart into it.' Boom! That's it! You don't learn this kind of leadership in the classroom—you learn it from coaching and by trial and error." Fisher found that Toyota's beliefs could easily be integrated with his own. "I always believed in including people in important decisions. I'm a Christian, a Catholic, and I believe in the Golden Rule—the essence of respect and trust. But I had never seen it practiced in business until I came here. Here is a country," he said about Japan in an animated voice, "that's non-Christian, and look what they do!"

## ALTERING THE ROLE OF THE UNION

The Toyota system's requirement of interdependence between management and labor, NUMMI's assurances of security and fairness, and a decision-making style that included everyone offered union members a chance to become participants rather than to be obstructionists. George

Nano said, "At GM, all they wanted was your back. They wanted you to check your brains outside. Here, they want our ideas. They'll have a *ne-mawashi* [a Japanese term meaning "open discussion"] with the union *before* they do something! I don't want to make it sound like we've died and gone to heaven. I mean, they don't invite us to their board meetings, but we don't use muscle to solve problems anymore."

Nano said that at GM the union had represented only the 5 percent or 10 percent of the union members who were perennially in trouble. He acknowledged that some of them had had real grievances, but the union's job had really been representing the "assholes"—a sympathetic term for team members who were always in trouble. But now, under the conditions created by a more cooperative, inclusive model of labor relations, the union's interest had begun to shift toward representing the majority of its members.

The turbulent union politics revolving around who should lead the local had not, however, disappeared. Though the Administrative Caucus (the original bargaining committee) still controlled the local when we went to work there in 1989, a dissident group called the People's Caucus was gaining popularity. This oppositional caucus charged the Administrative Caucus with "selling out" to the company. One day at lunch, a team member complained about the union. "Those committeemen have nothin' to do but stir up trouble," he told the others at the picnic table. "Nano and his guys tell us that if it wasn't for them we wouldn't have our jobs. But that's not true, it's because of the Japanese. They gave us our jobs." Another worker exclaimed, "The problem here is that there isn't no goddamned union, they're just like management! You can't tell 'em apart!" He crossed his fingers, "They're in bed together." A young worker sitting alone said quietly, "If the company treats you right, you don't need a union. Most of the guys here use the union just to bitch because that's the way it used to work. Guys that come in and do their work don't go to the union—it's mostly the assholes that do." He stuffed his leftover lunch into his sandwich bag as he got up from the table and said, "If those guys from the People's Caucus or whatever they call themselves got in here, they'd shut the whole fuckin' place down."

In fact, the People's Caucus won the presidency of the local and a majority of the committee seats in 1991, beating the Administrative Caucus for the first time. Bruce Lee interpreted the change in union leadership as normal, explaining, "It's not a perfect world, you know. It's only natural that ultimately there'd be another caucus. Some of these guys had been in power before, but now they were out. So what do they do? First they take on the system, but when that doesn't fly they take on the leadership."[15] Though the changes in leadership worried some managers and team members, the system itself stayed intact. Lee said philosophically, "When the opposition says 'This system sucks,' it falls on deaf ears. Nobody is trying to throw the system out. Sure, they've got some ideas about how to do this or do that, to tweak the system to make it better. But burn down the church to roast the pig? No, sir!"

Despite the roiling union politics, the local's constructive role is apparent throughout the plant—on the line conferring with suppliers about parts, in meetings with environmental regulators over emission controls, and in the development of training programs for its members with Bill Childs and his staff. One of the clearest examples of how labor's role is changing is best seen in the way disputes are settled. When GM ran the plant, thousands of grievances were filed each year. Roger Gallet said, "It was pure harassment. If you got into it with the union, they'd have somebody standing over you writing up grievances on the spot!" As this book went to press, only fifty-seven grievances were pending.

One reason for the small number of grievances is that NUMMI tries to settle conflict on a personal, face-to-face basis as quickly as possible. When GM ran the plant, the company labor relations representatives offices were separate from those of the union. But today company representatives and union representatives occupy the same space, and they always try to solve labor relations problems together.

One night I met with Neva Burke, a young company representative, and Jesse Hernandez, a union committeeman. Burke, a recent college graduate, was in her late twenties and had been with the company for only a few months. Hernandez appeared to be about forty, with black, slicked-back hair and aquiline features. He wore a blue-and-gold union jacket with PEOPLE'S CAUCUS stitched across the back, identifying him as a member of the dissident union faction.

They had been called into the plant to settle a grievance that was about to be filed by a group leader against one of his team members for loitering, or wandering around without permission. We took seats around a table in an office near the rumbling assembly line as the team member, Charlie, a husky young man dressed in gray overalls, walked in and sat next to Hernandez. He complained to Hernandez about the group leader; "This guy's been bird-dogging me since day one. He's got it in for me." The group leader shoved a formal corrective action statement across the table at Charlie, who stared at it and shouted back, "Goddamn it, I wasn't loitering! I was on company business, and I stopped for a minute to get a fucking Coke!" Hernandez, who had been quiet, flicked the corrective action away with his finger and told the group leader, "This isn't some goddamned prison. It's a free country. You're bird-dogging him, and I won't sign it. I'll take this to George Nano!" Charlie continued shouting across the table, "You're just trying to get me fucking fired!" Burke took control as she admonished, "That kind of language has no place here. Cool off, both of you." The angry discussion settled down, and within thirty minutes or so both sides agreed: the group leader would withdraw the formal action, and Charlie would ask for permission when he needed to leave his team. Charlie seemed relieved to have told his side of the story to both officials, and the group leader had calmed down. As Burke and Hernandez headed back to the office, they talked about the two, agreeing that Charlie was a good employee but that the group leader needed some counseling to learn how to be a better manager.

Only a few years earlier, when GM had been running the plant, the idea that a company and its union might have a common interest in the workforce would have been heresy. But as we walked back to the office, Hernandez explained that at NUMMI he could not survive by sticking up for only those members who were always in trouble. "It's not the assholes who get you elected here. It's the other ninety-five percent," he said, "It's those you never hear from." Neva Burke added that any company has a certain number of employees who are always in some kind of trouble and that it is easier, cheaper, and better for morale to accept the fact, and to work to rehabilitate them. She said, "This is a small place, and we know them by name. Counseling's the key. When we see a pattern, we sit down with them and straighten them out. People *do* shape up."

NUMMI's success hinted at the possibility of a new relationship across all of American industry, but its significance had still not dawned on GM, which remained mired in adversarial human relationships. One day, a General Motors vice president was on his way from Detroit to Los Angeles. The corporate jet landed in Palm Springs to pick up former treasury secretary and GM board member George Shultz to give him a ride. As the plane climbed, clearing the steep San Bernardino Mountains, Shultz asked the vice president, "How's NUMMI doing?" "It's doing very well," the vice president assured him. "Well, if *it's* so successful," asked Shultz, "why isn't GM doing better?" The vice president sheepishly recalled his automatic answer, which revealed GM's deepest problems: "*It's how NUMMI treats its people!*" he stammered.[16]

# CHAPTER FOURTEEN

# THE MAKING OF
# A NEW COMPACT

NUMMI's TURNAROUND has been nothing short of spectacular. In 1993 NUMMI's Toyota pickup truck, Toyota Corolla, and Geo Prizm were ranked the best compact vehicles built in the United States. In 1994 its Geo Prizm was ranked higher than any other American-built car ever rated by J. D. Power and Associates. NUMMI was lauded in union magazines as having "changed into a worksite unlike any other in the UAW's experiences." *Newsweek* called it "a model of industrial tranquillity," and *The Wall Street Journal* reported that NUMMI "has managed to convert a crew of largely middle-aged, rabble-rousing former GM workers into a crack force that is beating the bumpers off Big Three plants in efficiency and product quality."[1] In a recent team member survey, 93 percent said they were proud of the job they do.[2] Most former GM workers we talked with said they would not go back to work for GM even if it reopened across the street.

How was such a turnaround accomplished? How was it possible to convert one of the worst GM plants into one of the most productive auto plants in the world? Even as late as 1988, the reasons for NUMMI's turnaround were unclear to its own employees. Bill Childs, who had played a leading role in the company's conversion, quipped. "We know what goes in and what comes out. But what goes on in the middle remains somewhat of a mystery to us."[3]

There is no question that the GM-Fremont shutdown and the wave of plant closures that swept America in the early 1980s sent a powerful message to the factory workers who were losing their jobs in record numbers. Though generations of autoworkers had taken factory work for granted, suddenly the prospects for such high-paying jobs become dim. Hundreds of NUMMI employees told us they had worried about whether they would ever work in an auto plant again. There can be little doubt that the fear of long-term, mass unemployment helped persuade the UAW to deviate from traditional work rules to try Toyota's new system. Bruce Lee said, "I felt that maybe there was an opportunity to get our people back to work. There were a lot of unknowns, but if the opportunity presented itself and we were able to get ourselves back to work, we needed to be prepared to do things differently. We had to be prepared to say, "The old GM days was a chapter in the book that's gone. But there are other chapters, and we're in a position to write them."[4] By itself, however, fear is not enough to account for NUMMI's achievements, which have now been sustained for more than ten years.

There is limited merit in the popular theory that NUMMI's success stemmed from the fact that its workforce had been carefully selected. As mentioned earlier, 80 percent of the original workforce had worked in the old GM plant, and only about 300 of the 3,000 applicants for jobs at the joint venture had been rejected outright. But even if we accept this theory, how are we to account for NUMMI's continued high performance, now with a workforce twice the size of the original one?

The answer is that NUMMI's *transformation* was due mostly to the introduction of Toyota's lean production system. But NUMMI's *success* ultimately stemmed from the creation of a new "third" culture that, like the HP Way, gave guidance to day-to-day behavior. The culture that emerged was neither completely American nor completely Japanese. Rather, it was a hybrid that combined the best qualities of both General Motors and Toyota and allowed American workers and managers to reject their old conflict-ridden relationship and create a new and productive one.[5]

The conditions were ideal. The seriousness of the undertaking and the dire consequences of failure forced the union and management to recognize their mutual interdependence. This new realization—that they were in the same boat—was revolutionary. For the first time each side had had to consider the effects of its actions on the other! Second, management and labor consciously committed themselves to creating a secure workplace based on fairness, mutual respect, and trust. But these qualities would have become little more than hollow slogans, much as they had at Douglas Aircraft, unless they could be embedded in the system of work. The Toyota production system reinforced these human qualities by requiring NUMMI's employees to work interdependently and respectfully with one another. Only in this way was NUMMI able to begin to forge the elements of a new culture that would ultimately replace anger and hostility with trust and mutual respect.

Such a comment might lead one to wonder "If 'lean production' is so simple, why aren't all manufacturers converting to it?" The answer is that such a conversion is both risky and difficult. A dynamic system such as NUMMI's requires workers and managers to constantly adjust to changing conditions, and it is far more difficult to manage than a traditional mass production system is. During several months of working on the assembly line, I began to detect a cyclic pattern: management would set goals for quality and productivity and press hard to meet them. Once the goals were met, the workers and managers would tend to ease off and relax, which would cause quality to suffer. After a while it became clear that every drive for improvement ended in a leveling off and a downward cycle. Some veteran autoworkers interpreted these downturns as a return to the old GM days, which generated anxiety and grumbling. What seemed miraculous, however, was how team members and managers were rejuvenated as they worked to reverse each cycle. Slowly but surely, trust and mutual confidence were earned as employees struggled through these cycles of change.

Accepting Toyota's principle that quality must come first is a long, slow process that often runs against the grain of conventional thought. Only after an acceptable level of quality is reached can full production be achieved. Whenever a new model is introduced, NUMMI shuts down its line for a few weeks to allow time for training and to achieve acceptable quality levels. Only then is *takt* time adjusted to increase production. But it takes time, working under pressure, for team members and managers to learn that they must be in control of the process before productivity can be increased. When the pressure from top management gets too great, however, lower-level managers often fall back on the old ways. "It's an old pattern," Mike Mulleague said. "I learned it at GM, and I'll tell you, nobody ever kicked my ass for failing to meet production quotas!" He added, "When the pressure's on, half of the people in this place will revert to their old ways, pushing cars out the door. I'm no exception."

## TRUST UNDER PRESSURE

NUMMI's kind of trust is not an abstract concept—rather, it develops from working together productively under tension. I saw its benefits one day when a group meeting blew up. A manager had demanded that Roger Gallet eliminate a job on the line without first consulting his group. During the morning break Gallet informed his team members, with whom he had worked for a number of years, that he had already made the change. The meeting instantly turned into pandemonium. One team member shouted angrily, "You know, we've got a stake in this place too! This is a lot of shit! Why weren't we consulted? Aren't we important?" Another team member blurted out, "Management's got to learn to play by the rules. It's not GM, you know, a one-way street. I don't want to see this place fold, but this is sure as hell no way to run a plant." As "Greensleeves" began to play, signaling the end of the break, the meeting broke up without resolution. On the way back to the line one of the team members commented to another, "This isn't like Roger. He must be being pushed [by] the higher-ups." The other team member responded, "Yeah, but it doesn't make it right. He's got to know how we feel."

At the end of the shift, Gallet called an impromptu meeting and explained, "I was under pressure this morning, and I didn't want to hear what you had to say. I'm sorry." The group's mood shifted, becoming more relaxed and positive. A team member whispered, "Well, at least he's honest." She added, "You know, Roger's really okay. We cut him some slack." Afterward, some of the team members tried to soften the morning's harshness by touching Gallet on the arm and making friendly comments as they went to their lockers. It became apparent how the trust that had been established between Gallet and his group over the years was playing an important role by absorbing conflict and redirecting energy.

When a manager falls back on old patterns and turns authoritarian, he or she invariably provokes an angry response from team members that diminishes trust. At one point, management announced a policy that groups should rotate jobs every two and a half hours to reduce injuries, level out the workload, and counter boredom. In one meeting, as the manager discussed the policy, some members voiced heated objections because some of them preferred to do just one job. As the tension built and the manager began to lose control, he put one hand on his hip and with the other pointed at the fifteen assembled team members, blustering, "We're going to rotate whether you like it or not! Management is not going to tolerate the defects coming from this group. And if you don't perform, you might not be around much longer!"

Hands waved as team members asked to be recognized, but he ignored them. An angry feeling spread across the group as a woman shouted, "Why not find out what the majority wants? Let me tell you, sir, you're gone a good deal of the time, and you don't know what the hell goes on here." Others yelled, "Who the hell do you think you are?" The group leader backed behind the table and assumed a defensive posture, putting both hands on his hips. Facing the group, he said, "There are some things you vote on and some things you don't. There is a time to get input, but I don't have to take a vote on it or get your blessing. You'd never get consensus from this group anyway. My role is to *give* you information! Rotation! We're going to have it!"

He stalked off, but the team members stayed behind, talking angrily in small groups. One man said, "You just can't get the American out of the manager. Jesus, it's getting just like GM. I thought the Japanese owned half of this plant. Must be the other half!" What little trust might have existed had quickly been obliterated by this angry exchange. But when word of the meeting spread, NUMMI's response was to counsel the group leader in more effective ways of fostering participation and handling conflict. His performance has improved, and he still works at the plant.

## FORGING A THIRD CULTURE

As we noted earlier in this chapter, it was the creation of a third culture that had enabled NUMMI to make such a radical transformation. I am convinced that if GM alone had set out to re-create this plant, it would surely have failed. Not only was GM's mass production system unable to meet the market's demands for low cost and high quality, but the beliefs that had been imprinted on its managers, union leaders, and rank-and-file workers were too deeply ingrained to allow the kind of change that was necessary. Most employees at NUMMI agree. As Gary Convis said, "The Japanese have been a critical factor in what we've accomplished. It's not until you work with them, learn the principles from them, that you begin to understand how they see the world and how they feel. You know, this system can't be learned from a book. My understanding keeps deepening, and my commitment to managing in a more open way gets stronger. It has evolved over time from seeing why they do things how they do them. So the idea that we could have learned what we have without the Japanese is absurd."

GM's seasoned, experienced workforce provided a hospitable environment for the Japanese contributions. NUMMI's tolerant atmosphere, in which differences of opinion are accepted and valued, proved to be another important ingredient. The joint venture inherited a workforce of individuals who had known one another for many years. Though racism and sexism can be found in any organization, NUMMI's employees (more than 50 percent of whom come from minority groups) get along with a relatively low degree of friction. This tolerance, which stems in part from old friendships, has helped unite this multicultural, multiethnic workforce, often bridging serious conflict. In fact, employees speak proudly of the plant's diverse workforce, commenting that the differences between people are a source of strength. Jesse Palomino, a UAW committeeman, explained, "You know, this place is a blend. We have Mexicans, blacks, whites, Japanese, men, and women." Palomino tapped his head. "And we all think a little differently. That's *gooooood.*" Sherry Ward, a veteran autoworker, was also proud of NUMMI's multicultural workforce. She said, "When the plant first opened, *Fortune* did an article saying that workers came from the barrio and the ghetto. You know, I felt bad. I look at my friends here—middle-age people I've known most of my working life—and I don't see them that way. Hell, after reading that article, I'd be afraid to come in this place! You know, we're the pride of America—autoworkers, middle class. We're a culturally diverse group—isn't that the way it *should* be?"

## POINTS OF CONVERGENCE . . .

While the tolerant UAW workforce offered fertile ground from which a new culture might grow, the Japanese and the Americans had to discover whether or not they had enough in common to make it work. As it happened, NUMMI's new operating philosophy suited both sides. Employment security was a concept that both the Japanese and the Americans liked. Toyota's inclusive decision-making style was quickly embraced by both management and the union. NUMMI's union leaders respected Toyota coordinators' detailed job knowledge and their readiness to roll up their sleeves and get their hands dirty. Also greatly respected was the self-discipline that the Japanese brought to their work. One manager marveled at how the Japanese analyze a problem. "They'll sit there and spend hours on it," he said, "asking hundreds of 'whys' until it's solved."

## . . . AND DIVERGENCE

Little by little, the Japanese and Americans found that they shared some fundamentally important views. They managed to integrate two different cultures around some fundamental concepts such as employment security, mutual respect, and trust. Still, the Japanese communitarian beliefs frequently conflicted with American individualism.

Hayao Kawai, a Jungian analyst and professor of education and Japanese studies at Kyoto University, once explained to me the basis of the Japanese communal spirit.[6] Japanese children, he said, are raised according to a maternal principle to be open to others, who are seen as the source of all nourishment. But the Japanese communitarian spirit has deeper roots. "In the East we think of ourselves as related to everything—animals, plants, and humans," Kawai explained. "This table is no different than you and me. By saying 'I,' we separate ourselves from each other. So rather than saying 'I love you,' I might say only 'love.' That's enough. We don't like to use 'I' and 'you.' Often if you ask a Japanese 'What do you think?' he'll say, 'Don't know.' "[7]

Kawai described how Japan's ancient animistic religions conceived of the center, where Christians place God, as nothing. In this way the center is kept open, allowing the entry of other religions, with which life can be harmonized and balanced. For this reason, said Kawai, "Nobody wants to be at the center. Whenever the emperor takes power, it leads Japan into trouble." This inclusive maternal principle, he said, manifests itself in the all-embracing concept of lifetime employment.

This Japanese concept of self as part of a larger community reveals itself in numerous ways at NUMMI. One day in the assembly offices, one of Toyota's senior coordinators explained how he had first seen the difference—in how Americans and Japanese compete in sports. He said, "Here in America, the competition is among individuals, but Japan competes as a group. If you look at how many gold medals Americans got from Olympic Games, you can easily see just how capable and skillful each American is. In contrast, Japanese as individuals cannot compete with Americans at all."

The coordinator, who has spent a good deal of time in American friends' homes, extends this view to the company, saying that Japanese workers pool their efforts to produce a better product. He explained, "The most important thing is the extent to which each individual joins his effort in the company he or she serves. It is a competition of a company's product, not an individual competition. Each Japanese individual is far less strong than each American, but when they join their efforts, it is stronger. American individualism is not bad if you look at it from the perspective of an individual. However, it is big trouble for a company or for industry."

Interestingly, the clash over communitarian and individualistic values shows up most clearly around the very points on which Japanese and Americans can most easily agree—employment security, participative decision making, and plant discipline, for instance. It seems as though an invisible line divides the two. When it is crossed, tempers often flare.

For instance, when NUMMI first started up, "Greensleeves" would play before each shift and Toyota coordinators would lead the Americans in warm-up exercises designed to loosen up their muscles and enhance the group spirit. Over time, interest in the exercises died off, though the music still played. One team member who appreciates the Japanese influence at the plant nevertheless quit the exercises, saying "They just went too far." She laughed, "I mean, we're *Americans*. We're not robots!"

Some Americans also said that Japanese people's loyalty to their employers goes beyond what they can feel comfortable with. One manager explained how in Japan employers develop loyalty early by taking on high school age youngsters as interns. He said the children know that if they work for Toyota they'll be taken care of. He added, "We don't have anything like that here. It's not the same type of commitment. That's why the Toyota model in its pure form wouldn't work here at NUMMI."

But Toyota coordinators say that, lacking a strong group consciousness, American companies are at a disadvantage when competing with the Japanese. A young Toyota coordinator expressed concern with the distance he feels exists between American workers and their employers. He said, "Japanese workers make a lifetime commitment to their employers, but Americans lack this sense of 'belonging-ness.' American workers exercise individual choice, but by working as individuals, knowledge cannot settle down."

He continued, explaining how the Japanese family fosters collective, or communal, effort. He said of the typical Japanese household, "It's like the aircraft carrier that supports the fighter." An American manager commented that he thinks the Japanese commitment to the employer and American individualism are inherently incompatible. "I understand, but most of us put our families first. We work to live, not live to work. I don't think the American worker will ever be like the Japanese. I just don't think that model would ever work here."

Sometimes the tension between these two opposing beliefs surfaces as Toyota coordinators press the fine points of the system and unknowingly transgress the line between the two national cultures. For instance, after one shift a senior Toyota coordinator was training a group of managers in standardized work. Suddenly he squatted down to count some trays filled with screws, bolts, and nuts. According to the standardized work parts sheet, six trays should have been on the left and two on the right. He loudly counted out the trays one by one, using exaggerated arm movements to draw attention to his point: "One, two, three, four, five, six, seven, eight, *nine!* Chart says six plus two equals eight, but I counted *nine!*" In mock disbelief he exclaimed, "How can this be?" As the managers listened, a team leader nearby responded angrily, muttering under his breath about the Japanese attention to detail: "Picky, picky. They'll find mistakes like a fly finds shit. Works great in theory, but not down here!"

Some American workers fear they may lose their individualism by conforming. "Personal Touch" parties, NUMMI's equivalent of drinking sake after work at Toyota, were established to help build a sense of fellowship. One night at a gathering at a popular Mexican restaurant, a group from Chassis was drinking and blowing off steam. A team member I'll call "Ramon" left early after angrily denouncing the company and the team concept, and the conversation turned to him. Ramon was known as a complainer who did as little work as possible and was counting the days until he could retire. Team members agreed that Ramon thought he'd get attention by complaining. "Like the squeaky wheel gets the grease?" a young new team member asked innocently. "Not exactly," said the group leader. "In Japan, the sticky nail gets the hammer! By God, Ramon's lucky we're Americans. If this were Japan, he'd get clobbered!"

## FINDING COMMON GROUND

What is significant is how NUMMI has managed these differences, successfully steering around seemingly intractable problems and focusing energy on critical issues on which the Japanese and Americans must find agreement. Nowhere is this more evident than in the way Toyota introduced the production system to the American workforce. Higashi said that at first the Japanese coordinators at NUMMI had not known how to approach the Americans and that they had had to resist the urge to transfer the process in its pure form. A senior Toyota coordinator reinforced Higashi's view, saying that he had found it hard to transfer the method the way he had expected to. At Toyota, he said, he had simply explained how to do something and team leaders had followed without question. "But at NUMMI," he said, "I didn't get the same reaction." He explained that he had had to learn how to compromise since he could not force his way onto the American workers. "I could not transfer the Toyota way in its pure form. The new way had to be localized. It had to fit correctly with American ways. Otherwise team members simply refuse to participate. It took a year for me to discover a way to get the Americans to agree with me. Once they did, it became possible to join our efforts."

Osamu Kimura said the cultural exchange has worked both ways: "Despite our differences as Japanese and Americans, we found that we share many important similarities." Kimura was a serious executive, but he had a personable manner that managers and team members appreciated. During union negotiations he would often play poker and drink with the union leaders. He worried, however, that language obscured the fine points of communication that are so critical to building relationships. Kimura explained, "Practical language, discussing quality or cost, is not so difficult. But jokes at dinner, which are an important means of communication, are most difficult. Americans sometimes say that Japanese are very shy and do not like to joke. But that is not true. It's just that most American jokes end very quickly, with a fast sentence or two. Americans laugh, but I cannot understand! Because of the language, we cannot join in those areas! So sad."

But the gap was being narrowed, and many Japanese coordinators believed that their personal relationships with their American colleagues were helping them understand the American culture. One compared GM and Toyota to oil and water and NUMMI to a small salad bowl: "Unless you mix them well, the oil and water will never become dressing. NUMMI is like a small salad bowl—a big one would never work—and communication is the way to mix them. It takes a while to mix them to make a good dressing."

## THE DURABILITY OF NUMMI'S SYSTEM

The joint venture has successfully weathered pressures that have caused other enterprises to founder. Since the late 1980s, Toyota has gradually recalled its NUMMI management and technical team, which today includes Iwao Itoh (NUMMI's fourth president) and about twenty-five managers and coordinators. However, Toyota began to scale back its presence at NUMMI only after being assured that its key principles had been successfully diffused and that the American management team had learned to manage the dynamic system. Like his predecessors, Itoh is conscious of the fact that the system needs continuous reinforcement to keep workers from slipping into complacency. He said, "My greatest challenge is to make sure that both managers and team members truly internalize the concepts. That is the key to successful diffusion."

With few exceptions, the original American management team remains nearly intact, though there have been substantial changes in the union. In the 1991 election Tony DeJesus lost his seat as president, and in the 1994 election George Nano lost the bargaining committee chairmanship to People's Caucus leader Richard Aguilar. Charles Curry, who succeeded DeJesus as president, won by representing the People's Caucus, though he joined the Administrative Caucus a few months later. In 1995 Curry was replaced as president by Leo Garcia, a leader of the People's Caucus, and Bruce Lee retired as regional director.

As noted earlier, NUMMI remains efficient and the quality of its products continues to rise. The internal quality audits done by Toyota, GM, and NUMMI over the last few years were validated in May 1994, when NUMMI's Geo Prizm was given the highest J. D. Power and Associates rating ever given to an American-built vehicle. In 1994 NUMMI had its most profitable year ever.[8] These facts have not escaped Toyota's attention as it continues to invest in the joint venture's expansion. The FTC also took note of NUMMI's importance when, in late 1993, it set aside its original order that had limited the joint venture to a twelve-year life. The Commission explained that it had made the decision because of the evidence that NUMMI was helping General Motors "to reap the benefits of gaining first-hand experience with an efficient production system."[9]

Despite its success, NUMMI's status as a joint venture makes it vulnerable—a condition faced by USS-POSCO and other joint ventures that depend on the uncertain world of international trade and politics. Just recently, fallout from the 1995 U.S.-Japan auto trade talks threatened to impose steep tariffs on parts imported from Toyota, which would have raised NUMMI's costs by a half-billion dollars. Dennis Cuneo said, "It was only through a frantic last-minute lobbying effort that we escaped the administration's 'hit list,' " which could have doomed this vibrant company.

## CONCLUSIONS

NUMMI's case is especially significant because it reveals that an organization's culture can be fundamentally altered. As we have seen in each of the companies, a force great enough to induce change, or "unfreeze" the organization, must lead any effort at transformation.[10] Such a force must be powerful enough to cancel out individuals' natural fears of letting go of their core beliefs, but it cannot be so great — as it was at Douglas Aircraft — as to paralyze the organization's ability to act. For instance, NUMMI's union leaders and team members had to suspend their long-entrenched beliefs that management would take advantage of them before they could learn Toyota's principles. Their past experience with time-and-motion studies — which had been used by management to increase output at workers' expense — made it difficult for them to trust that standardizing work and setting *takt* time were anything more than a prelude to a speedup. Dissident voices from within the union, not the most muted of which was that of Victor Reuther, brother of UAW founder Walter Reuther, warned of the disaster that would surely befall American labor if its leaders cooperated with management.[11] However, once NUMMI employees began to believe that they would not be abused and that they would share fairly in the fruits of the company's success, they could begin to embrace the system's principles and let go of their old, dysfunctional beliefs. Still, changing some beliefs has been hard. As one American manager concluded, "Maybe I'll get seventy or eighty percent of the way in my lifetime, but I'll never be perfect!"

This is an especially hard transition to make because such beliefs, which have been reinforced by experience for years, give direction and security to individuals as they navigate through their daily lives. They are not given up easily, and it is little wonder that considerable force is required to induce change of this kind and to sustain it over time.[12] In this case the impetus came partly from the shutdown and the resulting unemployment but more from two added factors: NUMMI's commitment to treating its workforce fairly and Toyota's integrated production system, which demanded participation, mutual respect, and trust. There is little doubt that without these twin incentives for change, little progress could have been made.

Also crucial was the way in which Toyota assumed a dominant voice in the joint venture and took full responsibility for teaching the Americans how to implement and manage its potent production system. Toyota's role offers some important insights into advantages that foreign partners can bring to joint ventures, a lesson lost at USS-POSCO, where U.S. Steel forced its South Korean partners into a subordinate position.[13]

Toyota's managers resisted the temptation to forge ahead with a unified vision of how the system should be implemented in its pure form; instead, both the Japanese and Americans learned as they went. By adopting a "go-slow" attitude, both sides remained open to points of resistance as they arose and were able to steer around them. By tolerating ambiguity and searching for consensus, Toyota's managers established the beginnings of mutual respect and trust with the American workers and managers. Toyota's attitudes stand in sharp contrast to those of Mazda when it established a plant in Michigan in 1988.[14] Mazda's assembly plant was not a joint venture, though it had some characteristics similar to NUMMI's because of its agreement to hire an all-union workforce. However, Mazda failed to lay sufficient groundwork and to establish a mutual cultural understanding with the American workers. Mazda had little understanding of the American unions' belief structure, and the unionists were suspicious of their Japanese bosses' motives. The UAW local adopted a confrontational attitude toward Mazda's management and resisted the introduction of Mazda's production system. Grievances mounted, and Mazda, in the hope of avoiding negative publicity, ordered its workers not to speak publicly. Mazda's tactics only confirmed the union leaders' worst fears. Cooperation and teamwork broke down as the UAW's New Directions, a wing of the union that opposes cooperation with management, won control. Thus, despite Mazda's hopes of a cooperative and profitable venture with its unionized American workforce, the company's failure to examine both its own and the UAW's beliefs and assumptions led into a morass of conflict that in all likelihood could have been avoided.

Finally, NUMMI contributes significantly to our narrative in yet another way. Its story leaves little doubt about the vital role played by the way in which work is organized. It was the day-to-day influence of Toyota's production system that gradually welded NUMMI's workforce and its managers into a single team. The case of Douglas Aircraft, by contrast, is a stark reminder of what happens when the production system is ignored. NUMMI clearly demonstrates how the principles of new human relationships must be embedded in how an organization conducts its daily work to achieve a true cultural transformation.

NUMMI hints at another important issue — that producing successful products leads to expanded opportunities for employees and managers alike. NUMMI's impressive ten-year record has been a microcosm of that principle. However, it has been created on a rising tide of sales and investments by Toyota. Just what would happen if Toyota's sales or its investments in NUMMI were curtailed, or if NUMMI's managers and workers became complacent in their success, is an open question. It is an issue that transcends NUMMI, however, and one that we will examine in detail in the final chapter.

# PART VI

# RESTORING PROSPERITY

# CHAPTER FIFTEEN

# TOWARD A CULTURE OF COOPERATION

LET US NOW RETURN to the beginning of our story. Remember how Korean steelmaker Yoh Sang Whan warned that without a vibrant economy the United States would be destined for stagnation and decay? Recall his belief that America's industrial problem is a "culture" problem? As we toured the four companies, it was hard to miss the truth in his observations. We learned firsthand how managers and workers had grown complacent during the postwar economic boom. We saw how their attitudes had been shaped by a system of work that had fostered self-destructive beliefs and habits. Over time, they had become unable to respond effectively to an economy that had suddenly changed, and they could not adapt quickly enough to avoid the devastating consequences.

Thousands of men and women—managers, engineers, and hourly workers—had lost their security and their high-paying jobs at Douglas Aircraft, U.S. Steel's Pittsburg Works, Hewlett-Packard's Santa Clara division, and the GM plant at Fremont as these companies slashed their payrolls to survive. The evidence is stark, and the message is clear. There is little doubt that unless American industry finds a way to break out of its insularity and foster new and productive employee relationships, the future will be bleak.

Nevertheless, as we probed deeply into these companies, we found compelling evidence that something new was being born. We could see the outlines of a new compact being forged, however fitfully, between workers and managers as they strained under the crushing forces of change. This new compact may seem elementary at first because it seems like common sense, but make no mistake: it goes to the heart of everything that is wrong with American industry. It suggests a new set of assumptions by which managers, union leaders, and workers can be guided into the future. It is also a harbinger of the change that is sweeping through America, and it carries powerful suggestions for redesigning public-sector organizations—notably education.

The compact's implications change what we mean by "human resources," redefining it to stand for the ability to work interdependently and cooperatively, to participate in decision making, and to develop mutually respectful, trusting relationships. It places the highest priority on being able to learn how to learn. These qualities are the antithesis of those that were created by the mass production system of the past, and many observers have doubted whether managers and workers could adapt to the new reality. But, incredible as it may seem, by breaking with mass production and adopting new, flexible production systems, these companies have actually *produced* these necessary human qualities. Naturally, not everyone can rise to the challenge. Still, as we have seen, the ingredients are now at hand to begin building a new economy, and those who can grasp the opportunity created by this massive economic transformation will prosper.

During our examination of the four companies, we witnessed this new compact in its infancy. We saw how increased competition and uncertainty were forcing managers, union leaders, and workers to learn how to work cooperatively with one another across the traditional boundaries that had previously separated them. Each had to break with tradition and take on increased responsibility. Managers had to disregard the harsh lessons taught by mass production and learn how to treat their employees fairly, according to mutual agreements. Union leaders had to risk being called "Judas goats" and learn to cooperate with managers. Working interdependently required managers, union leaders, and workers to learn to treat one another with respect. Slowly, confidence developed that each side would live up to the new covenant. To be sure, the four companies we researched progressed at an uneven pace.

Our findings repudiate the increasingly popular view that the work of America can be done by nomadic employees who wander, without allegiance, from one company to the next. In fact, the evidence we have collected suggests just the opposite. The companies that will be the leaders of tomorrow's economy will be the ones that treat their employees like assets today. This requirement is rooted neither in romanticism nor in morality. Rather, it is being imposed by the self-interested demands of survival. In the uncertain conditions of the new economy, successful companies will have to depend on a core of loyal employees who know how to work cooperatively and act decisively as though with a single mind and body.

## A NEW PATH TO PROSPERITY

But how can American industry throw off the cultural legacy that produced such awesome wealth and power? How can the heroic images of tough industrialists such as Andrew Carnegie and Henry Ford, or militant labor leaders such as John L. Lewis and Walter Reuther, be abandoned? The answer is revealed on the shop floors, in the union halls, and in the executive suites of the companies we studied. After seeing what we did, could anyone still believe that conflict and mistrust should define the relationship among managers, union leaders, and workers? Can there be any doubt that it will take the collective effort of all employees to get America back on the path to industrial preeminence? There is no doubt in my mind.

But it will not be easy. It will mean rewriting the social compact that has governed the course of American history and that has been reflected in our industrial relations for the better part of a century. Since Plato, philosophers and social critics have argued that the relationships between the citizen and the state, and between employers and employees, should be regulated by mutual obligation.[1] Under America's pluralistic form of government, the common good was to be voiced by the people. Founding Father James Madison wrote that the purpose of America's pluralistic form of government was to express the public good—the welfare of the peo-

ple—which would be established by the push and pull of differing interests.[2] But these founding principles were defeated by the pursuit of self-
interest and produced just the opposite—bitter, destructive human
relationships.

In this sense, the new compact is conservative: it arrives at the same
conclusions reached by philosophers such as Plato, Thomas Hobbes, and
John Locke hundreds of years ago. Its central premise is that the relationships between management and workers must now be governed by mutual obligations. Adam Smith spelled it out more than two centuries ago
in *The Wealth of Nations*, noting that wealth has a vital purpose beyond
satisfying individual wants.[3] Instead, he said, wealth is necessary to provide
the state with the means to pay for public services. In today's context,
Smith's view translates as follows: without a vibrant and expanding economy to provide a rising standard of living for *everyone*, America will surely
deteriorate.

Success in this new and unpredictable environment can only be assured by the mutual effort of managers and workers, plus the creation of a
new social framework to hold it together. A pervasive sense of mutual
obligation must be at the center of such a new compact. Employees must
be secure in the knowledge that they are important to their company's
well-being, that they will be treated fairly (under terms of employment to
which both employees and employers agree), and that they will share
fairly in the fruits of their labor, also to be spelled out in such agreements.
And to the degree feasible, they must be secure in their jobs. Only in this
way will a vibrant, expanding economy provide a rising standard of living
for everyone. As we are beginning to realize, America's industrial success
has become everyone's business.

## ESTABLISHING A NEW COMPACT

Reversing a century of hostile labor relations and replacing them with a
new compact that says "We are all in this together" is no easy task. True,
reengineering a corporation can be reduced to "three easy steps," but the
reality is that 85 percent of reengineering projects fail.[4] Our own experience shows that bringing about this kind of change requires a galvanic
force that will alter the underlying (and usually unacknowledged) beliefs

that have historically guided industrial behavior. Organizations that successfully transform themselves seem to discover the following five principles.

## 1. *Unfreezing*

I remember the sad sight of USS-POSCO's shuttered rod and pipe mills, which once employed thousands of steelworkers. In 1990 they stood empty, their windows broken, tall grass growing in the doorways. The dilapidated buildings were grim reminders of how in their struggle U.S. Steel managers and union leaders had become blind to their collective interest. A similar kind of myopia had nearly destroyed Douglas Aircraft. John McDonnell, chairman and CEO of McDonnell Douglas, acknowledged that he wished he had moved to reform the giant subsidiary more quickly. But he also marveled at how Douglas Aircraft's managers had failed to see the warning signs until it was almost too late. Success had blinded them to what was happening in the outside world, which had abruptly changed. McDonnell was surprised how impenetrable the Douglas mind-set had been even though employees must have sensed they were on the brink of disaster. In similar fashion, GM had actually had to close its Fremont plant before the cycle of destructiveness could be broken. And—though far less dramatic but equally painful for the employees who lost their jobs—Hewlett-Packard's Santa Clara division had to face imminent failure before it could respond. The lessons taught by these companies are clear: a powerful discordant note that signals "change or perish" must penetrate deeply into individuals' consciousness before any progress can be made.

Kurt Lewin and Edgar Schein understood this years ago when each wrote about the difficulty of shaking organizations out of their fearful paralysis.[5] The seemingly simple act of bringing everyone together in a threatened organization and agreeing on mutual obligations is one of the highest forms of leadership. Doing so is supremely difficult. It is crucial, however, because companies that are unable to achieve this first step cannot take strategic action and are condemned to making only limited changes.

## 2. *Discovering Mutual Obligations*

Some companies, such as Hewlett-Packard, inherit a productive culture. Hewlett-Packard was endowed with strong human bonds that enabled Santa Clara's managers and employees to redesign the division radically—no matter what happened, they knew they were in it together. The HP Way, generous profit sharing, and stock option plans had already established the concept that the employees were the company's owners. This fact helped Santa Clara's engineers to take responsibility for learning how to work with customers and its managers to take responsibility for making vital business decisions.

But what about other companies that are not as fortunate as Hewlett-Packard? Can mutual obligations be created, especially in unionized companies, where management and labor have always been antagonists? One has only to look NUMMI and USS-POSCO to find an answer. At NUMMI, managers and UAW leaders alike knew that their survival depended on their ability to transform the old GM plant. They took full advantage of propitious conditions to consciously establish a collective mind-set from the beginning. The management team was selected largely on applicants' willingness and ability to adopt such a new vision. The UAW leaders recognized the opportunity to try something new and helped pioneer a revolutionary concept in American industrial relations—the idea that management and the workforce could work more productively and profitably as partners than as adversaries.

A similar cultural conversion at USS-POSCO took longer to take root. When we began working at the plant in 1990, angry steelworkers and union leaders were doing everything short of sabotage to prevent the company from progressing. But just four years later, we saw compelling evidence that a new outlook was emerging. For the first time, a labor-management team had jointly launched quality improvement projects in the plant, steelworkers were regularly taking trips to visit customers, and steelworkers had been put in charge of product-related customer relations. For the first time in the joint venture's history, steelworkers and managers agreed that their collective efforts were needed to help improve quality, efficiency, teamwork, and customer satisfaction.[6]

## 3. *Establishing a Climate of Security and Fairness*

But for employees to cross this historic divide, they must be confident that their jobs are secure and that they will be treated fairly if conditions worsen. Consider what happened when John McDonnell took the necessary but harsh step of firing 2,500 managers at Douglas Aircraft. The shock waves that emanated from the mass firings, and the layoffs that ultimately cost the jobs of 40,000 men and women, all but paralyzed this once proud company. Under these conditions it became impossible to take any but the most limited steps.

On the other hand, Hewlett-Packard's Santa Clara employees expected that management would not show them the door after the division was redesigned to run with fewer employees. Most had internalized the HP Way, which spells out mutual obligations and expectations, and it gave them assurance that management would help them find jobs elsewhere in the company if necessary.[7] In 1993, although two thirds of Santa Clara's employees said they were worried about being laid off from their jobs, most reported that they felt confident they would be treated fairly.[8]

Similarly, having been seriously jolted by the GM shutdown, NUMMI employees committed themselves to learning the Toyota production system. It meant setting aside mistrust and taking responsibility for improving the production system, even if it meant working themselves out of a job. It was clear from the beginning that change of this kind would be impossible unless the employees felt reasonably secure. Gary Convis, now NUMMI's senior vice president, explained, "Employment security is terribly important to a system like ours. But the real revolution is that team members have learned to expect to be treated fairly. That's what really makes this place tick." What Convis referred to was NUMMI's flat wage rate, a profit-sharing system that treats team members equally, and a fair and equitable conflict resolution process. Just as HP employees had taken the tenets of the HP Way to heart, NUMMI employees have now begun to create a culture of mutual obligation, security, and fairness.

## 4. *Internalizing the Principles*

But these concepts will remain abstract if they are not internalized by managers and workers. How else can employees be expected to give up the dysfunctional beliefs and behavior created by the mass production system and master the new ones? As we have seen, this kind of transition is difficult, and there must be something more than fear to induce employees to embrace the new pact. The answer, however, is surprisingly simple. As companies make the switch from mass production to what are now being called "high-performance" work systems, the flow of effort is reversed.[9] Instead of pushing huge volumes of standardized products down the assembly line and out the door, these production systems start with the customer's needs and work backward down the line all the way to the suppliers of the most rudimentary parts. Becoming responsive to customers' changing requirements by means of a flexible but tightly linked system produces a "pull" up and down the chain of human activity. Managers and workers learn that they must work cooperatively for the common good—a discovery that actually generates interdependence and ultimately mutual respect and trust.[10]

## 5. *Welcoming Conflict and Developing Trust*

Working interdependently across boundaries naturally leads to conflict. But when that conflict is well managed and employees have confidence that they will be treated fairly according to agreements already established with management, they learn to disagree and express unpopular points of view without making personal attacks or threatening to strike or walk out. As individuals learn that differences can be successfully resolved without the threat of force, conflict is transformed into a creative process that generates confidence and trust. In a turbulent environment, that trust becomes a critical resource, because it helps to absorb the continuous shocks of change.

Of the companies in our study, NUMMI is perhaps the most vivid example of such a transformation. We saw how both managers and workers had learned to use conflict creatively as they took responsibility for product quality, as well as for continuously improving the system. Not surprisingly, working in a constantly changing environment requires employees to make fast decisions under pressure. At the same time, they expect to be included in the decisions that affect them. It is a hard balance to strike correctly. Managed right, it produces a strain that tests the durability of the new human relationships. The tension produces cycles of change that are difficult to manage because they upset employees' "natural" rhythms. When goals are met, employees tend to relax, causing defects to increase and quality to suffer. When quality declines, management exerts corrective pressure, which stresses the whole organization. When the pressure gets too great, managers and employees tend to fall back on their old behavior. More than once at NUMMI we found ourselves in the middle of pitched verbal battles. But the company and the union managed the boundary between healthy conflict and destructive behavior carefully, because they knew that without mutual respect their system could not operate. Over time, through trial and error, managers, union leaders, and team members have developed (and are continuing to develop) confidence in one another and trust that they will be treated fairly and with dignity.

## RECASTING THE UNION'S ROLE

Union leaders often worry, with good reason, that "lean production" systems will spell the end of trade unionism. After all, how many have watched companies all but dismantle their workforces under the banner of "restructuring" or "reengineering"?[11] But our study leads to a different conclusion. Far from diminishing the union's role, this emerging compact between labor and management casts the union in a whole new light. The union continues to function in its traditional role of representing its employees and balancing management's power, but it now also becomes an instrument of productive change. Under the new assumptions of mutual obligation and cooperation, the union's focus shifts. In the years of mass production's heyday, the union's confrontational tactics were entirely rational.[12] Visible, angry conflict with management symbolized the lack of a common interest and the absence of fairness. Conflict reminded workers that management could not be trusted and were out to strip workers of everything they valued—secure jobs, good wages, and control over their working conditions.

The new compact, however, shifts labor's interest from antagonizing

management with grievances brought by a minority of workers to representing the majority of the workforce. The need for cooperation is an incentive for the union to resolve conflict quickly and fairly, and the
symbolic value of confrontation all but disappears. The new compact also
changes the concept of collective bargaining. Traditionally, after negotiations were concluded, labor and management walked away from the bargaining table and reassumed their adversarial positions. Then, the
grievance system functioned as the chief means of keeping antagonisms
alive and visible. It was an expression of a failure of human relations. But
under the new compact the relationship between labor and management
becomes more constructive. The union takes on a broader set of interests,
including not only the traditional ones such as safety, promotion standards, training, and pensions but also new ones such as child care, education, and environmental issues. For instance, both NUMMI and
USS-POSCO discovered that their unions could be powerful allies in representing the company in public forums. Who better than union leaders
to speak about the need for more jobs when NUMMI needed environmental agencies' approval to expand? Who better than union leaders to
speak for USS-POSCO's employees' welfare when the company was
threatened by a potentially devastating decision by the International
Trade Commission?[13]

But making this transformation is difficult. Changing from adversaries to allies refutes the basic principles of labor relations. We saw at
Douglas Aircraft, USS-POSCO, and NUMMI how union leaders had felt
the sting of being called backsliders and sellouts when they took the first
steps to cooperate with management. Suspicion of collaborating with the
company is buried just as deeply in rank and filers' bones as authoritarian
instincts are lodged in managers'. Unions' representative form of government and the turmoil of union politics also slow change and inject a certain sense of unpredictability into the process. No sooner does one group
assume leadership and head in a new direction than an opposition group
advocating a return to the old ways forms. Thus, trying to reshape the
union while being accountable at the polls is every bit as daunting as re-
forming management. To succeed, elected representatives must demonstrate that they have their members' interests at heart. Working with a
company under these conditions is not easy, because any move to coop-

erate with management can be quickly interpreted as selling out. In an untrusting environment, cooperating with the company may be political suicide.

## THE "TEACHING" ORGANIZATION

Transforming this powerful industrial culture requires continuous education and training to help managers, union leaders, and workers arrive at a new and inclusive vision and to exchange their traditional adversarial relationships for cooperative ones. In fact, the companies we investigated that succeeded could be called the "learning organizations" about which so much has been written.[14] But remarkably, what this study shows is how, in the transformational process, they actually become "teaching organizations." They produce both the knowledge and the human qualities needed to function in a fast-changing environment.[15]

### 1. *Altering the Structure of Work*

The secret, as we have seen, lies first in creating a new management-worker relationship and then altering the production system to exert a "pull" throughout the organization. It is an axiom that *until the production system is altered, no progress can be made.* As we saw most dramatically at Hewlett-Packard and NUMMI, when a production system is thoroughly redesigned, every employee is pulled into an inherently unstable environment in which each has to learn rapidly how to adapt. Learning—or the lack of it—carries tangible consequences for everyone.

John Dewey, probably America's most renowned educator, once wrote about how experience shapes education.[16] According to Dewey, it was not until a student could form a meaningful question from experience that education could truly commence. Later, Swiss psychologist Jean Piaget demonstrated how children's curiosity led them to construct their own knowledge, which in turn influenced their behavior.[17] In much the same way, little useful learning could start in these companies until the very structure of work was changed. Once the structure was altered, however, employees were naturally led to ask new questions, the answers to most of which they found on the job.

For instance, Hewlett-Packard's redesign required engineers and workers to learn how to work interdependently and to take responsibility for decisions that had formerly been made by managers. When the company's Santa Clara division created self-managing teams and charged them with meeting their own revenue targets, engineers had no choice but to learn how to design their software to appeal to customers. Manager Bruce Greenwood said, "When we started out, my bosses just figured it would happen automatically. But it didn't, because working with customers was a foreign idea for our engineers. We also found out they couldn't learn it until they sweated it. It's not their natural tendency. Formal training and role playing are too artificial and abstract, and they have no real consequences." Hewlett-Packard senior scientist David Chu explained that unless concepts like joint customer product design and accountability are actually experienced, they are not internalized. Chu said, "Intellectual knowledge by itself does not necessarily induce changes in behavior because painful changes can be avoided."

## 2. Providing Just-in-Time Training

The "pull" principle also ensures that training is provided just in time, when it is needed. For instance, at NUMMI, especially in the early years of the joint venture, no one knew what kind of training would be needed. Gary Welters, a group leader, said, "Classroom training just wouldn't make sense out here on the floor, because we're breaking new ground every day. When problems come up, they have to be solved on the spot." For instance, trusting team members to stop the line when they see a defect is critical to NUMMI's production system. Though team members intellectually know that they should stop the line, some fail to do so out of the old fear that they will be disciplined. One day Welters explained the theory of stopping the line to his group and then sent team members back to work to put the theory into practice. Welters wanted to see if the lesson had been learned. He stood unnoticed, watching a Corolla with an obvious defect head toward a team that had previously resisted stopping the line. At the moment one of the team members saw the defect and reached up for the *andon* cord, a wide grin broke out on Welter's face. He said proudly, "I just wanted to see how they'd handle it. If you explain the principles and give them some room, they'll do the right thing. The key to it is responsibility. If people feel that they're responsible, they'll do the right thing. Group leaders who aren't trained right can blow it away in an instant by reaming out a team member. You've got to give them the freedom to fail."

On the other hand, as we saw in the early years at USS-POSCO, if work itself is not altered, training is of little value. In 1990, though the modernization had begun, conflict raged between management and the union and few substantive changes could be made in the operation of the older mills. Training in statistical process control had little value, because when operators returned to their jobs nothing of substance had changed. I remember how in 1990 one steelworker complained, "All I do is take these numbers here and put them there. Someone picks up the charts, and I never see them again." However, by 1994, when management and the unions had begun to work more cooperatively and steelworkers knew they had to learn statistical process control to satisfy the customer, training had greater value.

Douglas Aircraft was another case. John McDonnell and his executives assumed that training could lead the transformational effort, but, as we saw, even though Douglas employees said they had enjoyed the TQMS training, few of the concepts could be applied because the way aircraft were built remained fundamentally unchanged.

An important lesson to be drawn from our study is that, by itself, training cannot alter the deep cultural imprint of mass production. To do so requires something far more profound. Years of hands-on research have convinced me that training can support, but cannot lead, a transformational effort. It must be tailored to the job, it must be provided at just the right moment, and it must carry real consequences. Nevertheless, many executives and union leaders continue to hold the illusion that formal classroom instruction—which is often unrelated to actual job requirements—can lead an organizational transformation. The reasons are many. Training, like education, has intrinsic value, and many executives and union leaders believe in its inherent virtue. It is also a humane way to persuade employees to change their most deeply held beliefs in a way that avoids unpleasant conflict. But as we have also seen, nothing changes until the production system also changes, thus requiring the new principles to be internalized by workers and managers alike. In the absence of fundamental changes in a production system, the power of this kind of training to alter years of mistrust and skepticism is terribly limited. Even worse, training itself is often confused with substantive change, diverting attention from the more fundamental issues of fashioning a compact of cooperation and redesigning the production system.

## A NEW SOCIAL FRAMEWORK

But even after the production system is altered and these new principles are internalized, the newly created human relationships remain fragile. Trust and mutual respect can vanish in the face of pressures that pit an individual interest (job security) against the collective interest (survival of the company): imagine the consequences if NUMMI or Hewlett-Packard were to lay off large numbers of their employees. Given the turbulent world economy, such a prospect can never be dismissed. USS-POSCO Vice President Bill Haley put it bluntly when he told his union president that he hoped layoffs would never happen again but that he knew "There may be a cold, dark day when we have to say 'one hundred of you have to go.' " Christoph Buechtemann, a senior social scientist at RAND and expert on European work systems, explained, "Mutual obligations and fairness may not be voluntarily sustainable because the trust required is inherently fragile as long as one side can default without penalty. By itself, trust is not enough. In a volatile environment, 'trust,' 'mutual obligation,' and 'fairness' are never guaranteed and their interpretation can be highly controversial when conditions change. There must be some institutional arrangements to force both parties to negotiate to achieve a proper balance between individual and collective interests."[18]

Though existing labor law creates a social framework within which such agreements can be structured, it is an adversarial one that blinds both sides to their mutual interest. Congress's recent refusal to grant unions more power, organized labor's massive losses of membership, and the inability of President Clinton's Commission on the Future of Worker-Management Relations to offer a new legal and social framework are evidence that the traditional labor relations are failing.[19] Bill Usery, who served on the commission, told me recently, "I am completely despondent about the condition of labor relations in this country. It is the most difficult time I have ever experienced in my forty-three-year life in labor relations. It all comes down to our inability to agree on ways to balance collective rights against those of the individual."[20]

Our research has revealed how such a balance can be struck voluntarily, but can it be reinforced by popular will? Perhaps. But in America, where individualism still reigns, such a new social and legal structure can only follow a massive cultural change.[21] Whether or not these changes ultimately carry government sanction, their implications for an uncertain future remain clear. A new social compact is needed to create the human resources that will steer America back to industrial preeminence.

## THE UNCERTAIN FUTURE OF WORK IN AMERICA

Here we run into a problem. Once companies embark on this new path and everyone seizes responsibility for improving quality and reducing costs, management confronts a dilemma: it becomes possible to produce more goods of higher quality at lower cost with fewer employees. Author Jeremy Rifkin claims, "As many as 90 million jobs in a labor force of 124 million are potentially vulnerable to displacement."[22] What is to be done with employees who are no longer needed? How can employees who work themselves out of their jobs be reemployed?

One answer is that companies like NUMMI and Hewlett-Packard will grow as they become more productive and competitive and will produce more good jobs for their employees. But what about the other companies—even industries—that are not so fortunate? Employees displaced from shrinking companies or industries will need to find employment elsewhere. But will our economy grow and prosper with enough good jobs for all, or are we facing a future of maintaining a large adult population who will never work again? Are we, as Rifkin claims, facing the end of work as we have known it?[23]

The signs are not hopeful. Though newspaper headlines trumpet "U.S. Widens Its Competitiveness Lead" and "We're No. 1 Again," the recent economic recovery does not inspire much confidence. The numbers of high-paying manufacturing jobs continue to decline, and wages continue to fall.[24] By late 1993 worker productivity had increased at the fastest rate ever in seven years, and manufacturing costs were continuing to decline.[25] But three million manufacturing jobs disappeared between 1979 and 1992.[26] And between 1950 and 1993 the percentage of nonagricultural manufacturing jobs was cut in half, plummeting from 34 percent to 17 percent of total employment.[27]

The reason for the decline is that companies are investing in technologically advanced manufacturing equipment (investments in capital equipment have nearly doubled since 1984), which, as we have seen, enables them to run with fewer employees.[28] Policy analyst Richard Barnet reports that between 1979 and 1992, "The *Fortune* 500 companies presented 4.4 million of their employees with pink slips, a rate of around 340,000 a year."[29] When all businesses are included, the annual loss of jobs rises to 600,000.[30] Anthony Carnevale, chairman of the National Commission for Employment Policy, an independent think tank that reports to the president and the Congress, says that during the postwar economic boom change was "the worker's friend" because so many who lost jobs went on to better jobs and higher pay. But today, says Carnevale, "change has increasingly been associated with dislocation and declining opportunity."[31] The evidence suggests that such layoffs will continue through the 1990s, and, as for their impact, *Business Week* calls the layoffs "the most unsettling and disruptive event in Corporate America."[32]

The facts are that there are simply not enough high-wage manufacturing jobs to go around and that the impact of this predicament has been absorbed mainly by the young and poor families. According to one estimate, there are six times the number of working-age adults in poverty than the number of job openings at above-poverty wages.[33] Economists Lawrence Mishel and Jared Bernstein note, "The economy is failing most Americans, and not simply because of the early 1990s recession: we are in the midst of a long-term erosion of incomes and opportunities."[34] Richard Barnet describes visiting automated plants in the United States and Europe: "The scarcity of human beings on the factory floor in these places is spooky." He concludes that "steady jobs for good pay are becoming poignant memories or just dreams for more and more people."[35]

There is more truth to his assertion than most of us would like to believe. The layoffs have now spread beyond production workers into the ranks of professionals and managers. Now the jobs that are disappearing in record numbers are the better, higher-paid, white collar jobs. According to *The New York Times*, "In a reversal from the early '80s, workers with at least some college education make up the majority of people whose jobs were eliminated, outnumbering those with no more than high school educations. And, better paid workers—those earning at least $50,000—account for twice the share of the lost jobs than they did in the 1980s."[36] To be sure, even though there has been a net increase of about 27 million jobs in total employment since 1979, the chief growth in the economy has been in lower-paying service-sector jobs. In the decade between 1979 and 1989 more than eighteen million low-paying service-producing jobs were created—fast-food cooks, waiters and waitresses, guards, and janitors, for example.[37] Even people who work at these jobs full time qualify for the national poverty standard.[38]

At the same time that employees are working longer hours and earning less, the wage gap between the "haves" and the "have-nots" is widening.[39] The disparity in employees' incomes is particularly stark when they are compared with executives' soaring salaries. American CEOs are paid twice as much as CEOs in most major industrial countries (their average total compensation was $993,000 per year in 1994). And even the most conservative estimates show that on average they are paid an astounding 180 times more than manufacturing production workers are—a difference greater than in any other industrialized nation.[40] Now, in early 1996, the trend seems to be accelerating. "New CEO pay figures make top brass look positively piggy," says *Business Week*.[41] At the same time, the percentage of individuals in America earning less than $10,000 per year has mushroomed from 12.8 percent of the workforce in 1969 to 22.4 percent in 1989.[42] The median wage, adjusted for inflation, is nearly 3 percent lower today than it was in 1979. Although average household income grew 10 percent between 1979 and 1994, 97 percent of the new income went to the "upper fifth."[43]

The economic signs are unsettling. But there is yet another, more intangible but no less significant, dimension to the problem. As good jobs disappear, they remove not only good wages from society but also a primary means by which men and women find meaning in their lives. Work has long been regarded as virtuous in its own right because it bestows purpose and identity.[44] These humanizing virtues are delineated throughout

American literature. Many books extol the inherent goodness of work—
Louisa May Alcott's *Work,* Jane Addams's *Twenty Years at Hull House,* Horatio Alger's *Mark the Matchboy* and *Andy Grant's Pluck,* Robert Ward's
*Red Baker,* and many others.[45] Indeed, these images became real for me
during the course of this study, when Joe Stanton, a third-generation steelworker, took me on a tour of the Monongahela valley, where he had
grown up. As we stood facing the Monongahela River, staring at the rusting remains of the once famous Homestead Works, Stanton, who had
been the union's financial secretary, exclaimed, "We were steelworkers,
and we were proud of it! As a union man you were somebody in this town.
Steel was life to everyone around here, but look at it now." Over the last
five years I have listened to similar stories from other steelworkers, autoworkers, and aircraft mechanics, who, like Stanton, were worried about
what would happen to them if their industries vanished.

Their worries are real. No one knows whether a large number of
men and women will simply become unnecessary to produce what we
consume. Nor do we know how we would support a class of permanently
unemployed citizens, victims of what has come to be known as "shed-
ding."[46] Jeremy Rifkin warns, "This steady decline of mass labor threatens
to undermine the very foundations of the modern American state. For
nearly 200 years, the heart of the social contract and the measure of individual human worth have centered on the value of each person's labor."[47]

But how do industries grow, and where will new ones come from?
What we do know is that the answers will be found only as the new economy unfolds. The Alfred P. Sloan Foundation has invested millions of dollars in the country's best universities to answer the question. Hirsh Cohen,
a mathematician and former IBM vice president who is leading the effort,
admitted that the answers are elusive. "How do we maintain a high level
of 'good' jobs with increasing productivity?" he asked. "If we had some
new industries like semiconductors, computers, and electronics were in
the fifties, we would see where to go. Where are they? Can they all be in
services, entertainment, or information?"

Perhaps new economic growth will come from "clusters" of industries, such as complexes of automakers and suppliers that band together to
take advantage of proximity and a common infrastructure.[48] Or growth
may come from new structural arrangements such as the North American

Free Trade Agreement (NAFTA), the European Union (EU), or the General Agreement on Tariffs and Trade (GATT), as MIT economist Lester Thurow suggests.[49] Future growth may come from whole new industries such as nanotechnology or biotechnology, brand-new materials such as powder metal, or startling new discoveries that no one has yet imagined. "The truth is," writes John Rennie, editor in chief of *Scientific American*, "that as technologies pile on technologies at an uneven pace, it becomes impossible to predict precisely what patterns will emerge. Can anyone today truly foresee what the world will be like if, for example, genetic engineering matures rapidly to its full potential? Can anyone guess what a 21st-century factory will look like?"[50]

## CRUCIAL INGREDIENTS: LOYALTY, COMMITMENT, AND TRUST

While we lack answers to Rennie's first question, we do know that the companies that will flourish in this new and dynamic environment are those that are adaptable. This adaptability will depend heavily on a loyal, contributory cadre of employees who can act as though with a single mind, and it is through the exchange of mutual obligations that managers and workers form this necessary bond. Carnegie-Mellon University professor Herbert Simon, who pioneered organizational theory and artificial intelligence and who won the Nobel Prize in Economic Science in 1978, believes that such loyalty is fundamental to our very survival. He questions what motivates employees to work to maximize firms' profits: "Why will employees work hard if they can gain almost as much by loafing?"[51] The answer, he claims, is self-preservation, because "each human being depends for survival on the immediate and broader surrounding society."[52] Thus, it is society and its organizations from which we derive our safety and nourishment. Simon writes, "Companies work well, when they do, by securing the loyalties of their employees—not in the absence of economic rewards, but in addition to them—so that employees identify with the company's survival, growth and profit, making it the 'we' of their decision-making processes."[53] Thus, he concludes, "Companies succeed when they harness to their goals the human capacity for forming strong group loyalties and identities."[54]

Others too, provide insight about the growing importance of loyalty and commitment. For instance, James Womack and Daniel Jones, coauthors of the best-selling book *The Machine That Changed the World,* envision "lean enterprises"—individuals and companies synchronized to act as a single unit—that will form "value streams" in which families of products are created, produced, sold, and serviced.[55] They describe how such flexible and dynamic arrangements must depend on employee commitment. "Unless all members of a value stream pull together, it may be impossible for any one member to maintain momentum. Even if one member makes a lot of progress in becoming lean, neither that member nor the stream as a whole will reap the full benefits if another member falls short."[56] In other words, a single weak link can doom an entire enterprise.

There has recently been a renaissance of interest in workplace loyalty, commitment, and trust. In fact, a search of one of the country's leading libraries turned up an astonishing 7,391 citations in business journals on trust and employee relations published since 1990.[57] In one notable example in an article that recently appeared in the journal *Human Relations,* MIT professor Charles Sabel argues that trust—the mutual confidence that no one will exploit another's vulnerability—is fast becoming essential as markets become more volatile and fragmented, technological change increases, and product life cycles become shorter. Trust is crucial, Sabel insisted, because companies find it too costly to refine product design to the point where production can be executed in simply sequenced steps.[58] Instead, companies are becoming increasingly dependent on their blue-collar workers and their suppliers to use their own judgment. He observed that, in these conditions, "any party can hold up the others—most ruthlessly by simply enticing a collaborator into dedicating resources to a joint project, and then refusing to dedicate the necessary complementary resources until the terms of trade are renegotiated in its favor. If trust is absent, no one will risk moving first."[59] RAND social scientist Francis Fukuyama goes a step further, arguing that the contribution of trust to economic and social development has been greatly underestimated by economists and that in the twenty-first century social capital, represented by trust, will become every bit as important as physical capital.[60]

But the truth is that no one knows if and when new job-producing industries will appear, what they will be, or from where they will come. However, it is plain to see how worldwide forces are now demolishing the traditional assumptions about economic development and, at the same time, creating new opportunities. Can there be any question but that we must be prepared to capitalize on these opportunities as they arise? It is only out of these opportunities that new industries will be created and sustained. But what can we do to take advantage of them?

## PRODUCING NEW HUMAN RESOURCES

Training is not the answer. It does not create jobs, and any policy that assumes it does makes little sense. Worse, this persistent myth diverts attention from the very real problem of how to generate economic growth and opportunity. Nevertheless, every administration in recent history has gone down the same blind alley. Most recently, the Clinton administration's Reemployment Act of 1994 and the 1995 Middle-Class Bill of Rights have assumed that training, pure and simple, will put Americans back to work and help them move up the economic ladder into higher-wage jobs.[61] Clinton proposes to revamp the federal unemployment and training systems and extend skill training to millions of men and women who find themselves out of work and have few prospects of returning to their old jobs when the economy improves.[62] The assumption, however badly flawed, is that men and women, who are now expected to change jobs seven or eight times in a lifetime, can be trained in new skills and will then automatically be able to succeed in the global marketplace. Labor Secretary Robert Reich claims that such legislation will provide workers and companies with "real skills leading to real jobs."[63] What jobs? This has been a familiar and politically popular refrain since the early 1960s. Billions of dollars have been spent on training, with the goals of reducing unemployment, poverty, and crime and increasing productivity, but there has been little to show for the effort.[64] Officials have pumped so much federal money into training in the past thirty years that it has become an industry of its own. To what end? Bill Greene, a retired liberal California senator from south-central Los Angeles, is furious at the way training has been treated as a handout for the poor. He said angrily, "Training's become one of the biggest hustles in the world. Everybody's hustling training money. The way money's spent and people's lives are toyed with should be an insult to the entire society. People have made millions on the backs of poor people, and I refuse to sit in a position of responsibility and see that happen."[65]

The truth is that training is simply good politics. It has an inherent political appeal because "training" conjures up images of Horatio Alger–like characters pulling themselves up by their bootstraps (with a boost from government), an image that reaffirms a bedrock American belief that hard work and determination pay off.[66] And until the recent voter revolt against government spending, job training was always politically safe because it got votes from Democrats and Republicans alike and took nothing away from powerful interests. It channeled badly needed money to the states, where it helped to solidify elected officials' political support among the training agencies that shared in the spoils. But, rhetoric aside, thirty years of federal initiatives have made it abundantly clear that the ability of job training to generate employment and promote economic growth is limited because society's problems lie so far beyond its reach.[67]

## EDUCATION HOLDS THE KEY

Can we wait for the new economy to arrive? Probably not. Every moment we delay compounds the social and economic costs. Consider the following statistics: Each year 2.5 million young men and women graduate from high school and crowd into the shrinking job market, largely unprepared for its demands. This is just the tip of the iceberg. Behind these students loom 50 *million more*, whose characters are being formed as they pass through our elementary and secondary schools.[68] These are America's future leaders and workers, but in school most of them will never learn the skills and abilities that are crucial to our economic and social well-being. Few will ever learn *how* to learn — how to take responsibility for decision making and teamwork, how to develop trusting and respectful relationships. Nor will most students even master the basics — reading, writing, and arithmetic. Figures from the U.S. Department of Education reveal that more than a quarter (28%) of America's fourth-graders ranked below standard in mathematical comprehension and skill.[69] An international assessment of mathematics and science found that American thirteen-year-olds were at the bottom when compared with students from eleven other countries when they were tested on addition and subtraction, solving simple mathematical problems, and interpreting data.[70] Another study found that a third of eighth-graders could not calculate the price of a meal from a restaurant menu, while a similar proportion of junior high school students could not write a coherent paragraph.[71]

For many years educational reformers firmly believed that the quality of the public schools could be improved with more funding. By the mid-1980s, billions of dollars had been poured into school reform, but little of substance had changed.[72] It has now been more than a dozen years since the National Commission on Excellence in Education released its ominous report *A Nation at Risk*.[73] The report left little doubt that education in America's public schools was deteriorating and warned of a "rising tide of mediocrity that threatens our very future as a nation and a people." A flurry of reports followed, each of which reached the same conclusion— that American public schools were failing their students.[74] Even today, while some individual reform projects succeed, the condition of public education remains bleak. Former *New York Times* education editor Edward B. Fiske writes, "Our national senses have been numbed by one horror story after another about the abysmal ignorance of our young people. . . . Even our best schools are failing to meet minimal international standards."[75] Fiske warns, "The country is paying a terrible price for the failure of its public schools. . . . The social cost is equally devastating. More than a quarter of students who start out in American high schools fail to graduate with their classes."[76]

Just as in industry, the problems could be overlooked as long as there was enough money to go around. But "funding is not related to school quality," writes economist Eric Hanushek.[77] Dropout rates have continued to soar, while student achievement has steadily dropped. The incidence of poverty, drug use, crime, and violence has risen alarmingly, and white middle-class families have fled the inner cities, taking the tax base with them. The spreading effects have been like a meltdown as the already struggling schools have taken on the responsibility for providing more and more of what society could no longer furnish. The result has been the beginning of a serious erosion in public confidence.

The public schools still continue to sidestep serious efforts at reform.

"The best reform efforts aim at the educational process—what happens between students and teachers—and at helping teachers by empowering them," explained Theodore Mitchell, vice chancellor of UCLA and dean of its Graduate School of Education and Information Studies. "Some schools are taking it seriously and are getting results. But most are just substituting process for real reform."[78] In their book *Tinkering Toward Utopia: A Century of Public School Reform,* Stanford University professors David Tyack and Larry Cuban acknowledge the public schools' remarkable resistance to change: "Educators have often paid lip service to demands for reform to signify their alertness to the public will. But their symbolic responses often protected school people from basic challenges to their core practices."[79]

## THE LONG SHADOW OF MASS PRODUCTION

Is it any wonder that schools deflect criticism and change? One has only to recall how General Motors, U.S. Steel, Douglas Aircraft, and countless other American corporations were swept to the brink of disaster before corrective action could be taken. Public schools were originally created in the image of American industry, and the latter's dubious heritage (mass production and adversarial human relationships) still remains at their core. Turn-of-the-century education reformer Ellwood P. Cubberley expressed it clearly: "Our schools are, in a sense, factories, in which the raw products (children) are to be shaped and fashioned into products to meet the various demands of life."[80] In his book *Education and the Cult of Efficiency,* education professor Raymond Callahan described how twentieth-century public schools had been formed from the same social impulses that had given rise to mass production.[81] In fact, by the early 1900s the principles of scientific management extolling the virtues of efficiency had already spread into the home and the church, and education was next.[82] According to Callahan, between 1900 and 1930 school administrators began to regard themselves as managers rather than educators. They learned the principles of scientific management so their schools could accommodate the huge numbers of immigrant children at low cost. The idea reached its peak (or its nadir, depending upon one's point of view) in 1908 in Gary, Indiana, where "platoon" schools became the rage.

These schools, which were organized much like factories, were dedicated to the elimination of waste. They ran on a tight schedule to ensure an efficient use of "plant and equipment." Classrooms were in constant use, and students moved from room to room in orderly fashion after each bell. The idea spread, but not everyone was pleased. Some, like one mother who withdrew her child from the Detroit schools, wrote that the long lines of children "looked to me like nothing so much as the lines of uncompleted Ford cars in the factory, moving always on, with a screw put in or a burr tightened as they pass—standardized, mechanical, pitiful."[83]

Not surprisingly, as teaching and administration were shaped by the principles of scientific management, the public schools began to exhibit many of the same characteristics that would later cripple American industry. The schools became bureaucratic, departmentalized, and impersonal, and they developed in virtual isolation from the larger environment. Authority followed a rigid hierarchical form, flowing from top to bottom. Education codes and procedures spelled out exactly how teachers were to be trained and certified. In time the schools became inflexible, absorbed with their own internal processes, and out of touch with the very parents and students they were supposed to serve.[84] Not surprisingly, this highly rationalized system of work created an underlying adversarial "us-against-them" culture that pitted teachers against administrators.

While organizing and operating schools like factories may have made sense when America was expanding and assimilating waves of new immigrants, the environment has changed irrevocably. No longer can young people afford to leave high school barely literate and lacking the ability to learn. Gone are guarantees of jobs in local auto plants and steel mills—the traditional passports to the middle class. Instead, as we have seen, graduates who are lucky enough to find a good job will be required to be able to learn continuously, work cooperatively and interdependently in teams, and take responsibility and initiative. It is difficult to imagine what will happen to the rest.

It is folly to think that without fundamental structural and cultural change, the public schools can produce students who have mastered the basics and who can learn. It would be like asking GM to design and produce a fuel-efficient, high-quality, low-cost small car in the 1980s. How are students supposed to learn these skills and qualities in schools that have been designed to promote just the opposite—docile behavior, rote learning, and individual competition?[85]

## HARNESSING THE FORCES OF CHANGE

The answer may be simpler than it seems. The same forces that are compelling American industry to replace mass production and its destructive culture with "lean production" systems and cooperative human relationships have now been unleashed on the public sector. Human service organizations—police departments, hospitals, colleges, and universities, to name but a few—that have remained insulated and protected from serious reform are now scrambling for their share of dwindling resources. But this is not just a simple matter of cost cutting. It is a matter of improving service, just as the "quality revolution" forced industry to improve the quality of American goods. And like the quality revolution, this "service revolution" is painful, costing hundreds of thousands of employees their jobs.

The evidence is visible everywhere. Police departments are streamlining police work while they struggle to abandon the traditional "command-and-control" culture in favor of "community policing."[86] Hospitals are being restructured, becoming more responsive to customers (patients) as they merge and compete with one another for shrinking insurance payments. Colleges and universities are being compelled to set priorities and make hard choices in order to reduce costs and improve the quality of the education they offer. Some are borrowing ideas from the private sector, such as total quality management (TQM) and responsibility-centered management (RCM), while others are establishing new (and at one time unthinkable) partnerships with one another to reduce redundancy and costs.[87]

Progress is slow, because it requires fundamental changes that can emerge only after the systems of production and the underlying cultures have been altered. We have seen just how wrenching this kind of change can be because of the massive force required to induce it. Remember the enormous effort that was required to transform NUMMI from mass production to "lean production." Recall what it took for Hewlett-Packard's

Santa Clara division to throw off its stifling management structure and teach its engineers and marketing representatives to work together on behalf of the customer. Think about the years it took USS-POSCO to create a new and productive culture around its "high-performance" technology and how Douglas Aircraft had to all but destroy itself to bring itself under control. There is little doubt that a similar and painful transformation of the public schools' very structure will be required. Like leading manufacturing companies before them, they will have to throw off the unproductive systems and the underlying culture that supports them. Another important lesson that can be taken from our study is that such changes cannot be produced by public mandate: they must be generated from *within* an organization. And, ominous as it sounds, such changes are nearly always brought about by an external threat.

To all appearances, the stage has been set. Money is running out. A growing number of states are finding that social demands are outstripping their abilities to pay. Yet even darker storm clouds are gathering as elected officials demand accountability from public service agencies for spending these increasingly scarce funds, and education is no exception.[88] It seems unlikely to me that in today's era of tight purses that voters will settle for anything less than fundamental educational reform. Whether education will get a "wake-up call" as American industry did a decade ago, or whether it can be restructured voluntarily, is debatable.

The advance of educational vouchers—an arrangement whereby parents receive public funds to spend at the school of their choice—may shake the public schools out of their paralysis. Though it is an idea that has been hotly debated for two decades or more, no state has yet voted to support a full-blown voucher initiative (though Minnesota has elements of one).[89] But the evidence suggests that conditions have changed and that half of all Americans now support the idea of choice in public schools (up from 38% in 1971).[90] In their book *Reinventing Education*, IBM chairman Louis Gerstner and his colleagues warn, "When half of Americans support vouchers, the public schools must respond or face the public's wrath."[91] Just as voters in California, Oregon, and Colorado abruptly slapped term limits on state legislators, vouchers could become a reality overnight. According to University of California, Berkeley, law professor John Coons, who has written extensively about vouchers, the initiatives have failed so far because they have been drafted poorly.[92] They have also become associated with extreme conservatism and the religious right. A new California initiative, Coons says, has been drafted more thoughtfully than the older version was. He claims that the new initiative will focus on advancing social concerns and that it will draw votes across the political spectrum.[93]

But even if a voucher initiative fails, other forces are lining up to force fundamental school reform. Public education is faced with a serious lack of public confidence at a time when state legislatures are trying to spread dwindling resources among competing demands—for jails, welfare benefits, and health care. There simply is not enough money to go around, and the inevitable result is that public schools are facing wrenching change. Whether we will seize the opportunity to make these changes remains to be seen.

## ALTERING EDUCATION AT ITS CORE

Lessons we have learned from industry can help restructure the public schools. I am not suggesting that education copy industry, and I am certainly not suggesting an "industrial model" of education. What I am saying is that there is much to learn from a close observation of companies that have already left mass production behind.

For instance, we have learned that no serious restructuring can take place if it is mandated from above. It must be embraced fully by employees at every level of every organization. Only in this way can the beginnings of a new social compact among teachers, unions, students, parents, administrators, and policy makers be fashioned. As in the companies we have studied, new mutual obligations will have to be spelled out, and all parties will have to be assured of fair and equitable treatment.

But as we saw, no fundamental changes can be made until the system of work itself is altered. For the schools, this means that teaching and learning must be completely redesigned. Just as workers, union leaders, and managers participated in altering production in the companies we studied, so must teachers, unions, administrators, students, and parents participate in redesigning the schools. Such a change, however, will require a profound cultural transformation to overcome the historical inertia. There is some cause for worrying that schools will once again get caught up in the visible process of change and miss this more fundamental point because actually going through a fundamental transformation is painful and distressing and employees avoid it if they can. Today there is a lot of talk in educational circles about "restructuring," but for the most part the ideas involved remain abstractions. Some advocate using total quality management and redesign concepts but leave the impression that educational reform can advance in a smooth, seamless fashion.[94]

I am not so sanguine. I have become convinced that the changes that were forced on industry and are now facing education can come only on the heels of a crisis. I am equally convinced that reforms cannot progress very far until a compact is created among administrators, teachers, unions, students, and parents. Only then will it be possible to agree on how the outmoded teaching and administrative systems, and the beliefs that underlie them, should be altered.

## AT THE CROSSROADS

But how can we establish a level of discourse that will transcend conflicting views and establish this new and productive direction? I think the answer has already been found, and it is right in front of us. Remember that, in the companies we studied, there had to be a recognition that something larger than individual self-interest was at stake? There had to be the discovery of a collective good that could be shared by management and labor. It was only then that a new discourse of cooperation could be established to bridge antagonism and define the common good.

Recall that, at the very beginning of this book, we discussed how rapid changes in the world economy had already begun to create the same conditions for cooperation — but on a grand scale. "Might" no longer makes "right," and former adversaries are now finding it necessary to cooperate to survive. What is hopeful in these developments is the possibility of reawakening the knowledge that voluntary acts are far more durable than those produced by coercive force. French philosopher Jean-Jacques Rousseau recognized this fact more than two hundred years ago. In his book *The Social Contract*, he wrote, "The strongest is never strong enough to be always the master."[95] What Rousseau meant was that "right" had to be derived from a principle other than force if mankind were to become truly free.

Could it be that in these companies we are seeing the re-creation of the timeless phenomenon of human adaptation that is applicable to all organizations in the throes of change? At one moment, we see mutual endeavor arising in an international economy that is racing headlong into the future. In the next, we see it as it existed in the small economies of two hundred years in the past. Might we be seeing the shaping of a new social agreement that recognizes the limits to individual self-interest and the creation of a new compact that stems from our interdependence? Perhaps. History shows us that cultural change is never invented; rather, it is always produced as an adaptation to a changing environment.[96] If I am right, and if what we have witnessed is a creative act by which the men and women in these companies and unions are reshaping our collective economic and social future, can we afford to ignore the lesson?

Perhaps, but only at our own peril. We are now standing at a crossroads, and choosing one direction over another will surely carry powerful consequences. We can blind ourselves to the past and to the need for a new sense of our collective self-interest. But such a choice can only plunge a growing segment of Americans into greater insecurity and an even deeper gloom of hopelessness. Casting millions of men and women adrift in a topsy-turvy world to be guided only by a "survival of the fittest" philosophy will certainly have disastrous consequences for us all.

The other choice is to recognize that we really have no other option. The only open road is one of aggresively reinvesting in hope for everyone. We have examined these companies and unions in microscopic detail and have seen what it requires to write a new social compact based on cooperation instead of antagonism. It will take courage to throw off the beliefs that have shackled us to the past so we can grasp the unmistakable fact of our interconnectedness. Only then can we begin to chart a new path that offers a reasonable hope of restoring prosperity.

# NOTES

## CHAPTER ONE: THE ECONOMIC ENGINE OF CHANGE

1. Yoh Sang Whan has since retired from POSCO.
2. According to *The Wall Street Journal*, March 12, 1993, Park was forced from office in 1993 after being charged with taking kickbacks from suppliers and embezzling company funds.
3. Lawrence Mishel and Jared Bernstein, *The State of Working America, 1992–1993* (Armonk, N.Y.: Economic Policy Institute, 1993), p. 203; remarks made by Michael Dukakis at the Human Resources Round Table for Senior Executives, UCLA, February 7, 1996.
4. Japan's acute shortage of production workers is forcing it to depend more and more on foreign workers, who are hard to integrate into the homogeneous Japanese society. Having achieved peak production, Japanese companies are being pressed to cut working hours so their employees can enjoy more leisure time and the fruits of their newfound wealth. At the same time, as the cost of investment capital has risen dramatically and real estate investments have soured, Japan's economic boom has subsided, at least for now. As its economic recession deepens and its managerial workforce ages, the big Japanese companies are being forced to reconsider whether or not they can afford to promise lifetime employment any longer. In Korea too, the lack of investment capital is stifling new-technology development, threatening the country's footing in the worldwide economic race. And as the Korean economy develops, ideological differences between management and labor flare up frequently, resulting in shutdowns and strikes.

5. See, e.g., Peter Drucker, *The Age of Discontinuity* (New York: Harper and Row, 1968); Michael J. Piore and Charles F. Sabel, *The Second Industrial Divide: Possibilities for Prosperity* (New York: Basic Books, 1984).
6. Interview with Jinnosuke Miyai, Tokyo, Japan, December 16, 1991.
7. See, e.g., James P. Womack, Daniel T. Jones, and Daniel Roos, *The Machine That Changed the World* (New York: HarperCollins, 1991); Harry Katz, *Shifting Gears: Changing Labor Relations in the U.S. Automobile Industry* (Cambridge, Mass.: MIT Press, 1985).
8. David Halberstam, *The Reckoning* (New York: Avon Books, 1986), p. 497.
9. Ibid., p. 30.
10. John Holusha, "Layoffs Are Just One U.A.W. Problem," *The New York Times*, January 24, 1982, p. 1.
11. Paul A. Eisenstein, "GM Workers in Doubt About Layoffs," *Christian Science Monitor*, vol. 84, no. 2, December 6, 1991, p. 6.
12. John Hoerr, *And the Wolf Finally Came: The Decline of the American Steel Industry* (Pittsburgh: University of Pittsburgh Press, 1988).
13. "Airbus Unveils Long-Range Airliner," *Los Angeles Times*, October 5, 1991, p. D2.
14. *McDonnell-Douglas Annual Report*, 1990.
15. Michael L. Dertouzos, Richard K. Lester, and Robert M. Solow, *Made in America: Regaining the Productive Edge* (New York: Harper and Row, 1989).
16. Ibid., p. 263.
17. "How American Industry Stacks Up," *Fortune*, March 9, 1992, pp. 30–46.
18. Charles W. McMillion, "Debt, There's a Better Way to Grow," *The New York Times*, August 16, 1992, p. 11.
19. Marvin Wolf, *The Japanese Conspiracy: The Plot to Dominate Industry World Wide—And How to Deal with It* (New York: Empire Books, 1983).
20. The Federal Trade Commission has recently launched an investigation into whether an Americanized form of the Japanese *keiretsu* serves to fix prices Japanese automakers pay for their parts and to shut out U.S. suppliers; see, e.g., "FTC Probing Japanese Auto Firms, Suppliers," *Los Angeles Times*, June 13, 1990, p. D1.
21. Peter Drucker, "The Changed World Economy," *Foreign Affairs*, Spring 1987, pp. 768–91.
22. *Economic Report of the President* (Washington, D.C.: U.S. Government Printing Office, 1990).
23. Dertouzos et al., *Made in America*.
24. S. Cohen and J. Zysman, "The Myth of a Post-industrial Economy," *Technology Review*, February–March 1987, pp. 54–62.
25. S. Cohen and J. Zysman, *Manufacturing Matters: The Myth of the Post-industrial Economy* (New York: Basic Books, 1987).
26. Dertouzos et al., *Made in America*, p. 40.
27. Richard J. Barnet, "The End of Jobs," *Harper's*, September 1993, pp. 47–52.
28. Ibid, p. 174; also see Barry Bluestone, "The Inequality Express," *The American Prospect*, Winter 1994, pp. 81–93.
29. Mishel and Bernstein, *The State of Working America*, p. 166; also see Stephen Rose,

*On Shaky Ground: Rising Fears About Incomes and Earnings*, Research Report No. 94-02, National Commission for Employment Policy, Washington, D.C., October 1994.

30. *California on the Verge of a Breakdown* (John Vasconcellos, Chair), Assembly Ways and Means Committee, Sacramento, Calif., June 30, 1994.

31. *Promoting Long-term Prosperity*, Competitive Policy Council, Third Report to the President and Congress, U.S. Government Printing Office, Washington, D.C., May 1994.

32. Lester Thurow, *Head to Head: The Coming Economic Battle Among Japan, Europe and America* (New York: William Morrow and Co., 1992).

33. P. Krugman, *Peddling Prosperity: Economic Sense and Nonsense in the Age of Diminished Expectations* (New York: Norton, 1994).

34. *The OECD Economic Outlook: Developments in Individual OECD Countries* (Paris, France: Organization for Economic Cooperation and Development, 1994), pp. 45–51; Joseph Spiers, "The Most Important Economic Event of the Decade," *Fortune*, April 3, 1995, pp. 33–40.

35. Brian O'Reilly, "The New Deal: What Companies and Employees Owe One Another," *Fortune*, June 13, 1994, pp. 44–52; Joseph Nocera, "Living with Layoffs," *Fortune*, April 1, 1996; Louis Uchitelle and N. R. Kleinfeld, "The Downsizing of America," *The New York Times*, March 3, 1996.

36. Jeffrey Pfeffer, "Competitive Advantage Through People," *California Management Review*, Winter 1994, pp. 9–28.

37. Jaclyn Fierman, "The Contingency Workforce," *Fortune*, January 24, 1994, pp. 30–36; "Temporary Employment Industry Working Overtime," *Los Angeles Times*, July 5, 1994, p. 1.

38. For some of the best writing on organizational culture, see Edgar Schein, *Organizational Culture and Leadership* (San Francisco: Jossey-Bass, 1989); C. Argyris and D. Schon, *Organizational Learning* (Reading, Mass.: Addison-Wesley, 1978); Benjamin Schneider, ed., *Organizational Climate and Culture* (San Francisco: Jossey-Bass, 1990); Joanne Martin, *Cultures in Organizations: Three Perspectives* (New York: Oxford University Press, 1992); Michael Owen Jones, Michael Dane Moore, and Richard Christopher Snyder, *Inside Organizations: Understanding the Human Dimension* (Newbury Park, Calif.: Sage, 1988).

39. W. Wilms, *Public and Proprietary Vocational Training: A Study of Effectiveness* (Lexington, Mass.: Lexington Books, 1975); W. Wilms, "Scientific Management, Education and the Erosion of Ideas: The Need for New Communities of Interest," *Educational Horizons*, Winter 1983, pp. 73–82; W. Wilms, "Training for Technology: A Questionable Investment," *International Journal of Educational Development*, vol. 8, no. 3, 1987, pp. 43–54; W. Wilms, "Proprietary Schools: Strangers in Their Own Land," *Change*, vol. 9, no. 1, 1987, pp. 37–51.

## CHAPTER TWO: THE CULTURE OF MASS PRODUCTION

1. Henry Ford, *Today and Tomorrow* (Cambridge, Mass.: Productivity Press, 1988; first published by Doubleday, Page, New York, 1926), p. 27.

2. For a sweeping account of the historical development of mass production, see

Siegfried Giedion, *Mechanization Takes Command: A Contribution to Anonymous History* (New York: Norton, 1969; first published by Oxford University Press, New York, 1948).

3. Ibid., p. 38.
4. Ibid., pp. 93–98.
5. Ibid., p. 93.
6. Ibid., p. 49.
7. Ibid., pp. 24, 114–115.
8. Karl Marx, *Das Kapital: A Critique of Political Economy* (New York: Modern Library, 1936), p. 384.
9. Quoted in Harry Braverman, *Labor and Monopoly Capital: The Degradation of Work in the Twentieth Century* (New York: Monthly Review Press, 1974), pp. 45–46.
10. Friedrich Engels believed that subjecting men to the routine of assembly work, where all of the creative thinking had already been done, would stunt their development. Thorstein Veblen, a noted early-twentieth-century social critic, warned that forcing workmen to conform to routines imposed by the machine would in the long run retard their ability to think for themselves. John Dewey, a foremost American educator, also decried the idea of mass production once it became apparent that jobs would be highly specialized and divorced from the final product. Like Marx, he firmly believed that the work of the hands reflected inner human development. He and other early-twentieth-century social reformers such as Jane Addams warned that mass production was inherently antidemocratic and that it would arrest human development, dividing society into two large classes from which those at the bottom could not escape. See Engels, quoted in Braverman, ibid., p. 49; Thorstein Veblen, *The Instinct of Workmanship* (New York: Macmillan, 1914), pp. 41–42; John Dewey, "A Policy of Industrial Education," *New Republic*, December 1914, pp. 11–12.
11. For a balanced account of Taylor's complex personality, see M. Weisbord, *Productive Workplaces* (San Francisco: Jossey-Bass, 1987), pp. 24–69.
12. Frank Barklay Copley, *Frederick W. Taylor, Father of Scientific Management*, vol. 2 (New York: Harper & Row, 1923), p. 84.
13. See, e.g., Horatio Alger, *Ragged Dick* (New York: Collier Macmillan, 1962).
14. Frederick Winslow Taylor, *Shop Management* (New York: Harper and Brothers, 1919), p. 147.
15. See, e.g., D. Montgomery, "Industrial Democracy or Democracy in Industry?: The Theory and Practice of the Labor Movement, 1870–1925," in *Industrial Democracy in America*, N. Lichtenstein and H. J. Harris, eds. (New York: Press Syndicate of the University of Cambridge, 1993), pp. 20–42.
16. William Serrin, *Homstead: The Glory and Tragedy of an American Steel Town* (New York: Times Books, 1992).
17. David P. Demarest, Jr., ed., *The River Ran Red: Homestead, 1892* (Pittsburgh: University of Pittsburgh Press, 1992), p. 78.
18. Interview with John Allard, Southgate, Calif., March 17, 1992.
19. Sanford Jacoby, *Employing Bureaucracy* (New York: Columbia University Press, 1985).
20. Ibid., pp. 230–231.

21. J. Hoerr, *And the Wolf Finally Came: The Decline of the American Steel Industry* (Pittsburgh: University of Pittsburgh Press, 1988).
22. Interview with Art Mullett, Sacramento, Calif., February 17, 1992.
23. *Statistical Abstract of the United States* (Washington, D.C.: U.S. Government Printing Office, 1991), p. 423; ibid. (1959), p. 239.
24. Interviews with M. Brody, Fremont, Calif., October 19, 1989, and February 10, 1992.
25. K. Lewin et al., "The Practicality of Democracy," in G. Murphy, ed., *Human Nature and Enduring Peace* (Boston: Houghton Mifflin, 1945); K. Lewin, *Field Theory in Social Science: Selected Theoretical Papers*, D. Cartwright, ed. (New York: Harper & Row, 1951); E. Mayo, *The Social Problems of an Industrial Civilization* (Boston: School of Business Administration, Harvard University, 1945).
26. K. Lewin, R. Lippett, and R. K. White, "Patterns of Aggressive Behavior in Experimentally Created 'Social Climates,'" *Journal of Social Psychology*, vol. 10, 1939, pp. 271–99.
27. Elton Mayo and George F. F. Lombard, *Teamwork and Labor Turnover in the Aircraft Industry of Southern California* (Boston: Bureau of Business Research, Graduate School of Business Administration, Harvard University, 1944).
28. Frank G. Goble, *The Third Force: The Psychology of Abraham Maslow* (New York: Pocket Books, 1970).
29. A. H. Maslow, "A Theory of Human Motivation," *Psychological Review* vol. 50, 1943, pp. 370–396.
30. Frederick Herzberg, Bernard Mausner, and Barbara Bloch Snyderman, *The Motivation to Work* (New York: John Wiley and Sons, 1959).
31. Douglas McGregor, *The Human Side of Enterprise* (New York: McGraw-Hill, 1960).
32. J. Gooding, "Blue Collar Blues on the Assembly Line," *Fortune*, July 1970, p. 70.
33. Braverman, *Labor and Monopoly Capital*, p. 33.
34. U.S. Department of Health, Education and Welfare, *Work in America* (Cambridge, Mass.: MIT Press, 1973).
35. Robert Blauner, *Alienation and Freedom: The Factory Worker and His Industry* (Chicago: University of Chicago Press, 1964).
36. See, e.g., Gooding, "Blue Collar Blues"; "The Blue Collar Worker's Lowdown Blues," *Time*, November 9, 1970, pp. 68–78; "Sabotage at Lordstown?" *Time*, February 7, 1972, p. 76; B. J. Widick, "The Men Won't Toe the Vega Line," *The Nation*, March 27, 1972, pp. 403–404; Barbara Garson, "Luddites in Lordstown," *Harper's*, June 1972, pp. 68–73.
37. Gooding, "Blue Collar Blues," p. 71.
38. B. Bluestone and I. Bluestone, *Negotiating the Future: A Labor Perspective on American Business* (New York: Basic Books, 1992), p. 17, taken from *Proceedings of the Special Collective Bargaining Convention* (Detroit, Mich.: UAW, 1967), p. 118.
39. T. Kochan, H. Katz, and R. McKersie, *The Transformation of American Industrial Relations* (Ithaca, N.Y.: ILR Press, 1994).
40. Bluestone and Bluestone, *Negotiating the Future*, p. 17.
41. Kochan et al., *The Transformation*, p. 156.

42. R. Cole, *Work, Mobility and Participation* (Berkeley, Calif.: University of California Press, 1979).

43. E. L. Trist and K. W. Bamforth, "Some Social and Psychological Consequences of the Longwall Method of Coal-getting," *Human Relations*, vol. 4, no. 1, 1951, pp. 33–38.

44. F. E. Emery and E. L. Trist, "Socio-technical Systems," in C. W. Churchman et al., eds., *Management Sciences, Models and Techniques* (London: Pergamon, 1960).

45. Louis E. Davis and James C. Taylor, eds., *Design of Jobs* (Santa Monica, Calif.: Goodyear Publishing Company, 1979).

46. R. Cole, *Work, Mobility and Participation*.

47. See Neal Herrick, *Joint Management and Employee Participation: Labor and Management at the Crossroads* (San Francisco: Jossey-Bass, 1990).

48. See, e.g., R. E. Walton, "The Diffusion of New Work Structures: Explaining Why Success Didn't Take," *Organizational Dynamics*, Winter 1975, pp. 2–22; R. E. Walton, *Innovating to Compete: Lessons for Diffusing and Managing Change in the Workplace* (San Francisco: Jossey-Bass, 1987).

49. Thomas Kochan and Paul Osterman, *The Mutual Gains Enterprise* (Boston: Harvard University Press, 1994).

50. J. Blasi and D. Kruse, *The New Owners: The Mass Emergence of Employee Ownership in Public Companies and What It Means to American Business* (New York: Harper-Collins, 1991); M. Conte, "Economic Research and Public Policy Toward Employee Ownership in the United States," *Journal of Economic Issues*, June 1994, pp. 427–437.

51. James P. Womack, Daniel T. Jones, and Daniel Roos, *The Machine That Changed the World: The Story of Lean Production* (New York: Rawson Associates, 1990); Martin Kenney and Richard Florida, *Beyond Mass Production: The Japanese System and Its Transfer to the U.S.* (New York: Oxford University Press, 1993).

52. See, e.g., J. Katzenbach and D. Smith, *The Wisdom of Teams* (Boston: Harvard Business School Press, 1993); Andrea Gabor, *The Man Who Discovered Quality* (New York: Times Books, 1990); Michael Hammer and James Champy, *Reengineering the Corporation: A Manifesto for Business Revolution* (New York: HarperBusiness, 1993); Warren H. Schmidt and Jerome P. Finnegan, *The Race Without a Finish Line: America's Quest for Total Quality* (San Francisco: Jossey-Bass, 1992).

53. See E. Appelbaum and R. Batt, *The New American Workplace: Transforming Work Systems in the United States* (Ithaca, NY: ILR Press, 1994).

54. Kochan, et al., *The Transformation*, pp. viii–ix.

55. *Fact-Finding Report: Commission on the Future of Worker-Management Relations* (John Dunlop, Chair) (Washington, D.C.: U.S. Department of Labor and U.S. Department of Commerce, May 1994).

56. "Dunlop Commission Reports," *Monthly Labor Review*, April 1995, p. 78.

## CHAPTER THREE: FROM BOOM TO BUST

1. For a detailed analysis of Douglas Aircraft, see Alan J. Harcastle, *TQM and Cultural Change: The Douglas Aircraft Story* (Ithaca, N.Y.: Cornell University Press, to be published).

2. Interview with Donald Douglas, Jr., Orange, Calif., July 21, 1993.

3. Frank Cunningham, *Skymaster: The Story of Donald Douglas* (Philadelphia: Dorrance and Company, 1943).

4. See, e.g., Arthur P. Allen and Betty V. H. Schneider, *Industrial Relations in the California Aircraft Industry* (Berkeley: Institute of Industrial Relations, University of California, 1956).

5. Elton Mayo and George F. F. Lombard, *Teamwork and Labor Turnover in the Aircraft Industry of Southern California* (Boston: Bureau of Business Research, Graduate School of Business Administration, Harvard University, 1944).

6. Telephone interview with James A. Moore, July 22, 1993.

7. Cunningham, *Skymaster*, p. 311.

8. Interview with John Allard, Southgate, Calif., March 17, 1992.

9. A retired Douglas engineer recalled how the engineers had remained loyal to Douglas even in the face of the sit-down strike. "In 1937 strikers broke down the plant's doors and tried to destroy the engineering department. But the engineers loved the company, and they loved old man Douglas. They fought the strikers back with chairs and anything else they could grab and ran them out of the building!"

10. J. R. Wilburn, *Social and Economic Aspects of the Aircraft Industry in Metropolitan Los Angeles During World War II*, unpublished doctoral dissertation, University of California, Los Angeles, 1971.

11. *Douglas Aircraft Company—A Brief History*, unpublished company document no. 4362, April 1991, p. 2.

12. Ibid., p. 3.

13. "The Passionate Engineer," *Time*, November 22, 1943, pp. 77–84.

14. Ibid., p. 82.

15. Ibid.

16. Ibid.

17. Interview with James Douglas, Cerritos, Calif., July 29, 1993.

18. "The Passionate Engineer."

19. Interview with John Allard, March 17, 1992.

20. Allen and Schneider, *Industrial Relations*, p. 26.

21. Ibid., p. 34.

22. John Mecklin, "Douglas Aircraft's Stormy Flight Path," *Fortune*, December 1966, pp. 166–173; T. A. Wise, "How McDonnell Won Douglas," *Fortune*, March 1967, pp. 155–235.

23. See "Douglas Aircraft's Stormy Flight Path"; "How McDonnell Won Douglas"; Dan Cook, "Flying High, Economy Class," *California Business*, March 1989, pp. 26–42; Ronald Henkoff, "Bumpy Flight at McDonnell Douglas," *Fortune*, August 1989, pp. 79–80.

24. Interview with Donald Douglas, Jr., July 21, 1993.

25. Robert J. Serling, *Legend and Legacy: The Story of Boeing and Its People* (New York: St. Martin's Press, 1992).

26. "Douglas Aircraft's Stormy Flight Path."

27. "How McDonnell Won Douglas."

28. "Douglas Aircraft's Stormy Flight Path."

29. Interview with Donald Douglas, Jr., July 21, 1993.

30. Ralph Vartabedian, "John McDonnell's Bumpy Ride," *Los Angeles Times*, December 1, 1991, pp. 18–52.

31. Interview with Donald Douglas, Jr., July 21, 1993.

32. "Bumpy Flight at McDonnell Douglas."

33. "Back From the Brink?" *The Orange County Register*, June 30, 1991, p. 1.

34. John F. McDonnell, "Five Keys in Perspective," unpublished paper, May 8, 1986, page 1.

35. S. N. McDonnell, "The Five Keys to Self-Renewal," internal document, McDonnell Douglas Corporation, June 12, 1985.

36. Ibid., pp. 2–3.

37. Ibid.

38. "Ex–UAW Aide Puts Douglas on New Tack," *The Wall Street Journal*, April 24, 1989, p. B4.

## CHAPTER FOUR: TQMS AND THE PROMISE OF RENEWAL

1. Telephone interview with George Nelson, July 29, 1993.

2. Interview with Joel Smith, Newport Beach, Calif., January 31, 1991.

3. Interview with George Nelson, July 29, 1993.

4. Interview with Joel Smith, January 31, 1991.

5. In 1988 Douglas had other facilities located at nearby Torrance, Palmdale, and Carson, as well as a flight-test center at Yuma, Arizona. Douglas also had manufacturing plants in Salt Lake City; Macon, Georgia; Melbourne, Arkansas; Norman, Oklahoma; Columbus, Ohio; and Malton, Ontario, Canada.

6. Building 13 is one of a number of buildings on the Long Beach site that had been designed and built in 1940–1941 without windows so it could be blacked out in the event of a nighttime enemy attack.

7. This was true in 1990. Today, the production time has been shortened to fewer than seventy-five days.

8. Interview with Joel Smith, Newport Beach, Calif., January 31, 1991.

9. *McDonnell Douglas Annual Report*, 1990.

10. Telephone interview with James A. Moore, July 22, 1993.

11. Ibid.

12. Ibid.

13. Ibid.

14. Interview with John McDonnell, St. Louis, Mo., November 12, 1993.

15. Douglas Aircraft internal document no. 89-GEN-21037.

## CHAPTER FIVE: DISASTER OR MIRACLE?

1. Interview with James S. Douglas, Cerritos, Calif., August 11, 1993.

2. Interview with John McDonnell, St. Louis, Mo., November 12, 1993.

3. "TQMS Discovery Training," Douglas Aircraft Company, McDonnell Douglas Cor-

poration, undated manual; "Structured On-site Training and Continuous Improvement—Leader Guidebook, Version 3.1," Douglas Aircraft Company, McDonnell Douglas Corporation, April 1990.

4. "1.7 TQMS Discovery Training Agenda, Version 1.4."
5. Interview with John McDonnell, November 12, 1993.
6. McDonnell Douglas Corporation, internal memorandum, August 1, 1990.
7. "Exec Behind Douglas Teamwork Approach Resigns Unexpectedly," *San Jose Mercury News*, August 11, 1990, p. 11-D.
8. "Roast Crow Anyone?" *Forbes*, January 30, 1995, p. 57.
9. Loren B. Thompson, "McDonnell Douglas Corporation: Commercial Aircraft Operations Are in Decline; MD Will Exit Business in the 1990s," National Security Studies Program, Georgetown University, Washington, D.C., October 23, 1992, p. 5.
10. Ralph Vartabedian, "Pentagon to Buy 80 More C-17 Jets from McDonnell," *Los Angeles Times*, November 4, 1995, p. A1.
11. "Air Force Sees More Orders for McDonnell C-17s," *Los Angeles Times*, September 7, 1995, p. 1.
12. James F. Peltz, "Top 10 Business Stories of 1995," *Los Angeles Times*, December 31, 1995, p. D-3.
13. "Hope in Long Beach," *Economist*, October 28, 1995, p. 72.
14. Adam Bryant, "Saudis Sign $6 Billion Deal with Boeing and McDonnell," *The New York Times*, October 27, 1995, p. C4.
15. John Mintz, "Boeing, McDonnell Discussing Deals," *The Washington Post*, November 17, 1995, p. D1.
16. "Roast Crow Anyone?"
17. Howard Banks, "Aerospace and Defense: This Industry May Be Shrinking but It Isn't Dull," *Forbes*, January 1, 1996, p. 80.
18. "McDonnell to Share Reversal of Fortune," *Los Angeles Times*, October 29, 1994, p. D1.
19. Telephone interview with Ron Berger, May 6, 1995.
20. *McDonnell Douglas Annual Report*, 1994, p. 12.
21. *McDonnell Douglas Annual Report*, 1994.
22. "Roast Crow Anyone?"
23. Ralph Vartabedian, "Right Stuff for Aerospace Industry," *Los Angeles Times*, June 28, 1995, p. 1.

## CHAPTER SIX: THE SHADOW OF ANDREW CARNEGIE

1. David Brody, *Steelworkers in America: The Nonunion Era* (Cambridge, Mass.: Harvard University Press, 1960).
2. David P. Demarest, Jr., ed., *The River Ran Red: Homestead, 1892* (Pittsburgh: University of Pittsburgh Press, 1992), pp. viii–ix.
3. William Serrin, *Homestead: The Glory and Tragedy of an American Steel Town* (New York: Times Books, 1992), p. 63.
4. Ibid., p. 68.

5. Steffi Domike and Nicole Fauteux, "The Fate of the Principal Characters," in Demarest, *The River Ran Red*, pp. 199–201.
6. Quoted in Serrin, *Homestead*, p. i.
7. John Hoerr, *And the Wolf Finally Came: The Decline of the American Steel Industry* (Pittsburgh: University of Pittsburgh Press, 1988), pp. 47–48.
8. *Employee Representation in the Iron and Steel Industry* (New York: American Iron and Steel Institute, 1934).
9. Ibid., p. 5.
10. Ibid., p. 10.
11. Harry A. Millis, *From the Wagner Act to Taft-Hartley: A Study of National Labor Policy and Labor Relations* (Chicago: University of Chicago Press, 1950).
12. Hoerr, *And the Wolf Finally Came*, pp. 184–185.
13. Serrin, *Homestead*, p. 258.
14. Ibid., pp. 250–252.
15. Hoerr, *And the Wolf Finally Came*, p. 252.
16. Interview with Art Mullett, Sacramento, Calif., February 2, 1992.
17. Hoerr, *And the Wolf Finally Came*, p. 106.
18. Ibid., p. 94.
19. Ibid., p. 95.
20. Michael L. Dertouzos, Richard K. Lester, and Robert M. Solow, *Made in America: Regaining the Productive Edge* (New York: HarperPerennial, 1989).
21. Ibid.
22. Interview with Thomas C. Graham, Pittsburgh, September 11, 1992.
23. Hoerr, *And the Wolf Finally Came*, p. 11.
24. *First Annual Good Will Celebration*, Columbia Steel Co. Pittsburg Works Souvenir Program, sponsored by the Tin Mill Employees, Columbia Steel Grounds, October 20, 1934; "First Tin Plate Mill in West," *P.G. and E. Progress*, Pacific Gas and Electric Company, San Francisco, April 1929.
25. Norman L. Samways, "Modernization at Pittsburg to Make USS-POSCO More Competitive," *Iron and Steel Engineer*, June 1987.
26. Interview with Dayton Lawson, USS-POSCO, Pittsburg, Calif., May 10, 1990.
27. Interview with Thomas C. Graham, Pittsburgh, September 14, 1992.
28. "Big Korean Steelmaker Presses Its Goals of Beating Japan," *The Wall Street Journal*, January 22, 1992, p. B4.
29. After an unsuccessful bid for the presidency of the Republic of Korea in 1992, Park was charged with taking kickbacks from suppliers and embezzling company funds, after which he resigned; *The Wall Street Journal*, March 12, 1993, p. A6.
30. "Big Korean Steelmaker Presses Its Goals of Beating Japan," *The Wall Street Journal*, January 22, 1992, p. B4.
31. Alice Amsden, *Asia's Next Giant: South Korea and Late Industrialization* (New York: Oxford University Press, 1989).
32. Telephone interview with William Haley, May 12, 1995.
33. Interview with Hiwhoa Moon, Seoul, Korea, December 24, 1991.
34. Yoh had been the top-ranking Korean at the Pittsburg joint venture where I first met

him in 1989. In 1992, however, Yoh left the company in the wake of the scandal surrounding Chairman Park, though he was never accused of any wrongdoing. His departure was apparently due to his long association with the chairman. These interviews took place between December 24 and 29, 1991.

## CHAPTER SEVEN: CULTURAL PARALYSIS

1. Michael L. Dertouzos, Richard K. Lester, and Robert M. Solow, *Made in America: Regaining the Competitive Edge,* (New York: HarperPerennial, 1989), p. 287.
2. Interview with Thomas C. Graham, Pittsburgh, September 14, 1992.
3. "USS-POSCO Awards Contract," *The Pittsburg* (Calif.) *Post Dispatch,* January 19, 1987, p. 1.
4. "The Controversy That Came with the Modernizations," *The Pittsburg* (Calif.) *Post Dispatch,* April 4, 1989, p. 1.
5. Jerry Cornfield, "Protesters Rally Before Plant Start-up," Antioch, Calif., *Daily Ledger,* April 6, 1989, p. 1; Terry Toczynski, "Unionists Rally at POSCO Fete," *Contra Costa Times,* April 7, 1989, p. 1; Kathleen MacLay, "Pittsburg Steel Plant Opens to Protesters," *Stockton* (Calif.) *Record,* April 7, 1989, p. 1.
6. "The Controversy that Came with the Modernizations."
7. Jeff Delline, "USS-POSCO Fined Again for Toxic Dumping," *San Francisco Chronicle,* September 6, 1991, p. C1.
8. The Controversy That Came with the Modernizations"; Henry Weinstein, "Jackson Joins Protest at Steel Plant," *Los Angeles Times,* March 20, 1988, A3.
9. Leonard Chuderewicz, "Shipping Dispute Poses Threat to USS-POSCO Efficiency" (commentary), *Contra Costa Times,* March 14, 1991, p. 8.
10. Daniel Levine, "Air Battle, Steel Firm, Union in Environmental, Labor Dispute," *Oakland* (Calif.) *Tribune,* March 5, 1991, p. B1.
11. "POSCO Ships Refine Emission Control System," *Antioch* (Calif.) *Ledger Post Dispatch,* March 1, 1991.
12. "Pollution Board Too Severe with USS-POSCO Fine" (editorial), *Daily Ledger/Post Dispatch,* April 25, 1991, p. 6; "Environmental Blackmail" (editorial), *San Francisco Business Times,* April 26, 1991, p. 12.
13. William Serrin, *Homestead: The Glory and Tragedy of an American Steel Town* (New York: Times Books, 1992), p. 326.
14. John Hoerr, *And the Wolf Finally Came: The Decline of the American Steel Industry* (Pittsburgh: University of Pittsburgh Press, 1988), p. 153.
15. Ibid.

## CHAPTER EIGHT: THE DAWNING OF A NEW ORDER

1. Today the antiquated 1,000-foot-long mill is stretched out in a dark shed like a battleship in mothballs, covered with years of heavy industrial grime. Emergency instructions can still be faintly seen through layers of grease and soot.

2. Interviews with Robert Guadiana, Pittsburg, Los Angeles, and San Francisco, Calif., between June 1988 and May 1993.
3. John P. Hoerr, *And the Wolf Finally Came: The Decline of the American Steel Industry* (Pittsburgh: University of Pittsburgh Press, 1988).
4. Ibid.
5. "UPI 1994 Employee Survey," unpublished report.
6. *Rank and Filer*, United Steelworkers of America Local 1440, December 1992.
7. United States of America International Trade Commission, "In the Matter of Certain Flat-Rolled Carbon Steel Products," Investigation Nos. 701-TA-319-354 and 731-TA-573-620, July 21, 1992; "U.S. Steelmakers Win Ruling on Trade," *San Francisco Chronicle*, December 1, 1992, p. C1.
8. "U.S. Industry's New Strength May Soon Weaken," *The Wall Street Journal*, June 3, 1993, p. 2.
9. Sung-il Juhn, *A Case Study of a Joint Venture Between the United States and Korea: USS-POSCO Industries*, paper presented at the Conference on an Industrial Alliance Between the United States and Korea, La Jolla, Calif., June 22–24, 1994.
10. Comments by William Baker, USS-POSCO, August 1993.
11. "UPI 1994 Employee Survey."
12. "Blending Cultures at Pittsburg, California," *Iron Age New Steel*, July 1994, pp. 16–20.
13. Interview with Bill Haley, May 13, 1994.
14. Ibid.
15. "Record Fine for Bay Pollution," *San Francisco Chronicle*, July 23, 1991, p. D1.
16. "Steelmaker Honored for Enviro-excellence," *Environment Today*, October 1994, p. 13.
17. "UPI 1994 Employee Survey."
18. Ibid.

## CHAPTER NINE: REMNANTS OF MASS PRODUCTION

1. Dana Wechsler Linden and Bruce Upbin, "Boy Scouts on a Rampage," *Forbes*, January 1996, pp. 66–70.
2. Ibid., p. 67; *Hewlett-Packard Company Annual Report 1994*.
3. *Hewlett-Packard: Manufacturing Productivity Division*, report no. 9-587-101, Harvard Business School, Boston, 1986; Michael Beer, Russell Eisenstat, and Bert Spector, *The Critical Path* (Boston: Harvard Business School Press, 1990); John P. Kotter and James L. Heskett, *Corporate Culture and Performance* (New York: Free Press, 1992).
4. "The HP Way," internal company document #5955-4709, 1980, pp. 1–80.
5. David Packard, *The HP Way* (New York: HarperBusiness, 1995), pp. 83–84.
6. Ibid., p. 93.
7. Ibid., pp. 126–127.
8. Ibid., p. 128.
9. Ibid.
10. Interview with Lyle Hornback, Santa Clara, Calif., October 19, 1993.
11. Interview with Jim Collin, Santa Clara, Calif., October 15, 1993.

12. David Packard, "The Corporation and Society: Allies or Antagonists?" a presentation to the Business and Society Seminar, February 25–27, San Francisco, 1973, p. 8.

13. Unpublished transcript of meeting between David Packard and Bay area division managers, February 11, 1974, Santa Clara, Calif. I have taken some liberties in editing the verbatim record to make it more readable, though I have tried to keep the meaning intact.

14. "Hewlett-Packard Rethinks Itself," *Business Week*, April 1, 1991, pp. 76–79.

15. Stephen K. Yoder, "A 1990 Reorganization at Hewlett-Packard Is Already Paying Off," *The Wall Street Journal*, July 22, 1991, p. A1.

16. Ibid.

17. "Hewlett-Packard Rethinks Itself."

18. Yoder, "A 1990 Reorganization."

19. Ibid.

20. Robert Levering, Milton Moskowitz, and Michael Katz, *The 100 Best Companies to Work for in America* (New York: New American Library, 1987), pp. 182–86.

21. Interview with Keith Ferguson, Santa Clara, Calif., October 19, 1993.

22. For another perspective on "terminal niceness," see Richard Tanner Pascale, *Managing on the Edge: How the Smartest Companies Use Conflict to Stay Ahead* (New York: Simon and Schuster, 1990).

## CHAPTER TEN: ALTERING THE SYSTEM OF WORK

1. Interview with Tom Vos, Santa Clara, Calif., February 18, 1994.

2. For an authoritative account of the use of work redesign at Hewlett-Packard, see Deone M. Zell, *Learning by Design* (Ithaca, N.Y.: Cornell University Press, to be published).

3. E. L. Trist and K. W. Bamforth, "Some Social and Psychological Consequences of the Longwall Method of Coal-getting," *Human Relations*, vol. 4, no. 1, 1951, pp. 3–38.

4. F. E. Emery and E. L. Trist, "Socio-technical Systems." in C. W. Churchman et al., eds. *Management Sciences, Models and Techniques* (London: Pergamon, 1960); Albert Cherns, "The Principles of Sociotechnical Design," *Human Relations*, vol. 29, no. 8, 1976, pp. 783–792; Marvin Weisbord, *Productive Workplaces* (San Francisco: Jossey-Bass, 1987).

5. In more recent adaptations, it has borrowed from the Toyota production system and from total quality management. In its newest configuration, it has become known as "reengineering," or "process redesign." But unlike TQM, which gets regular attention in the press as companies vie for the prestigious Baldrige Award, STS has remained largely unnoticed. Until the publication of Michael Hammer's book *Reengineering the Corporation*, top executives were generally unaware of its existence, and relatively few consultants know as much about it as they do about TQM.

6. Weisbord, *Productive Workplaces*.

7. Interview with Stuart Winby, Palo Alto, Calif., September 23, 1993.

8. C. H. Pava, *Managing New Office Technology* (New York: Free Press, 1983).

9. For a comprehensive view of Neil's plan, see "Vision, Purpose, Directions: SCD in the 1990s White Paper," unpublished paper, Hewlett-Packard, August 10, 1992.

10. Mark Allen, Jenny Brandemuehl, Peter Gaarn, and Deone Zell, *Santa Clara Division: Becoming a Customer-focused Division Through a Fast-Cycle Work Redesign,* Hewlett-Packard Company, Santa Clara Division, Factory of the Future, and UCLA's California Worksite Research Committee, September 21, 1993 (summarized version).

11. "Values, Guiding Principles, Key Strategies," memo from Marty Neil to SCD staff, February 22, 1993.


## CHAPTER ELEVEN: A PAINFUL TRANSFORMATION

1. For a thorough description of each step in the process, see Mark Allen, Jenny Brandemuehl, Peter Gaarn, and Deone Zell, *Santa Clara Division: Becoming a Customer-focused Division Through a Fast-Cycle Work Redesign,* Hewlett-Packard Company, Santa Clara Division, Factory of the Future, and UCLA's California Worksite Research Committee, September 21, 1993.

2. "Santa Clara 1993 Employee Survey," California Worksite Research Committee, University of California, Los Angeles, June 1993.

3. Readers who wish more technical information should see "Exploring the Modulation Domain," *Hewlett-Packard Newsletter,* no. 4, 5091-7714E, undated.

4. For more on oscilloscopes, see Garth Gelster, "What Your Oscilloscope Never Told You," *Electrical/Electronic Engineering and Technology Guide* (Cleveland, Ohio: Pennton 1992).

5. Interview with Tom Vos, Santa Clara, Calif., February 18, 1994.

6. Stephen K. Yoder, "A 1990 Reorganization at Hewlett-Packard Is Already Paying Off," *The Wall Street Journal,* July 22, 1991, p. A1.

7. Our 1993 survey indicated that despite H & P's commitment to employment security, 66 percent of all Santa Clara employees worried about being "excessed."

8. Telephone interview with Marty Neil, March 19, 1996.

9. Ibid.


## CHAPTER TWELVE: THE DISINTEGRATION OF MASS PRODUCTION

1. In a recent article, "Cultural Transformation at NUMMI," that appeared in the *Sloan Management Review,* Fall 1994, I estimated the workforce to be 50 percent the size of the original one. NUMMI's workforce has grown substantially over the last five years, and 65 percent is now the more accurate figure.

2. J. D. Power and Associates' rankings are based on customer satisfaction on more than a hundred items, such as squeaks, rattles, fit, and finish, in the first ninety days of ownership.

3. Federal Trade Commission, "In the Matter of General Motors Corporation and Toyota Motor Corporation: Petition to Reopen the Proceedings and to Vacate the Consent Order," docket no. C-3132, June 28, 1993, p. 12.

4. Telephone interview with Dennis Cuneo, May 12, 1995.

5. Comments by Jack Smith, San Francisco, May 6, 1994.

6. Comments by Tatsuro Toyoda, San Francisco, May 6, 1994.

7. Andrea Gabor, *The Man Who Discovered Quality* (New York: Times Books, 1991).

8. Ibid.

9. The founders' family name, "Toyoda," means "abundant rice field," while "Toyota" is a name that was chosen from a contest, though it has no meaning. According to the Toyota Motor Corporation's publication *Toyota: A History of the First 50 Years* (1988), "Toyota" was chosen because its *katakana* characters look like those for "speed," and the eight strokes it takes to make them signify good feelings about increasing prosperity.

10. Eiji Toyoda, *Toyota: Fifty Years in Motion* (Tokyo: Kodansha International, 1988), p. 109.

11. James P. Womack, Daniel T. Jones, and Daniel Roos, *The Machine That Changed the World* (New York: Rawson, 1990); Michael Cusumano, *The Japanese Automobile Industry: Technology and Management at Nissan and Toyota* (Cambridge, Mass.: Harvard University Press, 1985).

12. Eiji Toyoda, *Toyota*.

13. Koichi Shimokawa, "From the Ford System to the Just-in-Time Production System," *Japanese Yearbook on Business History*, vol. 10, 1993, p. 97.

14. Martin Kenney and Richard Florida, *Beyond Mass Production: The Japanese System and Its Transfer to the U.S.* (New York: Oxford University Press, 1993).

15. Yashuhiro Monden, *Toyota Production System* (Atlanta: Industrial Engineering and Management Press, 1983).

16. Taiichi Ohno, *Toyota Production System* (Cambridge, Mass: Productivity Press, 1988).

17. *Toyota: A History of the First 50 Years* (Toyota City, Japan: Toyota Motor Corporation, 1988).

18. Osamu Kimura and Hirosuke Terada, "Design and Analysis of Pull System, a Method of Multi-Stage Production Control," *International Journal of Production Research*, vol. 19, no. 2, 1981, pp. 241–253.

19. Interview with Dennis Cuneo, Fremont, Calif., December 20, 1994.

20. Interviews with William J. Usery, Jr., between March 19, 1992, and May 12, 1995.

21. Interview with Bruce Lee, Artesia, Calif., July 15, 1992.

## CHAPTER THIRTEEN: THE REVOLUTION OF LEAN PRODUCTION

1. Letter of Intent between the United Auto Workers and Joint Venture, September 21, 1983.

2. Interview with Dennis Cuneo, Fremont, Calif., December 20, 1994.

3. Federal Trade Commission, Dissenting opinion, December 22, 1983.

4. Interview with Kan Higashi, Tokyo, Japan, December 17, 1991.

5. Ibid.

6. Interview with Dennis Cuneo, December 20, 1994.

7. Interview with Bruce Lee, Artesia, Calif., January 21, 1994.

8. Interview with Tony DeJesus, Fremont, Calif., May 12, 1994.

9. Ibid.; also see Mike Parker, *Inside the Circle: A Union Guide to AWL* (Detroit: Labor Notes/South End Press, 1985).

10. For a comprehensive analysis of this period in California's economic history, see Philip Shapira, *Industry and Jobs in Transition: A Study of Industrial Restructuring, Work, and Displacement in California*, unpublished doctoral dissertation, Department of Urban and Regional Planning, University of California, Berkeley, 1986.
11. Michael Brody, "Toyota Meets U.S. Auto Workers," *Fortune*, July 9, 1984, p. 76.
12. Calculation by Dennis Cuneo, September 17, 1993.
13. Collective Bargaining Agreement Between New United Motor Manufacturing, Inc., and International Union, United Automobile, Aerospace and Agricultural Implement Workers of America, UAW, and Its Affiliated Local Union, 2244, July 1, 1991, p. 3.
14. Interview with Kan Higashi, December 17, 1991.
15. Interview with Bruce Lee, January 21, 1994.
16. Interview with Bruce Lee, Artesia, Calif., May 15, 1995.

## CHAPTER FOURTEEN: THE MAKING OF A NEW COMPACT

1. G. Raine, "Building Cars Japan's Way," *Newsweek*, March 31, 1986, p. 43; D. Buss, "'Gung Ho' to Repeat Assembly Errors," *The Wall Street Journal*, March 27, 1986, p. 32.
2. Team Member Survey, 1993 (internal document).
3. Interview with Bill Childs, May 2, 1988. While there have been other studies of NUMMI (see, e.g., Paul Adler, "Time-and-Motion Regained," *Harvard Business Review*, January–February 1993, pp. 97–108), ours was the first to be done as insiders.
4. Interview with Bruce Lee, Artesia, Calif., December 5, 1990.
5. This point of view was recently published; see W. Wilms, A. Hardcastle, and D. Zell, "Cultural Transformation at NUMMI," *Sloan Management Review*, Fall 1994, pp. 99–113.
6. Interview with H. Kawai, Kyoto University, Kyoto, Japan, December 21, 1991.
7. See also H. Kawai, *The Japanese Psyche* (Dallas: Spring Publications, 1988).
8. Telephone interview with Dennis Cuneo, May 15, 1995.
9. Federal Trade Commission, Order Granting Petition to Reopen and Set Aside Order, Docket C-3132, October 29, 1993.
10. K. Lewin, *Field Theory in Social Science: Selected Theoretical Papers*, D. Cartwright, ed. (New York: Harper and Row, 1951); W. G. Dyer, "The Cycle of Cultural Evolution in Organizations," in *Gaining Control of the Corporate Culture*, R. Kilmann, J. J. Saxton, and R. Serpa, eds. (San Francisco: Jossey-Bass, 1985), pp. 200–229; M. Beer and E. Walton, "Developing the Competitive Organization: Interventions and Strategies," *American Psychologist*, vol. 45, no. 2, pp. 154–161.
11. Mike Parker and Jane Slaughter, *Choosing Sides: Unions and the Team Concept* (Boston: South End Press, 1988).
12. W. A. Pasmore, "Overcoming the Roadblocks in Work-restructuring Efforts," *Organizational Dynamics*, vol. 10, 1982, pp. 54–67; J. Klein, "Why Supervisors Resist Employee Involvement," *Harvard Business Review*, vol. 62, no. 5, 1984, pp. 87–95; Beer and Walton, "Developing the Competitive Organization."
13. See V. Pucik, "Strategic Alliances, Organizational Learning, and Competitive Advan-

tage: The HRM Agenda," *Human Resource Management*, vol. 27, no. 1, 1988, pp. 77–93.

14. Much of this account is based on a highly publicized report by two journalists who, despite the book's title, had only limited access to the plant and collected most of their information during off-site interviews. See Joseph Fucini and Suzy Fucini, *Working for the Japanese: Inside Mazda's American Auto Plant* (New York: Free Press, 1990).

## CHAPTER FIFTEEN: TOWARD A CULTURE OF COOPERATION

1. *The Dialogues of Plato* (New York: Bantam Books, 1986); John Locke, *Concerning Civil Government* (Second Essay) (Harmondsworth, England: Penguin Books, 1986); Thomas Hobbes, *Leviathan, or Matter, Form and Power of a Commonwealth Ecclesiastical and Civil* (Chicago: Great Books of the Western World, Encyclopaedia Britannica, 1989).

2. Alexander Hamilton, John Madison, John Jay, *The Federalist Papers* (New York: New American Library, 1961).

3. Adam Smith, *An Inquiry into the Nature and Causes of the Wealth of Nations*, Edwin Cannan, ed. (New York: Modern Library, 1993).

4. "State of Re-engineering Report, 1994," CSC Index, reported in *The Economist*, July 2, 1994, p. 64. The journal reports that the two chief obstacles are "fear and turf-protection"—much the same conclusion as we arrived at.

5. Edgar Schein, *Organizational Culture and Leadership* (San Francisco: Jossey-Bass, 1985); Kurt Lewin, *Field Theory in Social Science: Selected Theoretical Papers*, D. Cartwright, ed. (New York: Harper and Row, 1951).

6. "UPI 1994 Employee Survey," unpublished report.

7. David Packard, *The HP Way* (New York: HarperBusiness, 1995).

8. "Santa Clara 1993 Employer Survey," California Worksite Research Committee, University of California, Los Angeles, June 1993.

9. For lack of a better word to describe the variety of new flexible work systems and methods to achieve them—including "lean production," sociotechnical systems design, reengineering, TQM, and others—I have borrowed a term first used by E. E. Lawler in 1986; see E. E. Lawler III, *High Involvement Management: Participative Strategies for Improving Organizational Performance* (San Francisco: Jossey-Bass, 1986).

10. It was NUMMI's third president, Osamu Kimura, who, with his colleague Hirosuke Terada, coined the phrase "pull system." See Kimura and Terada, "Design and Analysis of Pull System, a Method of Multi-Stage Production Control," *International Journal of Production Research*, vol. 19, no. 3, 1981, pp. 241–253.

11. Mike Parker and Jane Slaughter, *Choosing Sides: Unions and the Team Concept* (Boston: South End Press, 1988).

12. "The Pain of Downsizing," *Business Week*, May 9, 1994, pp. 60–69.

13. RAND senior social scientist Christoph Buechtemann warns, "This is a slippery slope: there are many instances in which unions and their political allies (e.g. Social-Democrats in Europe) have voted down environmental concerns or taken a hostile stance toward arms reduction, issues that may have a value for society at large, in the

name of preserving jobs. Such behavior, however, may produce externalities, which is one reason why the trend toward enterprise unions may be problematic if not backed by substantial institutional reform"; correspondence, February 1, 1995.

14. Peter Senge, *The Fifth Discipline* (New York: Doubleday, 1990); H. P. Sims et al., *The Thinking Organization* (San Francisco: Jossey-Bass, 1986); C. Argyris and D. Schon, *Organizational Learning: A Theory of Action Perspective* (Reading, Mass.: Addison-Wesley, 1978); Ikujiro Nonaka, "The Knowledge Creating Company," *Harvard Business Review*, November–December 1991, p. 97; David A. Garvin, "Building a Learning Organization," *Harvard Business Review*, July–August, 1993, pp. 78–91.

15. See for instance, Dorothy Leonard-Barton et al., "How to Integrate Work and Deepen Expertise," *Harvard Business Review*, September–October 1994, pp. 121–130.

16. John Dewey, *Experience and Education* (New York: Macmillan, 1963).

17. Jean Piaget, *To Understand Is to Invent: The Future of Education* (Dallas, Pa.: Penguin Books, 1945).

18. Christoph Buechtemann, correspondence, February 1, 1995.

19. In July 1994 Congress refused to grant unions more power by prohibiting companies from firing striking workers and replacing them with nonunion workers. Labor unions are also losing members at a rapid rate. For instance, the percentage of American manufacturing workers who belong to unions plummeted from 27.8 percent in 1983 to 18.2 percent in 1994. See Bureau of Labor Statistics, quoted in "Crossing the Lines: Scab or Survivor?" *Los Angeles Times*, May 15, 1995, p. 1.

20. Telephone interview with William J. Usery, Jr., May 12, 1995.

21. One model may be German work councils, in which workers are given stakeholder status—an inalienable right that cannot be taken away—and decisions about the terms of employment and the content of work are made after full discussion by both sides. See Christoph Buechtemann, correspondence, February 1, 1995; also see Thomas Kochan, Harry Katz, and Robert McKersie, *The Transformation of American Industrial Relations* (New York: Basic Books, 1994); *Fact-Finding Report*, Commission on the Future of Worker-Management Relations (John Dunlop, Chairman), U.S. Department of Labor, U.S. Department of Commerce, Washington, D.C., May 1994.

22. Jeremy Rifkin, "Vanishing Jobs," *Mother Jones*, October 1995, pp. 58–64; Jeremy Rifkin, *The End of Work* (New York: G. P. Putnam's Sons, 1995).

23. Ibid.

24. "U.S. Widens Its Competitiveness Lead, Study Says," *Los Angeles Times*, September 6, 1995, p. D-1.

25. Jonathan Peterson, "Economists Play 'Happy Days' as Many Sing Blues," *Los Angeles Times*, February 21, 1994, p. 1.

26. Mark Mittelhausen, "Manufacturing: It's Still the Industrial Age," *Occupational Outlook Quarterly*, Fall 1994, p. 4.

27. *Fact-Finding Report*, p. 6.

28. *Fact-Finding Report*, reported in Donald Nauss, "Factories Revel in New Industrial Revolution," *Los Angeles Times*, April 10, 1994, p. D-1; also see "The Pain of Downsizing."

29. Richard J. Barnet, "The End of Jobs," *Harper's*, September 1993, p. 48.

30. Stephen J. Rose, *Declining Job Security and the Professionalization of Opportunity*, National Commission for Employment Policy, Research Report No. 95-04, May 1995, p. i.

31. Ibid, p. ii.

32. John A. Byrne, "The Pain of Downsizing," *Business Week*, May 9, 1994, p. 61.

33. G. Lafer, "The Politics of Job Training: Urban Poverty and the False Promise of JTPA," *Politics and Society*, vol. 22, 1994, p. 351.

34. Lawrence Mishel and Jared Bernstein, *The State of Working America: 1992–1993* (Armonk, N.Y.: Economic Policy Institute, 1993), p. 13.

35. Barnet, "The End of Jobs," p. 50.

36. Louis Uchitelle and N. R. Kleinfeld, "The Downsizing of America," *The New York Times*, March 3, 1996, p. 1.

37. Mishel and Bernstein, *The State of Working America*, p. 174.

38. *Current Population Survey, 1993*, Annual Averages, Table 5 (Washington, D.C.: U.S. Department of Labor, Bureau of Labor Statistics, 1994).

39. *Fact-Finding Report*; Mishel and Bernstein, *The State of Working America*.

40. *Forbes* (May 22, 1995) reported that the average salary for executives of America's largest publicly held companies in 1994 was $993,000, up 11 percent from 1993; Mishel and Bernstein, *The State of Working America*, pp. 203–205; remarks by Michael Dukakis, Human Resources Round Table for Senior Executives, UCLA, February 7, 1996.

41. "Executive Pay: Gross Compensation," *Business Week*, March 18, 1996, pp. 32–33.

42. Paul Ong, "Economic Marginalization and the Rise of Inequality in Southern California," unpublished paper, December, 1994.

43. Louis Uchitelle and N. R. Kleinfeld, op. cit., p. 1.

44. Albert Schweitzer, *Out of My Life and Thought: An Autobiography* (New York: Holt, Rinehart and Winston, 1949); Thorstein Veblen, *The Instinct of Workmanship* (New York: The MacMillan Company, 1914); C. G. Jung, *Memories, Dreams, Reflections* (New York: Vintage Books, 1965); Herbert Read, *The Redemption of the Robot* (New York: Simon and Schuster, 1966).

45. Louisa May Alcott, *Work* (New York: Schocken Books, 1977); Jane Addams, *Twenty Years at Hull House* (New York: Macmillan, 1910); Horatio Alger, *Mark the Matchboy* and *Andy Grant's Pluck* (New York: A. L. Burt, undated); Robert Ward, *Red Baker* (San Francisco: Dial Press, 1985).

46. Paul Kennedy, "If Finance and Trade Can be Global, Why Not Workers?" (commentary), *Los Angeles Times*, December 19, 1994, p. B-15.

47. Rifkin, "Vanishing Jobs," p. 60.

48. Martin Kenney and Richard Florida, *Beyond Mass Production* (New York: Oxford, 1993).

49. Lester Thurow, *Head to Head* (New York: Morrow, 1992).

50. John Rennie, "The Uncertainties of Technological Innovation," *Scientific American*, September 1995, p. 58.

51. Herbert A. Simon, "Organizations and Markets," *Journal of Economic Perspectives*, Spring 1991, pp. 25–44.

52. Ibid., p. 35.
53. Herbert A. Simon, "Is International Management Different from Management?" working paper no. 94-1, Carnegie Bosch Institute, Carnegie-Mellon University, 1993, p. 4.
54. Ibid.
55. James P. Womack and Daniel T. Jones, "From Lean Production to the Lean Enterprise," *Harvard Business Review*, March–April 1994, pp. 93–103.
56. Ibid., p. 94.
57. These include Marvin S. Finkelstein et al., "Sharing Information Spawns Trust, Productivity, and Quality," *National Productivity Review*, Summer 1991, pp. 295–298; Mark Dogson, "Learning, Trust and Technological Collaboration," *Human Relations*, January 1993, p. 133–141; Mark Barenberg, "Democracy and Domination in the Law of Workplace Cooperation: From Bureaucratic to Flexible Production," *Columbia Law Review*, April 1994, pp. 753–983; Edward H. Lorenz, "Trust and the Flexible Firm: International Comparisons," *Industrial Relations*, Fall 1992, pp. 455–472.
58. Charles F. Sabel, "Studied Trust: Building New Forms of Cooperation in a Volatile Economy," *Human Relations*, September 1993, pp. 11–33.
59. Ibid., p. 12.
60. Francis Fukuyama, *Trust* (New York: Free Press, 1995).
61. The Reemployment Act of 1994 failed to come before Congress for a vote in 1994, being overshadowed by national health care, crime, and the congressional elections, though many of its provisions are included in the 1995 Middle-Class Bill of Rights.
62. Remarks of President Bill Clinton and Secretary of Labor Robert Reich at the presentation of the Reemployment Act of 1994, White House, Washington, D.C., March 9, 1994.
63. Ibid.
64. Wellford Wilms and Benson Munger, "Job Training Programs," *Encyclopedia of Educational Research*, 6th ed., vol. 2 (New York: Macmillan, 1993), pp. 672–677; Sar Levitan and Garth Mangum, *The T in CETA: Local and National Perspectives* (Kalamazoo, Mich.: National Council on Employment Policy/W. E. Upjohn Institute for Employment Research, 1981); Bart S. Barnow, "The Impact of CETA Programs on Earnings: A Review of the Literature," *The Journal of Human Resources*, vol. 22, no. 2, 1986, pp. 157–193.
65. Interview with Bill Greene, University of California, Los Angeles, October 21, 1986.
66. Wellford W. Wilms, "Captured by the American Dream: Vocational Education in the United States," in *Vocationalizing Education: An International Perspective*, J. Lauglo and K. Lillis, eds. (Oxford: Pergamon, 1988).
67. *National Assessment of Vocational Education* (Washington, D.C.: Office of Educational Research and Improvement, U.S. Department of Education, 1994). However, not all training programs have failed. Programs such as California's Employment Training Panel, which operate on a "pay-for-results" basis and target training directly at economic development, have been shown to produce high rates of job placement at low cost. For more information, see Richard W. Moore, Daniel R. Blake, and G. Michael Phillips, *Public Training with Private Efficiency: An Analysis of the Outcomes*

of California Employment Training Panel Programs (Sacramento, Calif.: E.T.D., 1994); Richard Moore, Wellford Wilms, and Roger Bolus, Training for Change: A Report to the Employment Training Panel, Training Research Corporation, Santa Monica, Calif., 1988.

68. National Center for Educational Statistics, Digest of Educational Statistics, 1993 (Washington, D.C.: U.S. Department of Education, 1993).

69. National Center for Educational Statistics, The State of Mathematics Education (Washington, D.C.: U.S. Department of Education, 1990), pp. 7–9.

70. Archie E. Lapointe, Nancy A. Mead, and Gary W. Phillips, A World of Difference: An International Assessment of Mathematics and Science (Princeton, N.J.: Educational Testing Service, 1989).

71. National Education Goals Panel, The National Education Goals Report, Executive Summary (Washington, D.C.: U.S. Department of Education, 1991), p. 14.

72. Eric A. Hanushek et al., Making Schools Work: Improving Performance and Controlling Costs (Washington, D.C.: The Brookings Institution, 1994).

73. National Commission on Excellence in Education, A Nation at Risk: The Imperative for Education Reform (Washington, D.C.: U.S. Government Printing Office, 1983).

74. See, e.g., John I. Goodlad, A Place Called School (New York: McGraw-Hill, 1984); William B. Johnston and Arnold H. Packer, Workforce 2000: Work and Workers for the 21st Century (Indianapolis: Hudson Institute, 1987); National Center for Educational Statistics, The State of Mathematics Education (Washington, D.C.: U.S. Department of Education, 1990).

75. Edward B. Fiske, Smart Schools, Smart Kids (New York: Simon and Schuster, 1991), p. 20.

76. Ibid., p. 21.

77. Hanushek, Making Schools Work.

78. Interview with Theodore Mitchell, University of California, Los Angeles, December 6, 1994.

79. David Tyack and Larry Cuban, Tinkering Toward Utopia: A Century of Public School Reform (Cambridge, Mass.: Harvard University Press, 1995), p. 4.

80. Ellwood P. Cubberley, Public School Administration (Boston: 1916), p. 338.

81. Raymond E. Callahan, Education and the Cult of Efficiency (Chicago: University of Chicago Press, 1962).

82. Outlook, August 12, 1911, p. 836; Shailer Matthews, Scientific Management in the Churches (Chicago: 1912), pp. 1–2.

83. Quoted in Callahan, Education and the Cult of Efficiency, p. 146.

84. See Kenneth G. Wilson and Bennett Daviss, Redesigning Education (New York: Holt, 1994); Fiske, Smart Schools, Smart Kids.

85. See Samuel Bowles and Herbert Gintis, Democracy and Capitalism (New York: Basic Books, 1986).

86. My colleagues and I are currently conducting studies of the Los Angeles Police Department, the University of California, Los Angeles, and teacher unions (and planning similar studies of health maintenance organizations), where evidence of these social forces is clearly visible.

87. Roger Benjamin, Stephen Carroll, Maryann Jacobi, Cathy Krop, and Michael Shires, *The Redesign of Governance in Higher Education* (Santa Monica, Calif.: Institute on Education and Training, RAND, 1993); also see "TQM: Will It Work on Campus?" *Change*, May–June 1993; David H. Entin, "Boston: Less than Meets the Eye," *Change*, May–June 1993, pp. 28–31; Edward Whalen, *Responsibility Center Budgeting: An Approach to Decentralized Management for Institutions of Higher Education* (Bloomington: Indiana University Press, 1991).

88. Louis V. Gerstner, Jr., et al., *Reinventing Education: Entrepreneurship in America's Public Schools* (New York: Dutton, 1994).

89. See John E. Coons and Stephen Sugarman, *Education by Choice* (Berkeley: University of California Press, 1978).

90. Gerstner et al., *Reinventing Education*, pp. 22–23.

91. Ibid., p. 23.

92. Telephone interview with John E. Coons, December 21, 1994.

93. Entin, "Total Quality Management," p. 9.

94. See, e.g., Jonathan Weisman, "Skills in the Schools: Now It's Business' Turn," and other articles that appeared in a special edition of the *Phi Delta Kappan*, January 1993; *Educational Record*, Special Focus: Total Quality Management on Campus, Spring 1993; Edward E. Lawler III and Susan A. Mohrman, *A New Logic for Organizing: Implications for Higher Education*, Center for Effective Organizations, University of Southern California, Los Angeles, Calif., April 1993; Kenneth G. Wilson and Bennett Daviss, *Redesigning Education* (New York: Holt, 1994).

95. Jean-Jacques Rousseau, *The Social Contract* (London: Dent, 1990).

96. Anthropologist Bronislaw Malinowski recognized this phenomenon more than seventy years ago, when he studied how ideas and practices diffused from people to people; see Bronislaw Malinowski, "The Life of Culture," in *Culture: The Diffusion Controversy*, G. Elliott Smith, Bronislaw Malinowski, Herbert J. Spinden, and Alex. Goldenweiser, eds. (New York: Norton, 1927), pp. 26–46.

# INDEX

## ABOUT THE AUTHOR

WELLFORD ("BUZZ") WILMS is a professor in UCLA's Graduate School of Education and Information Studies, where he has also been assistant dean and chair of the faculty. A recognized authority on education, job training, and economic productivity, Wilms holds a Ph.D. from the University of California, Berkeley, in education policy. He currently resides in Topanga, California.